1-4-76

Cruising the Pacific Coast, Acapulco to Skagway

Carolyn and Jack West

Cruising the Pacific Coast, Acapulco to Skagway

THIRD EDITION

Sea Publications, Inc.

First edition October 1966
Second edition May 1970
Third edition May 1974

ISBN 0-88403-007-5
Library of Congress Card No. 74-77092
Copyright © 1974 by CBS Consumer Publishing Division
of Columbia Broadcasting System, Inc.

SEA PUBLICATIONS, INC., NEWPORT BEACH, CALIFORNIA

Printed in the United States of America

Contents

List of Charts

Guides to cruising areas and harbor anchorages

When writing copy for the first edition of this book in 1964, we often wondered how many sailors and power boatmen might ever use it, or if the effort was strictly a labor of love. The answer was not long in arriving, with many favorable comments and a few suggestions about additional harbors and coves that could be included in later editions.

To the reader who might question a certain channel or facility described here, or point out a navigational aid or hazard mentioned which no longer exists—we can only answer that before the ink is dry on this edition, there will be some minor changes in what is reported. May we remind the reader that the Coast Guard finds it necessary to issue *Notice to Mariners* every week of the year to keep abreast of changing conditions; that navigational charts are constantly being revised by the Government; that the spelling of many points, harbor and island names on charts are often different from those in *Sailing Directions*. The chartlets of harbors or coves in this book are not drawn for navigational purposes. They are to supplement, or to give more detail to what is shown or described in the *Coast Pilot* and *Sailing Directions;* both of these publications should be aboard any boat cruising this coast, and *Cruising The Pacific Coast, Acapulco to Skagway* is not intended to take their places. The area sketches preceding each chapter are presented to help orient the reader with principal places along the routes being described. Fortunately the locations of bays, harbors, islands and rivers remain the same year after year, altered only slowly with man-made breakwaters, dredged channels and new facilities for the cruising yachtsman.

It was nearly 28 years ago that we first started searching for a cruising guide to Pacific Coast waters that would give boat owners some of the more intimate details of harbors, weather conditions, and facilities available. At that time we were commissioning our first, long-range, cruising boat, in Seattle. We were literally up to our Plimsol-line in problems—converting a war-surplus craft, repowering the ship with diesel engines, removing tons of military gear, replacing specialized electronic navigation equipment with units we understood and could use. It was a time we needed the help and guidance of others, and something more than copies of the *Coast Pilot* and *Radio Aids to Navigation* which listed every marine radio aid in the world. These were written mainly for the merchant seaman and deep-draft vessel operators, but what we wanted was information applicable to small craft. Nevertheless, armed with every chart and publication available, it was a successful passage, non-stop from Seattle to San Pedro.

We vowed then that someday we would compile a narrative guide for cruising the Pacific Coast—but only after we had cruised the areas and found for ourselves the pleasures, problems and conditions. Hence this third edition, considerably expanded over previous editions, combining our observations made during many trips, but organized in a geographical pattern as though it were a single trip from Acapulco, Mexico to Skagway, Alaska.

These pages reflect our findings based on more than 125,000 miles of cruising the Pacific Coast, aboard the first *Monsoon,* our second ship *Monsoon II,* and aboard friends' cruisers. The first *Monsoon* logged a distance of nearly twice around the world, and *Monsoon II* has logged somewhat more. All of this has been without professional crews—we being the Commodore and Captain of our ships.

Over the years we have written many thousands of words, in article form, for national boating journals. Each time we have felt, however, that much had to be omitted in the interest of confining a many-months' trip to a few pages of magazine size. Invariably, there would be letters asking for more information on weather, harbors, supplies available, and cruising conditions, indicating a growing interest in this area.

Any cruising region spanning a distance of nearly five thousand miles is expected to have wide contrasts in climates, scenery and cruising conditions. Few realize, however, that the Pacific Coast area has, in addition, even wider contrasts in the nationality of its discoverers. Included is the Spanish influence which predominates in the names given bays and capes from

Cape San Lucas to Cape Mendocino; the native American Indians whose stockades, forts and villages are still important landmarks along the Oregon coastline, northward into British Columbia and Alaska. Again, the Spanish who discovered the Strait of Juan de Fuca separating Canada and the State of Washington; the English who charted and named such islands as Vancouver, Whidbey and Bainbridge in Puget Sound and British Columbian waters; and the Russians and Scandanavians who first settled Alaska.

So international is the background of Pacific Coast cruising waters, it took Kaiser Wilhelm of Germany to act as arbitrator between the British and Americans to stop a near war between the two countries. The dispute arose over the location of the international boundary which the English claimed should be through Rosario Strait, to the east of the San Juan Islands, and the United States claimed should be through Haro Strait, to the west of the 172-island archipelago. Fortunately the near war was settled by Wilhelm and the boundary established through Haro Strait about 1890, when the present State of Washington was a part of the Oregon Territory.

Geographically there is little similarity between Atlantic and Pacific coasts, even on identical lines of latitude. On the western shorelines of Mexico, California, Oregon and Washington, nature has given us few natural harbors, clusters of protective islands or miles of inland waterways. The half-century lead in the development of East Coast waterways and harbors will never be equalled on the West Coast, due to the very nature of the coastline—notwithstanding the scores of man-made harbors that have recently been built or are scheduled for development.

Conversely, the Pacific shores have some startling advantages for the offshore sailor: uniformly deep waters, insect-free climates, absence of hurricane weather, except for a few months in the southernmost waters, the warm flow of the Japanese current which keeps harbors ice-free the year around as far north as Skagway, Alaska, and many delightful harbors unspoiled by tourism and its attending noise and confusion.

To those who have read some of the published reports of specific pleasure cruises along Pacific waters, and in so doing have decided "that's too rigorous, too hard-chancing for me"—let's first consider these factors: 1) did the author choose the most favorable time of year for his sail or cruise? 2) was he a seasoned navigator on a well-founded vessel, and was the boat of a proper type for the waters he plied? 3) did he visit a foreign country with prejudices stacked high on his shoulders? 4) did he overcrowd his boat with guests who were unacquainted with the sea?

The fable of the three blind men feeling diverse parts of an elephant who were asked to describe "what is an elephant like?" is perhaps analogous to a writer who, through ignorance or misinformation, is guilty of portraying an untrue picture of a visited land or body of water.

It is with this thought of writing informatively and objectively (after having "felt all of the elephant and having seen it visually") that we have prepared this book. We have purposely plotted our course from southeast to northwest because, with the exception of the Gulf side of Baja California's peninsula, this heading presents the more difficult run from a weather and sea condition standpoint. Shelter must be taken more often on a northwest run up-coast from prevailing winds and ocean currents. This heading will also take one into many harbors which otherwise he might delete from his itinerary when cruising down the coast with weather and seas behind him.

At the end of each of the three Parts of this book is a section covering: fuel, water and supplies; harbor facilities; communications; distances; customs procedures for foreign ports, and other pertinent data.

Whether your boat is power or sail, large or small, with or without a crew—the harbors, the people at them, and the grandeur of the Pacific Coast will be the same. So join us now, if you will, on this 5000-mile cruise from Acapulco to the upper reaches of the Gulf of Baja California, back down and around the Cape of Baja California, and northwest up the coast to our ultimate destination of Skagway, Alaska.

Carolyn and Jack West
San Pedro, California
March 1974

Part One

MEXICO / BAJA CALIFORNIA

UNITED STATES

San Diego

Ensenada

BAJA CALIFORNIA

San Felipe

Tiburon I.

Puerto Kino

Cedros I.

Guaymas

MEXICO

Mulege

Ballenas Bay

Loreto

Topolobampo

Gulf of California

Magdalena Bay

La Paz

Mazatlan

PACIFIC
OCEAN

Cape San Lucas

Tres Marias

San Blas

Cape Corrientes

Puerto Vallarta

Manzanillo

N

Zihuatanejo

Acapulco

W   E

S

200 miles

There are many highly varied reasons for seeking vacation along the shore of Baja California and the west coast of Mexico's mainland. For those who cruise or sail just for the water-borne interval, or for the boat-handling involved in getting there (or anywhere) and back, it offers just that. For the ardent fisherman, these Mexican waters are renowned for their angling rewards. For those seeking sunshine and warm waters during northern latitudes' winter season, this, too, is an asset in Mexican cruising.

Until the early 1940's, a half dozen pleasure boats per year were perhaps the total number that cruised from the States down to the tropical waters of Acapulco. Now many hundreds annually cruise to the Gulf, and a large number continue down the mainland to more southern points.

To know something of the inhabitants of Mexico, their temperament, customs and ways of life, is a definite asset in a visit to their land. Their lives are of slower pace than ours and if this fact is not taken into consideration nothing but frustration develops. If you plan in advance that every negotiation made in Mexico will take perhaps twice the time it would at home, then you will be in accord with the tempo. Don't fret. This cannot be changed. Sit on a curb and study your Spanish dictionary while you wait. Or relax with a beer in a cantina. Try to emulate your host's relaxation.

In the smaller Mexican harbor settlements it is customary to take ashore some small gifts, such as candy for the children or fishhooks for the men, many of whom depend upon fishing for a major part of their diet. In larger ports it is also customary upon arrival to engage an agent to handle customs papers and to act as supplies purchaser, translator, procurer of transportation, and, in short, to be an over-all representative. Arrange the

**There are several unnamed coves between Puerto Vallarta and
Cape Corrientes where fresh-water streams feed into Banderas Bay.**

business details first, what is expected of him, for how long and
for how many pesos. When in agreement, proceed to enjoy your
stay in port.

It is advisable to exchange U.S. currency for Mexican money
in the amount you anticipate spending during your stay in
Mexico. For some years the rate of exchange has been 12.50
pesos for one American dollar. Travelers' checks are accepted at
most of the resort hotels and at banks in larger cities, but
cashing a personal check, if at all possible, often involves long
delays. Food and staples are, for the most part, less expensive
than in the U.S. Gasoline; diesel fuel and engine parts, where
obtainable, will cost more than Stateside counterparts.

Whether or not one plans to fish in Mexican waters, it is
advisable to buy a fishing license at the start of a trip. The cost
is slight and because most people cruise south expressly to fish,
Mexican officials expect this added revenue. For those
intending to hunt, both gun and hunting permits must also be
obtained.

Wearing apparel for this area is basically informal. Take what
you will for an average temperature of 75 to 85 degrees, and
warmer wear for the windy coolness of the Peninsula's ocean
side. In some areas shore-going often involves precarious steps,

Yelapa's cove is a mixture of the old and new. Dugout canoes
share its tropical anchorage with modern power and sail boats.

ladders, etc., to docks or sometimes damp surf landings in a
shore boat. Consequently most women find slacks or culottes
more functional than a skirt. Dresses may be either too tight for
a wide step or too full for windy weather. Only at resort hotels
or at some of the major cities of the Peninsula and Mexican
mainland will commercial laundries and dry cleaners be found.
Easy-care cottons or acrylics are, therefore, the most practical
clothing materials for these southern climes.

Proper equipment and supplies for the boat will depend, of
course, on its size, type and proposed itinerary. Specific
suggestions in this category, as well as what shoreside facilities
are available at various ports, appear in the appendix at the end
of Part 1.

Tidal ranges run high in the upper Gulf with a fluctuation of
20 to 30 feet at San Felipe Bay, diminishing gradually to about

Typical Gulf-island anchorage. This is situated at the northwestern
end of Angel de la Guarda Island.

14 feet at Willard Bay and six feet at Puerto Kino. As the Gulf
widens to the south, tide ranges return to normal for the
latitude. Although the upper Gulf may be cruised the year
around, the summer and fall months are extremely hot and
muggy with temperatures averaging well over 100 degrees—fine
for fishing, but debilitating to the fishermen. December to June
is the best time to cruise the Mexican mainland and Gulf waters,
with one's itinerary so scheduled that his boat is out of Mexican
waters by mid-June. (See Appendix for a tabulation of the
monthly frequencies and velocities of tropical storms and
hurricanes.)

Because this volume is written as a cruising guide, rather than
an historical account, no attempt will be made to tell why

The only breakwatered harbor in the Gulf is Santa Rosalia, from which millions of tons of copper ingots or ore have been shipped during the past 90 years. Smelter slag was used to build the breakwater, completed in 1910.

Mexico is as it is today. And, of course, many travelers are disinterested in such "whys." But for those who are, and who have studied even a small part of Mexico's early tumultuous days, it will be apparent everywhere that progress has been made through the years; often times in amazing proportions, in light of four centuries of plundering and decimations.

From a geographical aspect, the towering mountain ranges of the west coast mainland remain aloof and impassive, with the old volcano at Colima, perhaps, an exception. It smolders occasionally, showering small black cinders across its green lap of coco palm and banana trees. Northward of Banderas Bay, at Ensenada de Chacala, a Mexican family drives a little herd of cattle into a palapa enclosure. Pale petals of the orchid tree drift around them like lavender confetti. Some 50 miles offshore from San Blas, prisoners are peacefully at work, some with their families, on Maria Madre Island, site of the Mexican Federal penal institution. Overall, a welcome period of calmness prevails—whether in the southern portion of the mainland or in the upper reaches of the Gulf.

Since its discovery in 1532, the Peninsula of Baja California has stubbornly resisted both industry and extensive colonization. This is due principally to its relative isolation and

The *Dorado* noses up to the stern of *Monsoon II* to provide a trans-
fusion of fresh water—difficult to obtain when in the upper
reaches of the Gulf.

general lack of fresh water.

From the United States-Mexican border south some 500
miles, there are several fertile valleys which, through rainfall and
irrigation, are now producing fairly extensive crops. A similar
though smaller subtropical zone at the southern tip of the
Peninsula produces excellent fruits and vegetables raised both
for local and for export trade. But most of this 1,016-mile-long
stretch of mountain and desert land, varying from 40 to 200
miles in width, is an arid yet spectacular wilderness. From
10,000-foot, snow-covered mountain peaks to the palm-fringed
river of Mulege (Moo-la-hay) down to its sear desert areas of
cactus and elephant trees, the Peninsula's topography is ever
awesome in contrasts.

It is only within the past three years that portions of this
erstwhile wilderness have been tamed. For decades only a
dream—but now a reality—Highway Numero Uno (Highway No.
1) is completed; a north/south road bisecting the Peninsula
from Tijuana to Cabo San Lucas, Baja's southernmost extremity. On the mainland side of the Gulf there are, and have been

One shrimpboat crew does the work for three. A common custom
in the Gulf. Only the center boat is under power while the outboard crews catch up on sleep.

for some while, good highways from the States which skirt the
Gulf, facilitating the launching of trailed boats at such ports as
Puerto Kino, Guaymas, Mazatlan and Puerto Vallarta.

To those who have read about and expect to find a chain of
harbors, resorts and marinas on both sides of Baja California, a
word of caution. In 1965 the plans were first announced and
early construction assured. They were repeated again in 1969,
with elaborate ceremonies in La Paz to which a group of
yachtsmen from the States were invited as guests of Mexican
industrialists and Government officials. As yet none of these
developments have taken place. For the many who enjoy the
serenity of quiet coves or the challenge of long runs between
anchorages, it is probably well that this proposed commerciali-
zation of harbors has not progressed at the rate some arm-chair
yachtsmen would prefer.

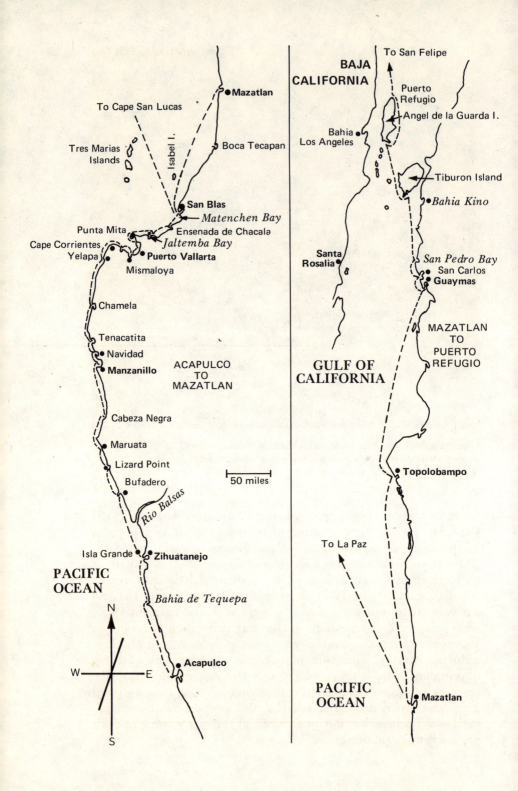

One cruises into Acapulco Bay, after many hours of viewing a nearly deserted shoreline, to an incredulous sight of contrast. One pink hotel rises mirage-like on a rocky pinnacle to overshadow another pastel-tinted giant structure. Blue jewels of swimming pools are splattered at random between mansion and castle, between jungle-green landscaping and more high-rise hotels. Power, sail and speed boats ply between the wide Bay's several anchorages and in and out of Acapulco's entrance channel.

On shore, at one hotel cantina, customers sit half-submerged on underwater bar stools. This wettest of bars affords sipping and swimming in aquatic ease. Airconditioning in all major hotels, homes and restaurants offers cool cocoons of respite from Acapulco's nearly year-round steaming heat. Even the "Ventilation Cut" due west of the city adds little to alleviate humidity. But there is no evidence of temperature deterring the growing numbers of spa-seekers wending their way south to Mexico's most popular seaside resort.

Despite the fact that Acapulco was discovered and subsequently occupied over four centuries ago, it is interesting to note that even a scant 34 years ago one sailor-writer noted*: "Acapulco...is an utterly dull town...no night life, no public amusements, no outdoor sports except a little boating. It could have good streets, but at present (1940) does not." The airplane of course is responsible for this mushroom growth of an erstwhile semi-neglected commercial port. Mexico City residents were the first in any numbers to make the quick trip by air to establish Acapulco's seaside resort as their own winter vacation retreat. Foreign visitors came later with money and plans to turn sleepy little Acapulco into a continental jet-set spa.

* *Forgotten Waters* by Randolph Leigh, now out of print.

Acapulco's landlocked harbor, looking northwest toward the
"Ventilation Cut", is the destination of the biennial San Diego
Yacht Club-sponsored sailing race. The Acapulco Yacht Club's
facilities are to the left of the boats at anchor.

Thus it is that famed Acapulco Yacht Club is actually a private club, with major ownership represented by Mexico City residents who consider it their personal playground. If a visiting boatowner is a member of a recognized U.S. or European yacht club, he may request a slip, plus use of this lavish facility, provided he is willing to pay the rather high fees involved.

There are, of course, other anchorage areas in Acapulco Bay, but no convenient means of reaching shore other than at the City Dock, or at a recently installed pier for securing a dinghy, some 200 yards north of the Yacht Club. The latter access is a guest landing constructed by a group of Acapulcanians who enjoy the company of visiting yachtsmen and who were concerned with the erstwhile paucity of guest facilities for those coming into Acapulco by sea. Informal conveniences offered here include a private beach area; a palapa-roofed entertainment center, with tables and chairs, where one may picnic, barbecue, play cards or simply rest in the shade on the bayfront. A shower and dressing room are also provided in an adjacent apartment

building. The fee for use of this facility is presently 50 pesos, or
$4. U.S. per week. For those wishing to spend some time in
Acapulco while living aboard their boat, it also offers a mailing
address, and a convenient access for the transfer of ship
supplies.

Many pleasure boats, traveling between Panama and the U.S.,
hasten their voyage by skipping small coastal coves and putting
in only at the major supply stops, such as Mazatlan and
Manzanillo. If time is that critical, so be it. However, such a
voyage precludes the enjoyment of visiting a host of delightful
coves and harbors along the Mexican mainland coast which we
have been fortunate in leisurely exploring. For the benefit of
those who may wish to do the same—or should need to seek
weather shelter along the coast between Acapulco and San
Blas—we'll recount a recent gunkholing cruise along this section.

It was early in March when we steamed out of Acapulco Bay.
Our destination for the day was a small bight about 70 miles
northwest called Bahia de Tequepa just north of the headland
of Morro de Papanoa. Along much of this coast, one may cruise
within a mile of shore; the better to watch an unending
procession of one vast coco palm grove blending with another;
thick green groves fronted with shining sea-swept sand, frosted
with breakers as far as eye can reach. Over all there was a
sweet-scented smoke in the air. Ashore, natives were burning off
their corn fields, and late afternoon offshore breezes carried the
smoke seaward. After a few seasons of corn crops the area's
poor soil is depleted and another swatch of wild vegetation
must be cleared and prepared for planting this staple product.
Corn is to Mexico what rice is to the Orient. Wheat cannot be
raised in any significant quantities in this climate. Nor is all of
this smoke veil caused by burning cornstalks. Sometimes
lightning sets underbrush and trees afire, and in some instances
marijuana growth is purposely burned in compliance with a
current Federal edict. But the smoke drifting out to sea was
pleasant—almost the sole reminder that one is actually
anywhere near civilization. The occasional settlements in the
area lie inland behind their coconut groves, usually near fresh
water lagoons, and completely hidden from our ocean-going
view.

Bahia de Tequepa is a small quiet anchorage, hugged on two
shore sides with palms and hardwood trees. Beside a huddle of
palapa-roofed houses a huge mound of turtle shells was

The Port Captain's office at Zihuatenejo has a commanding view
of the harbor through arched portals and palms that line the
beach.

burning. Turtle hunting was obviously one of the village's chief
industries, and pongas (dugout canoes) were in evidence all
about the Bay. We watched the crews depart the anchorage near
sundown, some with outboards on their ancient craft; others
skillfully wielding paddles. Some had inboard engines powering
larger dugouts, but steered with a sweep instead of a rudder.
Near the head of the Bay several new pongas were in the
building (or hewing-out) process. Each fashioned from a single
log, the ponga is the only safe and functional type of shoreboat
for Mexico's frequently heavy-surfed beaches.

The following morning we had a smooth 40-mile run up the
coast which took us past Bahia de Petetlan, then around Roca

A view from the top of one of Zihuatanejo's several hotels fringing
the bayfront. Here a funicular carries passengers up and down
from the hotel's beach to their rooms or to the open-air bar on the
roof.

Negra, a black rock islet that marks Zihuatanejo's entrance.
Moving into this idyllic sheltered harbor might well equal an
entrance to the storied Pearly Gates. Warm azure waters match
the sky. Above the circular bayfront climb evergreen mountains
where, toward afternoon, giant white cumulus boil up to
further frame this picture-postcard bay. We anchored near
Zihuatanejo's small-boat dock—a sturdy concrete structure, but
reserved for use by their local sport-fishing boats. Dinghies from
visiting craft are told to use the beach for shoregoing.

After siesta, between three and four in the afternoon,
open-air cantinas commence to churn music from jukebox,
Ashore we walked the hot sand beachfront to the Port
Captain's office, with our papers for his clearance. Along with
the school, his office is situated in one of Zihuatanejo's older
structures facing the sea. Many of the community's buildings
date back to the 1500's; only occasionally are they interspersed
with newer open-fronted stores and thatched-roofed hotels.
This is hamaca town. Hammocks are slung at convenient
intervals under huge branched shade trees, and are mostly
occupied with drowsing people seeking the sommulence of this
peaceful village.

After siesta, between three and four in the afternoon,
open-air cantinas commence to churn music from jukebox,

radio, or "live." Groups of laughing children troop back to school scattering dogs, chickens and pigs in their wake. Across the Bay to the south, another fine swimming beach, Playa de los Gatos, also comes to life with swimmers and snorkelers. Small boats dart in and out of its natural breakwatered beach. It was here during one afternoon's swim that we met a French-Canadian publisher and his son from Toronto. "When we left home two days ago," he told us, "it was 15 degrees below zero. When we flew into New York there was a 4 foot snowfall in the city. We thought we'd *never* get down here to thaw out!" The Canadians were counterparts of most of Zihautanejo's tourists, approximately a third of whom fly to Mexico City from the States to take a feeder line flight to this rapidly growing resort. Others, hotel owners tell us, come in their private planes or overland by car, and the remainder as we did by boat. Now when the deep-throated whistles of cruise ships announce their approach to Zihautanejo's beautiful harbor to disgorge hundreds of passengers who swarm through the village, it's time to leave with your own boat. The peace and quiet is shattered as though a bomb had been dropped.

It was only a ten-mile run from Zihautanejo up to Isla Grande's delightful anchorage. Although there is no settlement here, this well-protected cove is a popular haven for weekend pleasure boats. Our arrival came with Sunday and there were perhaps a dozen yachts or runabouts anchored near the island shore, many of whom had cruised up from Zihautanejo to picnic, fish, swim or water ski. Without a face-mask, one would miss the best part of a stopover at Isla Grande. Glass clear waters of nearly 90 degrees offer a spectacular view of exotic colored fish. As intricately marked as butterflies, these dainty denizens move past our facemasks in a never-ending parade. Striped, spotted, large and small, they swim kaleidoscopically before our little viewing window. The island itself is a birdland with nearly as many feathered varieties as we see in fins, while prone, afloat. During March, buds on the kapok tree are bursting white tufts of down, their branches mingling with the lavender orchid tree; and vivid as sunlight, the golden primavera adds its torchlike glow to lovely Isla Grande. Since our last visit to this island we have been told that sometimes it is "off limits" to visitors. It would be well to check with the Port Captain when getting clearance to leave Zihautanejo to see if this ruling is in force.

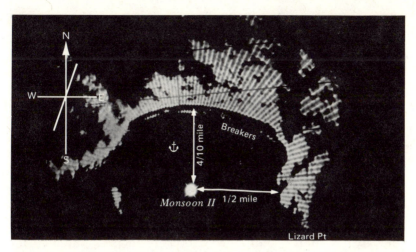

Ensenada de Pichilinquillo lies westward of Lizard Point, and provides good anchorage about 1/4 mile off the beach in five fathoms. Passage between the islet in the western portion of the bay and the mainland beach should not be attempted because there are numerous sunken rocks.

One of Mexico's longest and largest rivers, Rio Bolsas, empties into Bahia Petacalco at its northwestern extremity of Mangrove Point, 30 miles northwest of Isla Grande. An anchorage is eastward of this point but as there was no indication of shore access, we continued another three hours to inspect the cove protected by Bufadero Bluff. It was remarkable here to find a concrete pier and partial breakwater extending from the Bluff's southeasterly side. A lighthouse and small cluster of dwellings crowned the rocky point. "We tried to build a breakwater to give us a good boat anchorage," the natives told us, "but the sea would not let us." Indeed the sea cared little for man's puny attempts to divert its force. Surge near shore was such that only a ponga could negotiate the giant swells that heaved and sank under *Monsoon II's* keel. We backed down and made hasty retreat.

Twenty-five miles upcoast, Lizard Point anchorage proved to be calm and protected from prevailing northwesterlies. We dropped anchor in about four fathoms just northeast of an islet in the western part of the bay. Because this and other coves to be described later are charted as only miniscule indentations, we took pictures of our radarscope on the one- or four-mile range scale to illustrate best entrance and where we found good anchorage. Although we did not spend the night at anchor at the next two likely protections along this coastal area—Maruata and Cabeza Negra Bays—we did stay a few hours at each cove, again taking radar pictures of their anchorage aspects. And each stop, of course, gave us another chance to swim around the ship.

From Cabeza Negra, a 45-mile run brought us to Manzanillo and Santiago Bay. In past years we used to anchor directly in front of the Club de Yates which was situated only a few blocks from the center of town. Now, however, a new anchorage has been established in San Pedrito Lagoon, on the southeast of Manzanillo Bay. This was effected by cutting a canal through the long spit extending between the old anchorage area, and dredging a portion of the lagoon to depths suitable for commercial vessels to the south, and for a new yacht marina and clubhouse on the northly side. A launching ramp has also been built for trailed boats, near the new marina. Now, for the first time in Manzanillo's maritime history, both boats and ships can be better protected from tropical hurricanes which occur with regularity during the seasons of equinox.

Manzanillo has a population of about 26,000 people. Its aristocratic little city is steeped in the tradition of old Colonial days, in *dignidad;* cognizant of, yet not particularly catering to, the tourist. The feeling here is of its people's self-esteem and business preoccupation. Our guide drove us out to the perimeter of town where we saw fine modern schools and commercial buildings shoulder to shoulder with some of the older historic structures built in the 16th and 17th centuries. The compact business district was somewhat remindful of New Orleans, with iron grills or wooden fretwork decorating windows, balconies and doors. The marketplace was typical of most Mexican farm-mercados; a myriad of tiny stalls offered seasonal fruits, vegetables and native handiwork. We bought cantaloupes, tomatoes, mangos, fresh pineapple, papayas and eggs. And I finally had to buy a basket to hold my purchases together.

Before leaving Manzanillo Bay, we cruised across to Santiago Bay for a look around their "bay of wrecks" which we named the area reserved for dismantling obsolete tankers and freighters. With only the most primitive of tools and equipment, workmen were making slow inroads on cutting apart and moving piece by piece, serviceable parts of these old ships now

Typical grillwork seen in most of Manzanillo's private or public buildings speaks of early Colonial architecture.

destined for the scrapheap. In contrast to the dismantling of old ships on the north side of the bay are luxurious resort hotels and palatial homes on the eastern shore overlooking the entire harbor from a promontory.

One of the more popular excursions from Manzanillo is a trip out to the "Green Wave Beach", a half hour's drive south along the coast. This colorful giant wave rolls in regularly to an estimated height of 50 feet before thundering down on the beach. A spectacular sight for watching, but one not recommended for surfing.

From Manzanillo northwestward for many miles, the shoreline is interrupted with small river mouths, and both fresh and saltwater lagoons that run either parallel to or immediately inland from the coastal plane. *H.O. Sailing Directions No.153* only hints at the existance of these mangrove-shrouded waters, and charts seldom indicate their extent. All of this lends an air of exploratory excitement to one's initial discovery of these tropical indentures.

Along the highway outside Manzanillo, concrete sculptures of four
of Mexico's presidents are displayed; from left: Zapato, Juarez,
Morelos, and Hidalgo.

Bahia Navidad lies less than 20 miles northwestward of
Manzanillo. As we cruised into its cove to anchor we were a
little awed to see ahead on the beach a number of modern hotel
buildings with another under construction. Each contained a
possible hundred rooms behind a flat, austere facade. They
appeared to rear suddenly from the beach, fort-like, sternly
guarding La Barre Navidad. The anomoly was relieved only by
the more picturesque palapa-roofed dwellings huddled at each
extremity of this crescent white-sand beach. "This is the new
winter resort," we were told, "built primarily for those in
Mexico City who are trying to escape the overcrowded
conditions in Acapulco. It's very chic to winter here." Perhaps
so, we thought, as we toured the bayside in our tender, but
what a pity the architects had deviated so widely from
tradition.

We turned our backs on Navidad's new spa and pointed our
dinghy toward the southeastern end of the bay and the entrance
to a large lagoon. Fortunately for us, the tide was high, enabling
us use of our outboard through the winding shoals. Around a
bend in the channel we suddenly came upon what appeared to
be a wide lake. Fishermen were casting nets from their pongas,
villagers were paddling their ancient canoes to and fro from one
dwelling to another. Their weathered, water-fronting houses
could not possibly have been less than 400 years old. Across
from what appeared to be the remains of an ancient stone

A small channel from Navidad's bay leads into a lake-like lagoon where we step back in history many hundreds of years. Hand-hewn dugouts and thatch-roofed homes of the fishermen are in sharp contrast to the massive luxury hotels only a mile or so to the north.

breakwater, another arm of this wide lagoon extended several miles along a heavily wooded shore. Little ranchos and farm plots were partially discernible through the lush undergrowth. We stopped at one tiny boat landing where a native farmer was chopping wood. He had lived here 40 years, he told us, and wouldn't we like to come ashore to look around? A brown naked baby eyed us solemnly. Dogs, chickens, pigs, and goats started at us. Only the man smiled and bade us welcome. We stepped ashore—stepped back into long-lost chapters of history. At once I felt as strangely out of place as that cluster of so-called modern hotels back at Navidad's beachfront. We simply had no link with this man's timeless past.

Much later we retraced our outboard route to the Bay. Wind was up and tide nearly out. We just barely managed to get through a shoaling passage, then a rising surf, and finally into safe deep waters of the anchorage at Bahia La Barre Navidad.

Bahia Tenacatita, lying about ten miles to the northwest, is larger than Navidad. Its shore scene is once again one of dense palm groves, indigenous hardwood trees, stretches of corn and sugarcane; all lending a verdant background to beach and breakers. We tried out our rubber liferaft here for shoregoing, hoping that perhaps we could negotiate the surfline without having to resort to a native's ponga. We finally made the beach in an upright position, but we might just as well have body-surfed to shore. We were just as wet as if we had.

But we had a drier passage later when we took our dinghy back into Tenacatita's narrow, winding lagoon. The entrance lies half-hidden in the extreme northwestern end of the Bay, negotiable only at high tide. From an ample opening the crooked labyrinth often narrows to only four or five feet across. Mangrove trees reached high to arch across our water path which eventually turned into a virtual tunnel. Blue cranes, wood ibis and pure white herons nested and fed. We turned off our motor and rowed slowly, savoring the peace and stillness that pressed warmly about us. After an hour's slow passage we reached a cul-de-sac, the end of the line unless one had a machete to hack away the mass of entangling branches. Before retracing our way, we paused a while to eat our sandwiches and drink cold beer, listening meanwhile to a far away thundering surf, off to the west where lagoon meets the sea.

Our next port-of-call after Tenacatita, an approximate 20-mile span, was Bahia Chamela where a choice of anchorages offer shelter from various wind directions. U.S. Navy Hydrographic Chart No. 938 is particularly helpful in this bay. We stopped briefly just inside the Bay's southern point where the remnants of its 60-year old, and once thriving commercial port still stand. Ashore a few houses and a disintegrating dock are the sole reminders of better days. We found good protection may also be had in the lee of Isla Colorado, a small bird and cactus covered island in the center of Bahia Chamela. The most popular area, however, appeared to be at the Bay's northwestern extremity. This was attested to by several large shrimp boats that came into harbor each morning to anchor and to sort their previous night's catch.

It was from our anchorage at this end of Bahia Chamela that we set forth in the dinghy for a tour of nearby El Pulpito and La Perula, its tiny shingle beach. This north-bay indenture is not shown on charts nor mentioned in *Sailing Directions*. We learned the names from natives who live here. On shore, a man was cooking quantities of shrimp in 50-gallon drums, then spreading them on screens to dry in the sun. Just as we neared shore, a man came running down to meet us. "Come in," he called in English, "Welcome to La Perula. We are your friends. We will not harm you. You are among friends." As it had never occured to us that any of these people would be *other* than friendly, his reiteration seemed puzzling and amusing. Particularly so when we saw a second man running behind him, carrying a two-foot-long machete! The inconsistency was later cleared up during our visit with these and other natives at their little hillside casa. "Only lawbreakers used to live here. *Muy malo,* very bad here for many years. Now we are all good citizens. But we have a problem."

Our host Rafael Cedano had, it seemed, taken on a gigantic project: "We have no schools in or near Chamela," he told us. "Without schools there is no hope for Mexico". He talked at length of their plight and of his hopes that North American yachtsmen might be able to help them in their cause. Inspired by this conversation, we later started a campaign through newspapers and friends in California, and raised a school fund for Chamela that enabled a school for some 45 pupils to be opened the following year. Native landowners were pursuaded to donate some of their properties for school use at La Fortuna, and others set to work on the building's construction. Once such a facility is erected, the Mexican Government furnishes teachers as needed. Now, only a few years later, La Fortuna's school has 60 students—full capacity—and two additional schoolhouses have been built in the Chemela area with 40 to 50 children in attendance.

Rafael wanted to give us something to further impress upon us that they were friendly. We demurred. Our ship was well provisioned. He insisted. "Well, perhaps a couple of coconuts," we finally suggested. Rafael beamed. "Come for me on the beach this afternoon. I have no shoreboat."

What happened later was "Tipico". At four o'clock a whistle from the beach alerted us to the sight of a small parade with Rafael in the lead. A horse with elaborate trappings followed. The horse in turn led a burro carrying two hundred-pound sacks of coconuts on his back, while a native helper brought up the rear. Jack took one look at the surf, our low-freeboard dinghy, and the tremendous load of coconuts. He groaned. The tender swamped, of course, going ashore, and swamped again coming out through the surf with its load. But they finally made it back to our ship, a wet half-hour later. (I'll never mention coconuts again.)

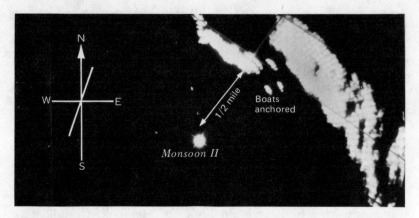

About 12 miles southeast of Cape Corrientes is Ypala anchorage
which is protected from all but southerly and southeasterly winds.
The extent of it is barely indicated on charts, but it is used by the
fishermen and U.S. owned boats who know of it. What appears as
an island due north of *Monsoon II* are hills with a valley separating
them from the mainland to the east.

Ypala is the last anchorage beyond Chamela before reaching
Cape Corrientes, the southern extremity of Banderas Bay. We
found its small cove filled to near capacity when we went in to
anchor. Besides our friends and recent cruising companions, the
Gould Eddys on *Y Como,* there were a dozen native fishing
boats and small (20- to 30-foot) coastal freighters. These carry
passengers and light cargo between Banderas Bay and an
assortment of remote villages situated along the coast to the
southeast. Ypala's anchorage hummed with activity. Aboard
their boats, natives were cooking dinner on charcoal braziers;
some were singing, others shouting greetings to crews of other
boats nearby. Ashore, men were working feverishly, cleaning
shrimp and packing it in baskets for delivery by ponga to other
boats at anchor. Later the big shrimp boats came in. With a
rattle of anchor chains and the bang of winches used to raise or
lower their net booms, their crews were celebrating the end of
another workday and adding to the general din. Due to the
usual water turbulence around Cape Corrientes, the protection
found at Ypala was obviously a welcome respite for all traveling
in the area. Although this noisy activity lasted most of the
night, we awoke the following morning to a nearly empty
harbor. Only *Y Como* and *Monsoon II* were left in Bahia Ypala.

The tropical beauty of Banderas Bay and its more popular communities of Puerto Vallarta, Mismaloya and Yelapa make this area a favorite stopping point for those cruising up or down the coast. Although few other places along the Mexican shoreline can equal the beauty of the apex and southern arm of Banderas Bay, these anchorages have been poor because of tremendous depths, with only occasional near-shore shelves, which necessitate bow and stern anchoring. Recently, however,

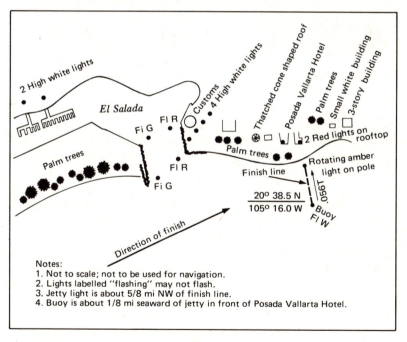

Notes:
1. Not to scale; not to be used for navigation.
2. Lights labelled "flashing" may not flash.
3. Jetty light is about 5/8 mi NW of finish line.
4. Buoy is about 1/8 mi seaward of jetty in front of Posada Vallarta Hotel.

A sketch of Puerto Vallarta's new *Terminal Maritima,* **used by contestants in the Del Rey Yacht Club—sponsored 1973 sailing race. This is a biennial event of growing interest. The Port Captain's office is in the modern circular building adjacent to the main pier.**

View from Port Captain's office in the terminal building, looking
northwesterly, across the new marina at Puerto Vallarta.

the Mexican Federal Government has completed a breakwater
across the entrance to Estero de Tomates at Puerto Vallarta,
and a protected harbor with slips and a safe anchorage area is, at
this writing, nearing completion. Fuel and water are readily
available, and access is easy to nearby hotels. The Port Captain's
office is in the terminal building, where arrival and departure
papers must be cleared.

Those unable to get a slip or stern-to-bulkhead space at the
new Terminal Maritima facilities can anchor on a 4- to 6-fathom
sand shelf that is a half-mile south of the Rio Cuate. A sounder
or lead-line is helpful to find the extent of the shelf and to
avoid anchoring on the edges of it which fall off to considerable
depths. Eastward and on the north bank of Rio Cuate is the
aptly named *Gringo Gulch*, with scores of homes mainly
occupied by state-side people. This river divides the business
section of Puerto Vallarta from the new residential and resort
developments further south of the river mouth. A small pier at
the north end of the beach in front of the resorts has been used

Our stern anchor is towed ashore in a hand-hewn log canoe by
obliging fishermen at Yelapa.

by tenders from cruise ships that seasonally disembark hundreds
of tourists to swarm through Puerto Vallarta. On our last visit
there, use of the pier as a dinghy-dock was prohibited.

Usually a stern anchor is necessary at this anchorage to keep
headed into the normal ground swell coming from the northwest. Almost without exception the services of native "ban-
dito" ponga-operators are needed for shore-going because of the
considerable wave action on the beach which is more than most
dinghies can survive.

Midway along Banderas Bay's southern arc, Yelapa still
dreams in its green-gold Eden, very much the same as it did 25
years ago. Its foreign habitués hope it will remain untouched,
and they plead with journalists not to write about it for fear
that zealous developers will wreck Yelapa's beauty, as has
happened at Puerto Vallarta, and to a lesser degree at
Mismaloya. With construction of major highways completed,
extending toward Manzanillo, and Guadalajara to Banderas Bay,
along with a new jet airport nearby, there is little likelihood of

Yelapa is perhaps the most tropical setting in all of Banderas Bay.
Bananas and other fruits are sent out by small boats to neighboring communities. On the far beach is a resort patronized by
gringos from the States and a thatch-roofed restaurant open to
visiting yachtsmen.

Yelapa's present semi-isolation being perpetuated.

The cove waters in both Mismaloya and Yelapa are deep to
within a hundred yards of the beaches. Even with bow and stern
anchors down, boats occasionally drift off the shelves and drag
around these picturesque coves. Normal daytime winds are
onshore and reverse their direction at night. For this reason we
have found more secure anchorages on the northwestern rim of
Banderas Bay. Scenery on this side is not as exotic as on the
south, but this is not always a paramount issue. Two north-bay
anchorages of particular note are La Cruz de Juanacosta, which
lies a mile or two northeast of Piedra Blanca, and the cove
formed by the northwestern protection of Punta Mita. At La
Cruz (as abbreviated by natives) there's a small group of palapa
thatched houses ashore near a lime kiln and, if winds are light
and little surf is running, one might have luck taking his dinghy
ashore. At least we did, with only minimal splash aboard.

For those cruising or sailing northwestward to a southern

point on the Baja California Peninsula, a direct heading can be
taken from Punta Mita past the Tres Marias Islands. Unfortunately the many fine coves on these islands are "off limits",
since the Mexican Government prohibits anchoring in them
because of the penal colony on one of the Islands. This is a
shorter approach to the Peninsula, but it by-passes what we
consider the most interesting 50 miles of this coastal span of
Banderas Bay to San Blas.

From Punta Mita we hugged the shoreline—a densely green
and heavily wooded terrain that sweeps up to the 3000-foot
peaks of the Sierra Vallejo Range. Evidence of abundant rainfall
and fresh-water streams and rivers dominate the landscape mile
after green mile. Groups of palapa huts, occasionally cattle or a
horse and rider wending their ways along the beach, appear with
regularity.

It was in this area that we were letting nothing ashore escape
our view. Before our start of this particular cruise, a friend who
had once been with the commercial fishing fleet told us of his
favorite cove "somewhere near Punta Raza." "I found it 20
years ago," he said. "There's an island in the center of the
anchorage, covered with palms, bananas and birds, and the
south end is protected enough for dinghy landings. I've
forgotten the cove's name, but I've dreamed of it ever since and
asked many cruising friends to stop there, but not one of them
has ever reported finding it." With such an intriguing description, we were determined not to miss it.

Within three hours from the northern tip of Banderas Bay we
had Punta Raza in view, and shortly thereafter rounded the
headland into Jaltemba Bay. Our issue of *Sailing Directions*
advised there was an 8-foot-high island lying about 2 miles
northeastward of Punta Raza, and 3/4 of a mile from shore. So
it was a definite surprise to find a large islet of at least 150 feet
in height right where the 8-footer was stated to be. But all other
notes coincided with those of our fisherman friend. We knew
we had at last found his favorite anchorage.

Our cruising companions, the Eddys on *Y Como*, were
already dropping their anchor when we brought *Monsoon II*
into Jaltemba Bay. After we had our hook secure, we joined
them aboard for lunch. "My copy of *Sailing Directions* calls this
island 80 feet high," Gould told us, "and I've already found out
from a native that it's called "Isla Penita de Jaltemba." We
wished for a surveyor's transit to find out the island's exact

At the rincon in one corner of Jaltemba Bay, natives prepare for an Easter-time Fiesta.

height, but all agreed it was certainly more than 8 or 80 feet from sea level to its green thatched top.

A fair-sized village lay on the Bay's southeastern shore, and Jaltemba's *rincon* (cozy corner) was a fine curve of beach to the south. There was a flurry of activity on the rincon. Little booths were being set up and covered with palm fronds. Outboards and runabouts were being launched from their trailers. Over all, music blared from a central pavilion. We took our dinghy ashore to watch their preparations for what turned out to be pre-Easter-week celebrations. Natives were trooping in from various outlying communities—all bringing additions to the fiesta, from watermelons to outboards, to baseballs. Meanwhile, the Eddys had taken their Boston Whaler over to the village shore and later reported they had been completely swamped in the surf. (As noted previously, the native ponga is the only way to go for a dry run ashore.) Waters surrounding Isla Penita proved to be a diver's or snorkler's dream. Colored coral crags and sea vegetation provided an ideal warm-water home for a variety of fish and crustaceans, and the islet itself, another birds home.

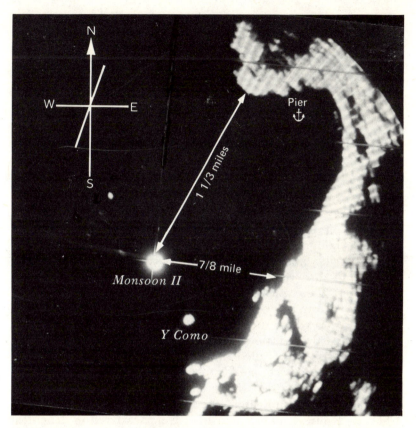

N
W — E
S
1 1/3 miles
Pier ⚓
7/8 mile
Monsoon II
Y Como

Ensenada de Chacala is an excellent anchorage, protected from all
but southwesterly winds. It is regularly used by the Mexicans but
seldom visited by state-side boats.

Our barometer was dropping that afternoon and a high, thin
overcast tempered the sun. "Do you expect a storm? Is this
normal weather for Jaltemba?" I asked a native. "Es el tiempo
de la luna" (it's the time of the moon), he answered me firmly.
We had heard that answer before, we reflected. Always it
seemed to satisfy those who spoke it. There was the moon each
night. It grew large and full, and weather performed in a certain
pattern. La luna shrunk to a thin crescent, and another weather
sequence followed. One could blame something or anything on
the moon. It was gratifying to have something visible to blame
or thank.

It was only an hour's cruise from Jaltemba northwest to

another tropical anchorage called Ensenada de Chacala. One of the most unusual sights in this area was tall stands of hardwood trees that forest the mountain slopes. Elsewhere so much of Mexico's timber has been depleted, felled through the centuries with no re-forestry program to renew this much needed product. There were even more trees shading the shores at Ensenada de Chacala where we found, in the bay's northwest corner, a modern concrete dock. Surrounding the dock along with a few wooden pongas were several 25-foot fiberglass double-enders, constructed along identical lines to the ancient dugout pongas. Some of the fiberglass boats were inboard and some outboard powered. We had not seen this new concept before and were much impressed with their manufacturer's foresight in constructing this lighter weight version of the indispensible ponga.

We hiked ashore that afternoon, past Chacala's little native village, up to a vantage point on a hill where we could look down on their pleasant harbor. Flowers, fruit trees and vegetation grew in prodigious profusion. The *amapa* or orchid tree was everywhere showering its pale petals down to hide the brick-red earth. A little boy shyly offered me a fruit I had not seen before. "It's called *anona*," he told me. This is the custard-apple, a sweet soft fruit with the consistency of a ripe fig. There were other fruits and vegetables at every hand. Whether wild or cultivated, there was no order to anything at Chacala. Houses, animals and trees were scattered in delightful abandon. We stopped to rest on a boulder that overlooked the Bay. A large goat wandered by to inspect my camera, then commenced rubbing her head on Jack's shoulder. He thought the goat was just being friendly. But later, to his itching sorrow, he realized she had been merely using him to scratch her flea-ridden head.

The Chila River empties into the ocean from a point about two miles northward of Chacala. All along the coast there were more clusters of palapa huts surrounded by the inevitable coco plantation and produce plot. Each tiny indentation had its own ponga launching beach where in calm weather a fisherman might put out to sea.

Only after we were nearing the wide entrance to Matenchen Bay, which lies immediately southward of San Blas, did the lush shoreside fertility dwindle to bald flat plains. At this time a northwest wind was increasing to a fresh 25 knots; our

Ensenada de Chacala is well-protected from prevailing northwest winds and affords good anchorage in 3 to 5 fathoms. It is one of the few anchorages where a small stone pier provides easy access to shore.

barometer was dropping noticeably and clouds were gathering over inland mountains. At sunset we dropped anchor in the northern end of shallow Matenchen Bay, glad to find protection behind the low-lying hills of Camaron Point.

Our original plan was to spend a day or two here in the vicinity of San Blas to see the remains of that historic town and its surrounding countryside. But now we felt indecisive. We were traveling alone at the time, on a schedule to meet a guest-couple a few days later at La Paz, a 360-mile run across the open Gulf. Whether by premonition or hunch, we decided to forego a local sightseeing expedition and depart Matenchen early next morning. When we weighed anchor at daybreak, thunder was rumbling and lightning crackling over 2300-foot Cerro San Juan. Our outbound course passed Isabel Island, a lonely rocky outpost 17 miles offshore and 40 miles northwest of Matenchen Bay. We noticed one seme-protected anchorage on the Island's southeastern side, but slowed only long enough to take pictures of its strange gargoyle-like north abutement. It was the last land we would see for the next 220 miles.

Rain poured a deluge the rest of the day, but winds on our stern afforded an easy ride. After leaving the Island we were alone on an empty waste of water. Neither bird nor fish nor boat was in sight at any time. We alternated watches through the rain-swept day and night; a night of heavenly fireworks—lightning, thunder and more rain. Once in the early predawn hours the moon burst up from a jet black mound of cloud ahead, startling us for a moment into thinking the cloud was land. The sight was so compelling we even turned on radar to prove the wildness of our imaginations.

Dawn brought back the sunshine and when we talked on radio with our *Y Como* friends on our 9 a.m. schedule, Gould reported that they had both bow anchors out in Matenchen Bay, along with every inch of chain. "Winds blew up to 45 knots last night," he told us. "You were lucky to have left this wild place. How did you know we were going to have this storm?"

Jack laughed. He stretched lazily in the sun-warmed pilot-house. "Well, I'll tell you, Gould; as the natives say, it was just 'el tiempo de la luna'." Which was, of course, only another way of saying we'd been lucky in our hunch.

To return to the mainland—for those who plan to go ashore at San Blas, it may be well to point out that Matenchen Bay is the only recommended anchorage. A native shore boat might be hailed here, or one could take his own dinghy to shore if surge is not too severe. Through the years, the old commercial harbor of San Blas has filled with sand, resulting in a dangerous bar across the original access. Gnats and mosquitos thrive here, too, most of the year due to the proximity of extensive lagoons and marshlands.

From Punta Camarones at Matenchen Bay, there is occasional bus or local taxi service into the community of San Blas, an approximate ten-mile drive. Although marine fuel is often scarce, most other supplies, such as pure water, food, and some engine parts, are available in this 5 to 6000 population village; however, such supplies would have to be lightered to the boat at anchor. The most noted excursion for San Blas visitors is a cruise by native boat up their jungle-shrouded river where herons, parrots and alligators share the lush tropical foliage, and snook, oysters and fresh-water shrimp inhabit the winding river. There are several good hotels and restaurants in town, all presided over by helpful and hospitable natives. Another interest here might be a hike around the crumbling ruins of Government buildings, a roofless church, and a few rusting cannon—all of which date back to the 1780's when San Blas was an important Mexican port.

For boats with itineraries leading from Matenchen Bay across to the Baja Peninsula, the crossing will angle into prevailing swells, affording a far more comfortable cruise to the Cape area or La Paz, than if one used Mazatlan as a departure point. A crossing from Mazatlan is usually in the trough and can be rather uncomfortable for a power boat. If one is heading up coast from the San Blas area along the mainland to Mazatlan, Isabel Island northwest of Matenchen Bay offers a better rest stop anchorage than anything along this flat, unindented shoreline. Perhaps it would be best to say that Isabel Island has the *only* anchorages between San Blas and Mazatlan, unless one has a very shallow-draft boat and the courage to attempt a bar crossing into Boca Tecapan.

As far as we know, there are few except local fishermen who take their boats into the shallow anchorages or inlets along the Mexican mainland between San Blas and Guaymas. With the exception of Mazatlan harbor, there is virtually nothing of interest in any of these small river mouth settlements, even if they did have safe accesses. The author-photographer team,

Looking northerly across the breakwatered harbor of Mazatlan.
Creston Island, lower center, forms the western side of the harbor,
atop which is one of the most powerful lighthouses in Mexico.

Anchorage for small craft is to the northwest of the breakwater
extending from Creston Island.

Spencer Murray and Ralph Poole, did cover this region several years ago in a 21-foot inboard/outboard cruiser, and subsequently brought forth their book *Powerboating the West Coast of Mexico**. It is an interesting and vivid account of their experiences, but not one to entice the prudent boat owner to follow suit.

Approaching Mazatlan, the 515-foot-high Creston Island on the north side of the breakwatered entrance is visible for many miles. At night, the lighthouse atop it can be seen for 25 to 30 miles in clear weather, and day or night the radiobeacon at the airport can be helpful. It is identified as MZT and is supposed to transmit on a frequency of 285 kHz (tho' most recently we have received it on 308 kHz). This beacon is situated about 4 miles north of the Creston Island lighthouse. Mazatlan is the most important harbor on the west coast of Mexico, with the Southern Pacific railroad serving it, as well as two jet-airports, highways, ferry service to La Paz, docks for ocean-going freighters and tour-ships, and a well-protected small boat harbor.

The entrance channel to Mazatlan is well-marked on charts, although the small boat harbor is not shown on detail chart No. 1024, last revised in 1965. This facility lies to port just inside the breakwater spurs of Creston and Chivos Islands. It is more than adequate for large numbers of visiting craft besides the fleets of sportfishing boats and others that are permanently based at Mazatlan. The Los Angeles Yacht Club-sponsored sailboat race, run every other year, turns this harbor into a festive area, with upward of a half-hundred yachts participating. As with other major ports, Mazatlan is a port-of-entry requiring customs' clearance on arrival and before departure. While it can be done by the boat owner, it is generally easier to have a broker, such as Bill Heimpel, handle the paper work. He also can make arrangements for fuel, fresh water or hotel reservations, if needed. Heimpel operates the Star Sportfishing Fleet, and those using his broker services may, for a small fee, rent one of his mooring buoys in the harbor and avail themselves of his well-maintained dinghy dock.

Besides being an industrial port, Mazatlan is also popular for vacationing and sportfishing. The city, now approaching 140,000 population, lies to the north of the small boat

* Out of print.

anchorage. It has many good restaurants, hotels and entertainment. Fresh produce and other galley supplies are readily available, and the market near the center of the city is typical of Mexican markets where virtually everything from sarapis to tequila can be obtained while grocery shopping. For those heading on northwest to Guaymas, or across the Gulf to the Peninsula, this is the logical "last chance" supply stop for fuel, food and boat gear.

There is a large fleet of shrimpers based here, with the result that the port has a number of well-equipped shipyards, with ways that can handle up to 1000 tons; machine shops able to effect engine repairs; electronic service facilities, and marine supply stores well-stocked with basic lines of equipment.

Heading northwest toward the upper reaches of the Gulf, Topolobampo might be considered as another opportunity for shoregoing. It is about 212 miles above Mazatlan, with only a few lagoon entrances used by native fishermen in the intervening distance. None are recommended by ourselves or by *Sailing Directions*. In fact, *Sailing Directions* devotes a full page and a half of alerts and cautions to those entering Topolobampo's harbor through a number of miles of tricky and shifting channels. Some dredging has been done in the channel, mainly of benefit to the cross-gulf ferry that runs between Topolobampo and La Paz. Most boatmen prefer visiting this port and neighboring Los Mochis by means of the ferry, with their boat safely anchored in La Paz—letting the ferry's experienced crew do the work.

Moving northwest toward Guaymas, there will be little to see ashore for nearly 190 miles. As is pointed out in *Sailing Directions*, the coastal waters of Sonora, Sinaloa and much of Mayarit States are shallow, with depths of less than ten feet recorded, in some areas, even five miles out to sea. This is particularly true off the several river mouths where silt accumulates through the years, forming ever-changing sand bars and shoals. From Lobos Island, approximately 35 miles south of Guaymas, shoreside desert flatlands give way once more to a steadily rising mountainous terrain. Cape Haro marks the entrance to Guaymas Bay. Its great rocky bulk offers protection from northerly winds to the half dozen small coves lying to its northeast, before actually entering the harbor of Guaymas. For pleasure craft crews with only occasional duties or errands in Guaymas, any of these small bights, such as Catalina, Pitahaya

Guaymas Harbor offers easy access by dinghy to their commercial city center.

or Paz, are favored anchorages for overnight or extended stays. The commercial harbor is convenient for a small-boat, city-side landing at the stone bulkhead south of the Cathedral, but one should keep continuous watch of his depth sounder while selecting his anchorage. We have found certain spots that shoal to 7 feet.

Guaymas is the Gulf's largest port, but the extent of its commercial activities is so spread around the perimeter of its bayshore, that the overall aspect is more that of a quaint yet semi-modern town. New buildings intersperse the ancient; a huge Super Mercado offers everything from food and clothing to hardware and farm machinery. On curving narrow side streets, native goods are piled high in narrow stalls, and at harvest time there will always be a wagon or two, double-parked and piled high with melons and oranges, fragrant with ripeness.

Near the Muelle Fiscall (municipal dock) is the office of John Davidson, Broker. For many years he was known as "the yachtsman's best friend." He has now passed away, but his staff will serve the visiting boatmen. They will handle clearance papers in and out of Guaymas, order fuel, water and, if the boatowner wishes, collect his mail—all for a nominal fee.

Two miles southerly from the Guaymas waterfront is Las

Across the harbor from Las Playitas is an ancient and abandoned
jail. The area is now used by natives for repairing their fishing boats.

Playitas. Although there are insects at times around this
anchorage, it is still a popular harbor for cruising visitors to the
Guaymas area. There is good holding here in clean water, a dock
for dinghies, a restaurant and bar ashore which is a part of a
modest motel-resort, and taxi service is available within a
hundred yards of their well-maintained dock.

Another favored anchorage in the general area is San Carlos
Bay, approximately 16 miles northwest of Guaymas. This Bay is
completely sheltered from Gulf seas, and although strong winds
will whip across the surrounding hills, it is normally calm in the
Bay. An inner bay with an opening to it of only 150 yards or
so, has in it a marina that would do justice to any in the States.
Gasoline and diesel fuels are available from hoses, along with
water. Unfortunately the inner bay is shallow, and boats
drawing more than 5 feet should not use it. The facilities
include a launching ramp, well-patronized by Stateside trailed-
boat owners. Ashore there are excellent motels, a market
and the Club de Nautica Guaymas which serves excellent meals.

A small portion of the San Carlos Marina, situated some 15 miles
northwesterly of Guaymas. This is the only true marina in all of
the Sea of Cortez.

Heading northwest about 13 miles from San Carlos Bay the
next coastal anchorage is San Pedro Bay, just south of San
Pedro Point. When we were here recently, we met a group of
native fishermen who had brought their boats ashore to make
camp until fish-biting time in the evening. They told us there
was fresh water a short way inland, and many deer in the area.
The fishermen said they also fished around San Pedro Nolasco
Island, lying 8 miles offshore, but seemed unenthusiastic about

its only anchorage at the Island's southern end.

As is indicated both in *Sailing Directions* and on the charts of this section of the mainland coast, there is no safe anchorage beyond San Pedro Bay until in the lee of Tiburon Island, 70 miles to the northwest. A course laid from San Pedro Point to the southern end of Tiburon Island will clear a shoaling area that extends some five miles off Point Baja. Less than three fathoms of water were shown on our depth recorder when we passed 5½ miles off this Point, indicating that each year the shoal extends further seaward than is indicated on the chart. The Point is not easy to distinguish because of its low elevation, so extreme caution is necessary when approaching it.

Once past the Point, a course can be laid to Isla Pelicano in the center of Kino Bay, if that area is the destination. The entire Bay is shallow and offers little of interest except for the trailed-boat owner who brings his boat from the States and uses the launching ramps at either Kino or New Kino. Not infrequently the surf precludes launching, and days may pass before a lull occurs in the winds blowing into the Bay. The town was named for Father Kino, an Austrian Jesuit, who was one of the best astronomers and mathmaticians of his time. He was also an expert geographer and cartographer. Much of his chart work is as exact today as when he first mapped this area in 1697. In view of his outstanding work it seems pitiable that his name was not attached to a more important geographical area.

Tiburon Island, lying nearly 20 miles to the west of Kino Bay, is too far distant to give it protection, but under its eastern shores there are a number of satisfactory anchorages. Separating Tiburon Island and the mainland is a narrow channel which is aptly named—Canal del Infernillo—(Broadly meaning "no good.") With the ebb and flood of the tides—as much as 10 feet in this region—currents can reach 6 to 8 knots, creating whirlpools and overfalls in the northern part of the Canal. Except for small well-powered boats, it is prudent to go around the south and western sides of Tiburon Island. For many years the Island was inhabited by the Seri Indians, reportedly cannibals, but the Mexican Government has moved their dwindling tribe to the mainland where they now are living a more civilized existence.

Our most vivid memory of Tiburon was on a late afternoon while anchored in the cove just east of Monument Point, at its southern end, watching a spectacle of blue-footed booby birds diving for fish. They gathered in large groups at an elevation of 50 to 60 feet over the Gulf, hovering as long as 10 minutes, then at an apparent signal from their leader, folded their wings back, stuck out their necks, and dive-bombed straight into the water. The booby is reported to plunge 6 feet below the water's surface. Those fortunate enough to get a fish would then be pounced upon by the less fortunate; a splashing noisy struggle would then ensue until they all arose again, a great cloud of birds soaring back up to their sky-watch station.

Another excellent anchorage we found on Tiburon Island's southeastern end is called Bahia Perro (Dog Bay). Its name is not on the chart nor in *Sailing Directions*, although it is described in the latter as situated on the north side of the ½-mile-wide and one-mile-long peninsula which extends from Tiburon's southeastern end. Good anchorage, sheltered from prevailing winds, is found around the 5-fathom curve off the beach. When we were there, we found several commercial shrimp boats anchored for the day, as well as a group of sport fishing people camping on the beach. We took a gallon jar of tortilla-beans over to one of the shrimpers whose crew, in turn, presented us with some rare pink murex shells, a bag of shrimp and two fresh cabrilla fish. Needless to say, all of us enjoyed our evening meals!

It is to the west of Tiburon Island that the smaller midriff islands are situated. For the trailed boats launched at Kino, they offer protection and close-to-beach anchorages if crossing the Gulf to the Peninsula. These islands are from 15 to 20 miles apart, barren and uninhabited, with deep water within only a fraction of a mile of their shores. Fishing around the islands is superb, and for those whose primary object is fishing they have much to offer—but little to the larger-boat owner, mainly because of the water depths that make anchoring difficult.

On our most recent cruise in this region, we by-passed the anchorage at Willard Point on the western tip of Tiburon. Winds from the west made the coves between Monument and Willard Points undesireable, although with normal northwesterlies they would be good overnight stopping points.

The southeastern end of Angel de la Guarda Island gives protection from prevailing winds, with colorful bluffs rising to over 3000 feet, a few miles inland. A good landmark while approaching the island from the southeast is Isla Estanque (also known as Pond Island), which is separated from La Guarda by a reef of rocks that are awash at low tide. We found good holding bottom about a mile to the west of a prominent and chart-indicated rock—off a beach.

On previous trips we had explored the western shores of 42-mile-long Angel de la Guarda Island. We decided that it was time to visit its eastern side between Isla Estanque and Puerto Refugio. A protected anchorage was said to be in a bay lying about midway up the island, and easy clam digging was one of its attractions. After rounding Rock Point, we turned westward to skirt the shoreline of the bay; stayed on the 5-fathom curve; and after spending nearly two hours to cover the bay's perimeter of 12 miles, decided that the report was either incorrect or our eyes not sharp enough to find it. True, anywhere in the bay would be a fair anchorage for protection from westerly winds, but shore-going looked difficult through a considerable surf that was breaking on the beaches. A lagoon did exist at the northern end of the bay but it looked uninviting, and hardly the anchorage we were seeking.

Another 14 miles brought us to Puerto Refugio, on the northern end of the Island. This is a group of coves and a favorite area for those who cruise this far north. They are well protected, have inviting beaches and spectacular coloring along their shorelines. Here sunrises and sunsets are especially violent in both color and aspect. It's an awesome and cruel appearing place of great red slabs of jagged granite, occasionally white-pocked with bird guano, or with a thorned arm of cactus pointing toward the sky.

One morning we arose particularly early with color film in our cameras to record some of nature's artistry at dawn. Mejia Island, just north of our anchorage, was steeped in gold and crimson over its upper extremities, though bathed in blackness all around its base. The sight of it inspired one of us to write a picture caption: "A rugged range reflects its ramparts in a stunning mirror sea." Some months later, however, when the picture was published, the magazine's less-inspired editor had changed the caption to read, simply: "Sunrise on barren Mejia Island." Blunt testimony to the truth that "beauty lies in the eyes of the beholder." And similarly is the total effect of a cruise to this region. Some may say, "it's a barren land, too harsh and lonely." For others, it will generate the compulsion to return again and again.

At the far northern end of Baja's Gulf, utter silence first strikes the senses. At San Felipe, a trailed boat has just been launched. It bobs soundlessly under a hot morning sun. For a few moments the people aboard are motionless, shading their eyes against the glare. Blue Gulf waters shimmer off to an infinity of hazy purple ramparts. A barren shoreline, shading from gray to tan, sweeps up and away to recede in a distant horizon—the exact pale blue of the sky.

"You wouldn't exactly call this a 'marina,' would you?" the small-boat skipper finally spoke. "I guess this is what is meant by 'getting away from it all'." Although there were others in the harbor—native fishing boats, several outboards and our own heavy cruiser, there was still the feeling of our being mere props on an improbable dreamlike stage. From the violet-colored heights of 10,126-foot-high Calamajue Mountain, Baja's highest peak, down to San Felipe's hot sand shore, the scene appeared one of suspended animation. We felt as if transfixed in some nebulous mirage.

The trailed boat's engine started then and its abrupt sound shattered the still morning air. But the noise was only momentary. The boat gathered speed and moved swiftly southward, its sound and wake rolling up like a carpet behind it. Soon it was a speck—a gnat on a flat blue plate. San Felipe's little huddle of dusty dwellings closed their shutters and returned to sleep.

This solemn place is the trailed boat's principle access to Baja California's waters, now that a good road joins it with Mexicali on the U.S./Mexican border. Until the road was built, it was a vacation area available only to boats capable of the long ocean haul down the Peninsula's Pacific ocean side, around the Cape and up the Gulf some 800 miles. This, in fact, had been our

At San Felipe, tidal changes range as high as 20 feet. Local fishing boats seldom bother to anchor beyond low-tide mark, but visiting boats should do so.

route on our first trip to San Felipe. It was mid-April and we with our guests, Sue and Joe Kelly, had been cruising nearly a month before finally reaching this northern Gulf apex.

"And that fellow told me they just left Los Angeles three days ago." Joe waved an arm in reference to the cruiser now receding in the distance. "He said the first day they were here they caught a 40-pound grouper and two totuavas weighing over a hundred pounds apiece!"

We agreed with Joe that the small boat's occupants were lucky on both counts: their quick ingress to the Gulf, compared to our own, and their sizeable fish catch—though the latter was not surprising. Here in this giant fishbowl the waters are continually agitated from above and below. Besides the abundance of game fish, the sea teems with surface action. Dependent on season, gray whales, porpoise, huge manta rays and sea lions are ever surfacing and disporting themselves. Gulls, terns and cormorants vie noisily with the silent pelican, each trying to outmaneuver the other for fish or plankton.

In contrast, the bordering shores are quite devoid of life. A few transient native fishermen are in evidence at certain seasons but for the most part there is little left to indicate the Peninsula was so well-populated as historians* inform us, up to the sixteenth century. Scientists' Carbon 14 tests are now disclosing this northern region contains some of the oldest kitchen middens in the world, testifying to its vast Indian population living here in greatest numbers, two to six thousand years ago.

This year's trip was purposely cruised in mid-spring. Previously we had cruised the Sea of Cortez in winter months, November to February, and on two of them had spent Christmas in La Paz. Difference of opinion as to best weather and sea conditions encountered, and whether insects were a problem during warmer weather, prompted this later start for a first-hand comparison. For the Kellys it was strictly a vacation and an introduction to Gulf cruising; for ourselves, it was another combination business and pleasure cruise to gather more material for our various writing projects.

"Well, we've seen what the upper Gulf is like," we told the Kellys, "Let's haul up the anchor and do some harbor hopping on our way south along the Peninsula."

Sue looked up from the history book she had been reading. "Do you know what Father Jacob Baegert wrote in 1863?" she asked. "He said there was a tribe of about 40,000 Cocopaha Indians living around here then and that they were all nudists!"

Joe looked at Sue's bikini and laughed: "We're pretty close to that state right now, aren't we?" We were indeed all wearing our most scanty attire in the near ninety-degree heat which fanned out from the Great Sonora Desert to this north-Gulf location.

Once underway the slight breeze caused by our motion was welcome. We stretched our autopilot's remote control out through a pilothouse window and the four of us gathered on the

*Historical Outline of Lower California, Francisco Clavijero 1862;
Three Years Residence in Upper and Lower California, E. Gould Buffum 1850

foredeck—our favorite station to suntan, relax and yet remain on watch.

South of San Felipe, the first harbor of any consequence is Puertocitos, 50 miles down the Peninsula's eastern shore. A few fishermen with especially sturdy trucks and trailers launch their boats from this cove, but as the road worsens below San Felipe, Puertocitos is not the most favored launching ramp. Twenty-five miles further southeast the first small group of Gulf Islands comes into view, opposite two good refuge coves of Willard and San Luis Gonzaga Bay.

Gonzaga Bay, protected from the southeast, is the larger and more accessible of the two, but Willard anchorage offers protection from both north and south winds. We noticed several small boats at anchor in Willard Bay. From a campfire on the beach came the tantalizing odors of roasting seafood, wood smoke and sounds of singing and guitars. Such is the contentment available for cruisers here during periods of calm weather. A few months earlier in the season, we were told, there had been many days of northerly winds, famous for their ability to chop the sea to a froth and to play disquieting tunes through boat rigging.

This is not an area for night running for boats without radar. There are no navigational lights at all and some of the islets near the shoreline are scarcely awash at full tide. By day, however, the islands surrounding these headlands and coves offer an interesting exploration from a dinghy. Sanctuaries for birds and seals, these rocky ledges are often completely covered with living creatures, all of which break into protest when neared. Here we found for the first time that there are occasional barrages of insects; but with a wind shift, the annoying gnat cloud will vanish just as quickly as it appeared. With the close proximity of seal and bird life on these upthrusting piles of granite (depicted on charts as islets) it was not surprising to find their accompanying parasites.

About forty miles down the Gulf from Willard Bay, the second largest of the midriff islands loomed into view—Isla Mejia and Angel de la Guarda. Again we spent several days in the area, using the western basin of Puerto Refugio as our base anchorage. It is better protected from winds than the eastern basin.

In approaching the western basin, Sail Rock is a prominent landmark about two miles westward of the basin. It stands over

Elephant trees are indigenous to the Baja Peninsula and its offshore islands. This one rises from the rockey soil on Mejia Island,
opposite Angel de la Guarda Island in the upper Gulf.

160 feet high, and from a distance looks like the mainsail of a
sloop. Between it and the northwestern tip of Angel de la
Guarda is a dangerous reef which is not shown on charts, and its
exact position not detailed in *Sailing Directions*. There are no
reefs to be concerned with if a course is laid into the western
basin of Refugio north of a line between Sail Rock and the
anchorage.

It was during a morning of exploration in our dinghy around
the eastern basin of Puerto Refugio that we noticed, for the
first time in several days, we actually had company—human
company. Another 12-foot skiff was moving slowly around an
outcropping, a fishing line dipped from its side.

"Maybe a native," Joe guessed. "Let's go over and ask him

A chuckwalla on Angel de la Guarda Island carries miniature
radio transmitter on its back, permiting researchers to follow its
travels for food and water.

where the fishing's good." As we neared the other boat they
hailed us: "Hey there, Jack and Carolyn, where'd you come
from!"

We maneuvered our outboards closer and were surprised to
see our good friends, Dr. Kenneth Norris and his wife, from Los
Angeles. "We're here on a U.C.L.A. project," Ken told us,
"studying the habits of some of this native fauna. There are a
lot of chuckwalla or iguanas here on the Island. I've attached
radio transmitters to some of the animals to find out where
they travel, their diet and so forth." He told us the chuckwallas
are equipped with sacks on the sides of their bodies which store
water during the rainy season, for later consumption. During
the long dry months they are able to drink salt water and
convert it to fresh through their amazing built-in "conversion
plant." We made a date to meet again later aboard *Monsoon II*
to visit and hear more of the interesting findings of the
University's ecology researchers.

Several days later we moved on to anchor in the protection
of Bahia Los Angeles. Surrounded by 15 small islands and
situated on the Peninsula directly across from Angel de la
Guarda's southerly end, Los Angeles Bay is a popular rendezvous for those flying in or coming by boat. A fresh water spring,
an adequate landing strip and the protection of its ample bay
create a pleasant stopover point for visitors. The Antero Diaz
family have established a sport fishing resort here which is
steadily gaining popularity. Good food and clean but unpreten-
tious guest rooms or cottages are available with prior
reservation.

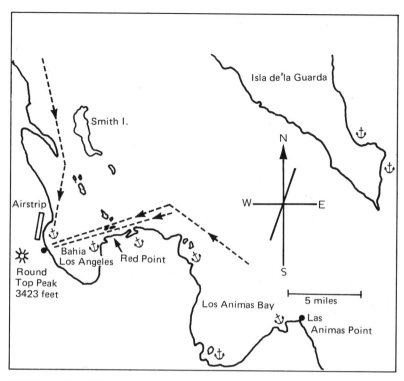

BAHIA LOS ANGELES
28° 55′ N lat; 113° 33′ W long.

Approach to this virtually land-locked 25-mile area harbor from
the southeast should be made between Red Point and two small
islets or between the two small islets and a larger island of reddish
color ½ mile north of the islets. Approach from the northwest
should be made between Smith Island and the low-lying, narrow
neck of land that projects southeastward from the mainland. The
two channels close-by Red Point have 20 to 30 fathoms of depth.
What appears to be a channel north of the large reddish island
lying ½ mile northward of the two islets contains many sunken
rocks with deep water close to them, and should not be used.
When entering the harbor from the northwest, proceed well
past the end of the narrow neck of land before taking a heading
to the anchorage, because a shoal extends for some distance.
Some 15 islands or islets lie between Smith Island, Red Point and
the bay. From the entrances, the bottom shoals gradually to the
beach, and anchorage can be made in 6 fathoms about ¼-mile
offshore. Anchorage may also be taken just to the south of Red
Point, in the Bay; this is often used during strong northeast or
easterly winds that would make the anchorage off the resort an
uncomfortable place to lie.

Bahia Los Angeles is the only settlement of any consequence in the upper Gulf's Peninsula side. Antero Diaz's 85' *San Augustin II*, shown on right, is often called for search and rescue missions, repair services, and many other mercy missions for those in need in this sparsely populated area.

Fifteen miles inland from Bahia Los Angeles and at an elevation of 1800 feet, lie the ruins of San Borja Mission. Built in 1760 by the Jesuits and native helpers, the Mission colony flourished for a few years, then dwindled and was finally abandoned in 1818. The community now consists of a few small ranches irrigated by several hot springs bubbling up from a palm grove. The great stone Mission church still stands, but vandalism has taken its toll, in a literal sense here, after its two ancient bells disappeared.

But while this inland settlement grows smaller, the Diaz resort is in the making at the bayside. Fast charter boats are available for game fishing; limited amounts of gasoline and water are available for visiting boats; a stone breakwater protects floats for dinghies from anchored craft or Diaz' own fleet of fishing boats. A launching ramp is available for the few brave ones who bring trailed boats over the rough road that connects Bahia Los Angeles with the new highway down the midsection of the Peninsula.

To the east of the Diaz' establishment are two excellent anchorages that are often passed by. The first is a cove to the southwest of Red Bluff about one mile, which affords protection from north and easterly winds, with an excellent sand

The modern houseboat is in sharp contrast to the decades-old dug-out canoes in the foreground at Bahia Los Angeles. Antero Diaz' charter fishing boats are at the floats protected by the stone sea-wall. A launching ramp between the dugouts and houseboat is one of the few along the peninsula.

beach for shore-going expeditions. The other is approximately two miles east of Red Bluff behind a peninsula extending on a northwest-southeast direction from the point on which Red Bluff is situated. Entrance to this land-locked anchorage is around the southeastern end of the peninsula, after which a northwesterly heading is taken to the inner basin. Neither of these anchorages is named in *Sailing Directions,* and barely indicated on the chart.

Another area often overlooked in this vicinity is Bahia de las Animas, eight miles southeast of Red Bluff. In the northern part of this bay are a number of islets and between them and a mile-long sand beach is a good anchorage. Within the next seven miles to the southern part of the bay are a number of bights that are inviting, as well as one just to the west of Las Animas Point—none of which are indicated on the large-scale charts.

The only human habitation in this area appears to be a small colony of Indian fishermen near the lagoon at the southwestern extremity of the bay. Later we saw some of them on tiny Raza Island, 14 miles to the east of Las Animas Point. When we approached the island and its cacophony of bird cries, we saw several of these timid fellows running across the island to hide with their loot of birds' eggs. On the shoreline of this flat, low island we found a functional rock jetty had been built to permit a small boat's access into an inner bay. This we used to take our dinghy into shallow water for closer inspection of the thousands

One of the many conical rock piles on Raza Island gives this Heer-
mann Gull a vantage point to guard his tiny plot of ground
reserved for egg-hatching.

of brooding gulls and terns, and to investigate the remnants of a rock fortress atop the island.

There have been several theories advanced as to the origin of these conical rock piles scattered across Raza Island. One theory holds these are burial headstones. Another insists the stones were piled in heaps to make more usable ground space for birds to lay their (nestless) eggs. Still another belief is that the Yaqui Indians had built the stone fort for their protection during the Spanish Revolution of 1910, and that they piled the rock cones for handy hurling down on their aggressors in an attempt to hold their island camp. Whatever the facts, the only certainty at present is that birds have claimed Raza as their own private hatching grounds. The Indians we had seen stealing gull and tern eggs were some of the last of these predators. On May 30, 1964, President Lopez Mateo signed a decree which established Isla Raza as a Migratory Waterfowl Sanctuary. Thus these birds which were threatened with extinction will now be able to perpetuate their species, fight though they do for brooding space on tiny Raza Island.

Raza Island is one of a score that are broadly termed the Midriff Islands. The largest ones are Tiburon to the east and Angel de la Guarda to the north. Proceeding southward, we cruised past razor-backed Isla San Lorenzo, but not without taking advantage of the 75-degree water and the small bights along the island for swimming and fishing—before reaching Bahia San Francisquito. The latter, the four of us agreed, is one of our favorite anchorages. It is a bay about one mile in width, with a smaller bay off its south-eastern shore, extending another quarter mile into the low-lying hills.

In mentioning Bahia San Francisquito, it might be well to state clearly and definitely at the offset that there is *no* fresh water available at this cove. During recent years there have been several published reports that potable water could be taken from this location. Obviously someone erred in the first published guide, and subsequent writers copied the erroneous report without having investigated the situation. It is true that San Francisquito is quite often used by small boats as a refueling station, but both gasoline and water put aboard there are from containers previously ordered and brought to the site by commercial or fishing boats, or overland by truck—just for this purpose. There *is* well water at El Barrill, a tiny rancho about 12 miles south of Bahia San Francisquito, but these wells

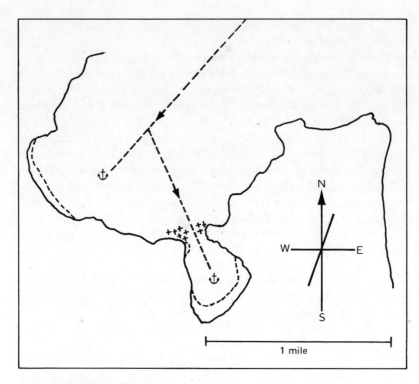

SAN FRANCISQUITO BAY
28° 50 N lat; 112° 52 W long.

Approaches to the 1-mile-wide San Francisquito Bay are deep,
with no out-lying rocks. The entrance to the bay ranges from 10
to 20 fathoms in depth, and gradually shoals toward the beach at
the southwest end. Within as little as 500 yards, there are between
3 and 5 fathoms of water. Holding is excellent, with a clean sand
bottom. Smaller craft can anchor in the smaller bay that opens off
the southeast side of the main bay. Care should be exercised when
entering it because rocks or ledges extend from either side of the
entrance and restrict the entrance to a channel of approximately
100 yards in width. Within the smaller bay there are from 2 to 4
fathoms of water up to within 150 yards of the shoreline.

are privately owned and one would need permission, of course,
to draw water from this source.

Despite its lack of facilities, however, San Francisquito is a
picturesque and sheltered anchorage. Its long, white beaches are
a delight for the shell collector: pink and white murex, Gulf
spiny murex, concha and variegated augur shells, beside many
we couldn't name—all were scattered with eye-pleasing abandon

along the strand. At one end of the beach we discovered a high pile of shucked pearl-oyster shells, indicating some pearling still exists. Near the shell pile was another mound of broken greenish rock laced intermittently with a deeper blue-green vein. This darker strata of semi-precious chrysocolla had been mostly removed from the dross by quarry workers and presumably shipped away for sale to gem polishers. It was obvious that both fishermen and miners had brought their separating chores here to the beach, to work at their trade in leisure amid peaceful surroundings.

Joe and Sue were our fish providers. (For some unaccountable reason, we don't care to fish—but are always glad to help eat the catch.) They came back to the ship one afternoon with two fine cabrillas and a surprising announcement:

"You'll never guess," they called, "we are all invited ashore for cocktails this evening!"

Inasmuch as we hadn't seen another soul in the three days we had spent at San Francisquito—not even a native fisherman—we laughed. "What's the punch line?"

"I mean it." Joe said. "Two couples in campers just drove in to the smaller bay and set up their awnings and stuff and asked us 'where are all the people?' "

"I told them 'we' were all the people. So they asked us over for martinis. I said we would bring the ice and they seemed surprised that we would have ice on our boat."

We didn't think of it at the time, but that would have made the picture. Eight people sitting around a contrived patio near the camper, tinkling glasses in hand—in the midst of the wilds—"Martinis on the Bush!"

There are several quiet anchorages along the 80-mile coastline between San Francisquito and Santa Rosalia, the one break-watered port on the Peninsula's eastern shore: Santa Teresa, just southwest of San Gabriel Point, which forms the eastern end of Bahia San Francisquito, San Miguel, San Carlos and Trinidad. The latter is a prominent headland, appearing like an island from some distance, but connected to the shore with a low sandspit. On both the north and south sides of the headland are good anchorages. To a lesser degree, San Miguel provides protection from either northerly or southerly winds on either side of the point.

We looked into them all with our usual time out for fishing and swimming. By now our foursome aboard found ourselves

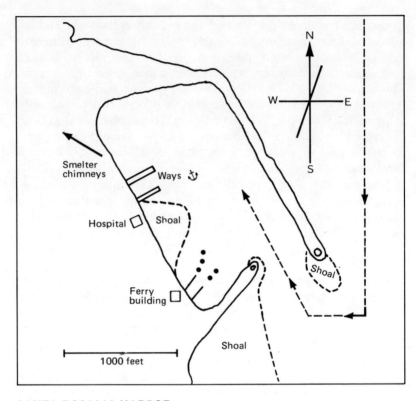

SANTA ROSALIA HARBOR
27° 20′ N lat; 112° 16′ W long.

The artificial harbor of Santa Rosalia is formed by the only
breakwaters of any harbor in Baja California excepting Ensenada.
It is 1½ miles northwestward of Santa Agueda Point, which should
be given at least ½-mile berth because of shoals. Similarly, the
southeast end of the seaward breakwater should be given a wide
berth because of shoaling that is not shown on available charts.
Lights are shown on the ends of the breakwater and the mole, but
a night-time approach to the harbor is not recommended. Once
inside the entrance, care should be exercised in picking a spot to
anchor because of shoals that exist. Vessels of up to 20-foot draft
are accommodated and are frequently alongside the wharf at the
northwest end of the harbor.

following the wildlife's habit of early to bed and early to rise.
Dawn was not to be missed; dawn, literally and emotionally, a
moving sight. From absolute stillness and with first light only a
loom in the east, there's a sudden splash. A gull crys, awakening
chittery land birds to voice. Another splash and more birds

Santa Rosalia's new terminal for the trans-Gulf ferry; to the right
of it is the beach used by those going ashore in dinghies.

shriek. Skies take on light and color as all the seascape turns to
action, rising in a small tumultuous crescendo of whirling, diving,
feeding, crying. The sun bursts over a far horizon. Its heat
distills a fresh, rich scent of desert and tideland. It's day. And
the birds' and fishes' breakfast frenzy subsides. Our cue to start
the morning coffee.

Hours before reaching Santa Rosalia, the brown plume of
smoke from the towering chimney of their smelter could be
seen. We later learned from Port Captain Rafael Elizondo that
since modernization of the smelter by the Mexican Government
(which acquired it from its French owners some years ago), this
concentration plant is one of only two such refineries in the
world, the other in the State of New Mexico.

Joe and the Port Captain found an immediate mutual bond:
they were both amateur radio operators. It was hard to tear
them apart from their "ham" session. But we had shopping to
do. We bought eggs, fresh fruit and tomatoes, excellent bread at
their French Panaderia (bakery) and a half dozen cans of
delicious Mexican mangos. Marine fuel is available here,
dispensed by tank truck from the wharf. Pure bottled water and
block ice made from purified water are also for sale at this port.

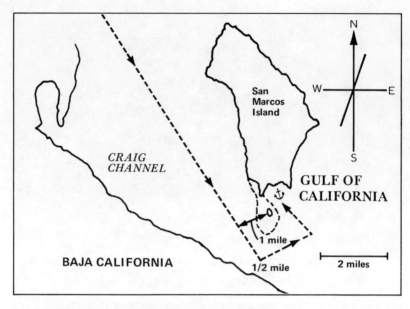

SAN MARCOS ISLAND, LOBOS ROCK ANCHORAGE
27° 11' N lat; 112° 05' W long.

When approaching this anchorage from Santa Rosalia or other
northwestern points, it is necessary to take a heading along the
west side of the island that clears Lobos Rock by approximately 1
mile, and continue past it until the mainland shoreline of Craig
Channel is approximately ½ mile distant. This is to give a wide
berth to a shoal area extending southward from Lobos Rock.
Course can then be changed to the northeast and later to the
northwest, heading toward the prominent bluffs. Anchorage in 2
to 4 fathoms, good holding sand, ¼ mile from the island shore
provides good protection from northwest prevailing winds. Tenders can normally be beached in the bay although it is a rock
beach, and if any swell is coming into the bay it is better to anchor
the tender a short distance offshore and wade into the beach.

After leaving Santa Rosalia, the first shipboard task was to
give the boat a thorough scrubbing with the fire hose, to rid the
fall-out dust from the smelter's smokestack. We then stopped
briefly at San Marcos Island. Although there is nothing of
importance on the Island other than its industrial gypsum
mining operation, we were anxious to make another attempt to
photograph some eagles on their nests that we had seen on a
previous visit. As we neared the Island's southern anchorage just
east of Lobos Rock, one eagle did appear at home on his lofty
nest perched atop a steep rock pinnacle. But just as I had the

Chivato Hotel at the northerly point of Santa Inez Bay serves fine
food and provides good anchorage, near shore, in all but south or
easterly winds. Airstrip lies to left, not shown.

bird within camera range, off he flew, disappearing as quickly as
his counterpart on the American dollar.

When leaving San Marcos Island's southern anchorage, it is
wise to plot a course toward the east to avoid the large shoal
area which extends south of the Island. When the shoal area is
at least a mile astern, one may then safely swing to starboard to
clear Chivato Point. To the south and west of the Point is Santa
Inez Bay, where the Chivato Hotel boldly stands on a rocky
point overlooking the Bay and into the full length of Bahia
Concepcion.

Access to this hotel is mainly by air, for which they have two
landing strips, or by boat. The anchorage is to the west of the
hotel, and further westward are miles of beach on which tons of
unusual shells have been washed during southeastern storms.

Under normal northwest wind conditions, the anchorage by
the Chivato Hotel is good, but if an easterly or southerly wind
comes up, there is better anchorage in the lee of the Santa Inez
Islands, or else south of Mulege in Bahia Concepcion.

Asuncion Bay

San Hipolito Bay

Ballenas Bay

Concepcion Bay

Chivato

Mulege

Pulpito Point

San Juanico

MEXICO

GULF OF CALIFORNIA

Pequena Bay

Loreto

Isla Carmen

N

W——E

S

Puerto Escondito

Aqua Verde

BAJA CALIFORNIA

50 miles

Santa Maria Bay

San Carlos

Magdalena Bay

Nopolo

Isla San Jose

Isla San Francisco

Isla Espiritu Santo

Ceralbo I.

La Paz ① ②

Muertos B.

Las Palma

PACIFIC OCEAN

Legend
1 Pichilinque
2 Las Cruces
3 Buena Vista
4 Palmilla Hotel
5 Hotel Cabo San Lucas
6 Baja Colorado Hotel
7 Hacienda Cabo San Lucas
8 Finisterra Hotel

③

⑥ ⑤ ④

⑦

⑧

Los Fr

San Jose del Cabo

Cape San Luca

Mulege and adjoining Concepcion Bay, near the 27th parallel, are rapidly becoming the Gulf's most popular mid-peninsula resort area. Four good airstrips welcome those flying in for fishing and hunting, and there are ample choices of protected anchorages for the boatman. This is a favored fishing area for trailer-size boats coming across from the mainland and for sport fishing craft kept year around in Mexico. From Guaymas on the mainland, it's an 85-mile cruise across the Gulf, and many make this run to Mulege in four to five hours.

On this particular afternoon we found the anchorage between Prieta and Sombrerito Point rather untenable from the afternoon northeast breeze. So we chose instead to take *Monsoon II* six miles across the Bay to San Domingo Point on the eastern shoreline where there is good protection from all but westerly and southerly winds. We anchored in 4 fathoms of clear water, and enjoyed a good swim around the boat, in company with a half dozen smiling and cavorting porpoises. This group were evidently the forerunners of a huge school which we watched later—after dark—when hundreds of these mammals churned the Bay into a brilliant display of bioluminescence. Long after midnight we heard them squeaking and splashing on their way out to the Gulf.

The next morning it took nearly an hour to return to Mulege in our little 7½-h.p. outboard powered dinghy, but as we all agreed—"what's the hurry?" We relaxed on our cushions and enjoyed the scenery while Joe and Sue took turns trolling.

It is only after rounding Sombrerito Peak (which looks like a huge hat topped with a lighthouse) and turning inland up the river, that the full vivid impact strikes one—Mulege, green as the Emerald City of Oz! Through a thick tangle of palms, mango and palo verde trees, little ranchos are visible at intervals all

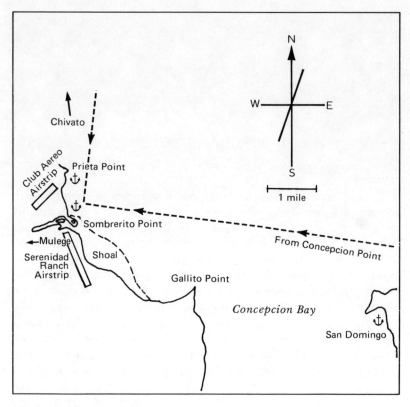

MULEGE ANCHORAGE IN CONCEPCION BAY
26° 53' N lat; 111° 58' W long.

The approaches to Mulege Anchorage are clear, and the bottom gradually shoals to the beach. Anchorage is normally taken between Prieta Point and Sombrerito Point, in depths of 4 or more fathoms, keeping Sombrerito Point about ¼ mile distant and to the southwest. A shoal extends off Sombrerito Point to the southeast as indicated on the chart. Once anchored, passage can be made with a tender up to the small docks on the banks of the Rosalia River. During high tide, local fishermen will take boats of up to 25 and 30 feet in length to the first of the docks, on the inside of Sombrerito Point, but shallow water and sand bars above that point restrict travel to outboard-powered boats. With care in picking the deeper water— ranging from 2 to 5 feet in depth—passage can be made up the river for 2 miles to the community of Mulege, through tropic tree-lined channels. During any degree of northeast or easterly winds the anchorage is uncomfortable, and anchorage should be taken further into Concepcion Bay, along either its southwesterly or northeasterly shores, depending on the wind conditions.

An estuary of the Rio Santa Rosalia provides a dinghy dock facility adjacent to *Club Aereo Mulege's* hotel and airstrip.

along the river edge. Snook and pargo jumped in the river. Natives were bringing their horses and burros to bathe and drink. We wondered why all Baja residents were not drawn here to live at Mulege with its miracle of fresh flowing water.

High above the village and above the river's dam, the ancient Misón de Santa Rosalia de Mulege sits alone, casting its benediction down upon this settlement spawned from the river's succor. Across from the mission stands the bleached white structural bones of Mulege's Federal prison. Its handfull of prisoners work at various trades on surrounding ranchos or in town by day, and return at sundown to retire behind the locked gates of Carcel de Cananea—their part-time prison.

Date growing is Mulege's principal industry. The Jesuits planted the date palms along the river banks early in 1700 when the Mission was first established. Since that time the groves have flourished, despite the many reverses of both this and other Baja Missions. Now flourishing, too, is tourism for tropical Mulege. Besides the small *Hacienda* hotel in town, there are two Gulf-fronting hotels: *Club Aereo Mulege*, situated on a hill just north of the river, and *Serenidad*, a beachside establishment. The latter two have their own airstrips, restaurant, pleasant hotel rooms and sport fishing boats for charter.

We stopped first at *Serenidad's* riverside small-boat landing, and walked across their excellent airstrip to the main building. Inside the cool lounge a group of exotic birds could be heard twittering in their outdoor aviary facing the bar. The desk clerk was busy with his radio, talking on the Unicom frequency to an incoming airplane.

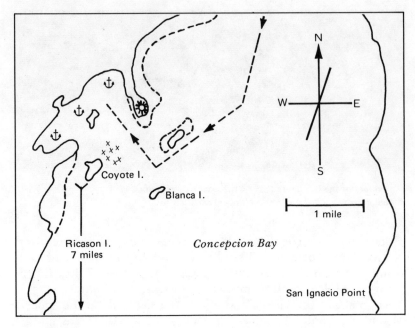

CONCEPCION BAY
26° 45′ N lat; 111° 53′ W long.

When proceeding southeastward down Concepcion Bay, it is well
to maintain a course mid-channel because of the shoals extending
toward it along most of the southwestern side of the Bay for the
first 9 miles from Sombrerito Point. Coyote Cove is an anchorage
well-protected from any winds, with sand bottom and sand
beaches. Approach to the bay should be taken by rounding the
islet that is southeast of the prominent 200-foot-high cone that
marks the northeast side of the Bay and then turning to the northwest. Coyote Island has a prominent group of rocks extending
from it to the northeast. Between the rocks and the 200-foot-high
cone there is from 5 to 10 fathoms of water. The road from
Mulege to La Paz skirts along the shoreline of the Bay.

"...wind's from the north, about ten m.p.h." he said. "We'll
have a jeep waiting to pick up your baggage." The pilot's voice
came back: *"Serenidad* Radio from N 259...roger; we'll want
two rooms, please, for a party of four. And, hey there, what's
for dinner?" The clerk smiled broadly, "Camarones, Senor. The
shrimpers are in! *Serenidad* off."

This is the comfortable and informal atmosphere at *Serenidad.* There are no telephones, no newspapers—yet VHF radio is

Hand dredging for clams in the shallow water to the west of
Ricason Island is done with a bucket held between knees.

in continuous operation, linking this small oasis to the planes
coming in or passing high in the sky.

The village of Mulege lies two miles inland, and as we found
the river too shallow that afternoon to take our outboard all the
way upstream, we took a taxi instead. Part of the road into
Mulege is the new highway that connects Santa Rosalia with La
Paz, and terminates at Cape San Lucas. Shopping for needed
ship's stores in Mulege was a delight in their recently built
supermercado; "super" in Mexican terms, but comparatively
small in ours, 'tho well-stocked with canned and fresh foods and
a wide variety of household necessities.

We spent the balance of the afternoon talking with the
villagers and taking pictures of the area around Mulege and the
Mission. We dined at *Club Aereo Mulege* that evening while
visiting with some of their guests. A party of four who had
recently flown in told us they were on their way down to the
Cape. Three tanned and bearded men sat at a table nearby
discussing their overland jeep drive down the Peninsula. Others
were boat owners, here for a few days of fishing. "Go to
Ricason Island if you want butter-clams," we were told. In prior
years Coyote Cove was the principal source of clams in
Concepcion Bay, but the new road and more tourists have
nearly wiped out those clam beds.

And clams there were at Ricason. We didn't know there
could be such an abundance of these tasty cockles. No rakes nor
shovels were necessary. It was merely a matter of scooping them
up by hand from their shallow sandy beds at low tide level.
Back aboard ship we prepared dinner—a banquet that evening:

clam cocktail, sivichi made from fresh cabrilla fillets, local vine-ripened tomatoes, langusta dipped in melted garlic-butter, and fresh papaya for dessert. In Concepcion Bay our ship's supplies of canned and frozen foods had few inroads.

The next day we took *Monsoon II* the length of the Bay, charting its depths as we cruised. At the far southern end, on shore, there's a dense forest of cactus "trees," ranging from 6 to 20 feet high. From the natives we learned there are great herds of deer living in the area, though how they forage through the spiney cactus branches is hard to imagine.

A few days later three couples flew down from Los Angeles in an Aero Commander belonging to a pilot friend of Joe's, who was to fly them home. Together we swam and explored the many beaches along Concepcion's westerly shore. One evening the men built a cooking fire on the beach and after several dinghy trips back and forth with supplies, we commenced another clam-bake. (However, the main course was clam Bordelaise instead of baked clams.) Someone forgot to bring the wine from the ship—a necessary ingredient for our entree. Someone else substituted bourbon. The clam melange had never tasted better!

By moonrise we were all still in our swim suits, eating a while and swimming a while, in the soft warm waters of the Bay. Storm and strife of world affairs seemed as distant as the stars—light-years away.

After a full week of exploration in Concepcion Bay, we weighed anchor and headed down the Gulf toward Loreto, the site of Baja's oldest Mission. This is about a 70-mile cruise, interspersed with several small anchorages along the way. From a distance, Pulpito Point appears as an island, because its 500-foot elevation is separated from the coastline with a low sandpit. There is excellent protection in the coves on either side of the Point, the best depending on wind direction. About 8 miles south of Pulpito is one of the most interesting and least-known anchorages along this entire stretch of coast—San Juanico Cove, just south of San Basilio Point. More than once we have gone by it without even noticing its existence, because from a mile or more offshore its deep indentations blend into the background hills. It is now our favorite overnight anchorage to break the run between Concepcion Bay and the Loreto area. While charts scarcely indicate this delightful cove, there is plenty of swinging room here for as many as 25 good-sized

One of the many small coves near Ricason Island, in the southwestern end of Concepcion Bay, sprouts a small huddle of palm
trees. A now-dwindling supply of butter clams may be found along
its beachline.

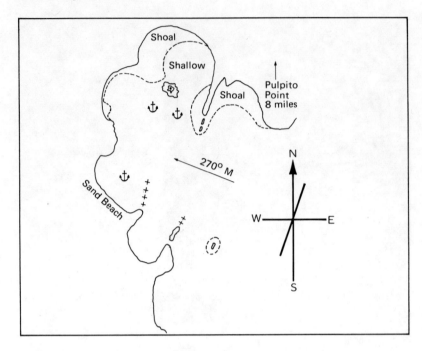

SAN JUANICO COVE
26° 23' N lat; 111° 26' W long.

Sailing Directions describe this cove as a small open indentation,
which is in considerable contrast to its actual configuration.
Except for easterly winds there is good anchorage in the northwest
part of it, in 3 to 4 fathoms of water. The southern part provides
protection from southeasterly winds, off a sand beach. To the east
of the beach are a group of rocks that extend out from it for a few
hundred yards.

boats at one time, as well as a mile or more of gently shelving
beaches.

The shortest route to Loreto is between the Coronados
Islands and the main coastline. There are actually two islands to
be considered—the largest to the east, and an islet close by its
southwestern end. The preferable course is midway between the
islet and the coastline where there are about five fathoms of
water at its shallowest point. Anchorage can be taken on either
side of the low sand spit on the southwestern end of Coronados
Island.

As we approach Loreto, the towering mountain range of
Sierra de la Giganta looms ever higher against a deep blue sky.

San Juanico Cove is studded with rock islets, offering good anchorages in a choice of locations, depending on wind direction. Exceptionally clear water and shallows toward shore beckon the skin diver for exploration.

On the Gulf horizon an early afternoon mirage builds a fantasy in pale ochre—a strange tan island with squared-off vertical cliffs. It hangs there in the distance, a fair height above water, resting on nothing whatsoever but air. Binoculars only magnify the apparition. Our charts deny its existence.

Three principal landmarks are helpful in anchoring off Loreto, in the open roadstead: the dome of the 275-year-old Mission Church about a half mile inland; the newly built (1970) Mision Hotel on the shore, and just to the north of it a commercial pier built some time between those years. South of the Mision Hotel a shoat extends along the shoreline for a number of miles, and as much as a half-mile seaward. Best anchorage is between the hotel and the pier, seaward of the pier as much as 500 yards. Dinghies can be tied to the pier, or, if the weather is calm, beached; invariably with the help of young lads ashore who are happy to earn a few pesos for their assistance.

Loreto is a Port of Entry, necessitating clearance with the Port Captain. His office is a short distance south of the new hotel, on the road that parallels the shore, or a taxi driver will find him in town if he is away from his office.

Baja California's oldest Mission, at Loreto.

Our first cruise to Loreto in 1950 coincided with the grand opening of Ed Tabor's Flying Sportsmen Lodge. Natives were then excavating for their Gulf-fronting swimming pool, using sharpened turtle shells for spades. The last tile was being placed on the patio floor and supplies of food and drink were being carried into the new kitchen. A fiesta was to start that night, destined to last well over two days. Families were coming in by horse and burro-back from ranchos miles distant. It was a memorable night of music and dancing, no more enjoyed by the natives than by our own group from *Monsoon*—prize winners

One of the oldest brick bread ovens on the Peninsula is shown
here, in Loreto. It has been used continuously since the early
1700's.

for having traveled the greatest distance to help officially open
the Lodge.

Since then a number of additional resorts have been built to
serve the ever increasing number of sportsmen who fly to Loreto
each season. Although the old Mission Cathedral, with its great
bells brought from Spain in the early 1700's, has been restored
after an earthquake, the community surrounding it remains

little changed over the years. True, a fine new school has been built; stores are better stocked than before; palms and vivid flowering trees are larger, casting longer shadows on hot white streets and dusty dwellings, but the community's only bread-baking oven, built centuries ago, continues to supply the needs of Loreto's inhabitants.

Eastward of Loreto lies Carmen Island. Its sharp bluffs rising to 1500-foot peaks are only occasionally broken with indentations that invite anchoring. Facing Loreto is one of the best coves—Puerto Ballandra. The rusting remains of a steel-hulled barge on the beach attest to its once-commercial activity, but it is the only evidence to spoil its beauty. Clear waters, white sand beaches and lush growth by the lagoon are there to enjoy.

It was here in Ballandra Bay that we were treated one night to a spectacular sight. The night was black and overcast. We were in our dinghy returning from visiting a friend's boat at the far end of the Bay. Once our eyes were accustomed to the darkness there suddenly appeared a myriad of darting brilliant flashes all about us in the inky water. Fishes and plankton all were vividly illuminated with firey bioluminescence as they flashed to the surface or shot down to depths of 25 feet. Brilliant green mingled with electric blue dots, or slashes of light; occasionally the glowing outline of a large fish shot by, sending a spray of tiny fish scattering before him. Finally we stopped our boat to drift, enthralled with the spectacle of this gleaming, teeming life beneath us. We called it "Ballandra's Ballet".

On the eastern side of Carmen Island is one of the largest salt-producing operations in the Gulf, at Salinas Bay. Protected from all but southerly winds, the Bay is a good anchorage and a convenient base for offshore fishing expeditions.

Although *Sailing Directions* has only a brief report of Puerto Escondito (Hidden Harbor), 15 miles south of Loreto and due west of the lower end of Carmen Island, it is the only completely all-weather harbor in the Gulf. Shallow-draft boats can go beyond the outer bay through a narrow channel which opens into a mangrove-rimmed inner bay. Here oysters abound; some on bordering rocks and others clinging to the mangrove roots at low tide level. Towering more than 4000 feet above Puerto Escondito are massive twin peaks of the Giganta Range, appearing as sentinels guarding the bay. A pier has been constructed in the outer bay in preparation for the day when

Northwest of the semicircular outer "waiting room" is the 30-foot-wide channel to the inner basin of Puerto Esconditio. Currents up to 4 knots run through the channel during tide changes; slack water should be awaited by cruising boats planning to negotiate it.

building commences of another luxury resort hotel and adjoining airstrip.

Two routes can be taken from Puerto Escondito to Agua Verde, about 25 miles to the south: along the shore of the Peninsula to Candeleros Point with Danzante Island to eastward, or around the outside of the island. Our choice is the outside route, as it is clear sailing directly to prominent Solidaria Pinnacle, which marks the northeastern entrance to Agua Verde. On Danzante there is a cove on its western side, about one mile south of its north end, which is a good anchorage, well-protected and with a sand beach for easy dinghy landing. If the route chosen to Agua Verde is to the west of Danzante Island, care should be taken in choosing the passage between the three Los Candeleros Islets that are between Danzante and Candeleros Point. The middle one of the three is the most prominent, and deep water is on both sides of it; but the passages between the northernmost and Danzante Island, and the southernmost islet and Candeleros Point "should not be attempted," according to *Sailing Directions*.

The waters of Agua Verde Bay are sheltered by outlying reefs and islets, and its shores kept green from subterranean springs seeping down from the two- to four-thousand-foot mountain peaks overshadowing the Bay. The best anchorage is in the northwestern corner of the Bay, with the reef on Point San Pasquel acting as a breakwater to any swells that may be coming

At Agua Verde many of the natives are now using fiberglass
replicas of the more frequently seen wooden dugout canoes. Palm
fronds are used to protect boats from the elements.

into the Bay from the east. Another protected area is a bight in
the southern portion of the Bay between the 350-foot hill and
the bluffs to the east. Ashore there is a small community, and a
new school for its children. The Bay also serves as access to a
few ranchos inland.

Another 35 miles southeast and opposite the midpoint of San
Jose Island, is Nopolo Point. Just to the west of the point is a
palm-green oasis surrounding a small anchorage. Natives call it
simply "Nopolo" (Nop-a-low) and have painted its name in large
white letters on a rock bluff. Neither H.O. No. 153 nor the
charts mention or identify this bay. It is a favored anchorage of
those who know the Gulf well and who enjoy shoregoing at
more primitive settlements. A several-generation family of
about 40 people with their cats, dogs, chickens and goats
comprise the populace whose lives are dedicated to fishing. This
is one of the very few native families on the Peninsula whose
women-folk take active part along with the men in fishing. This
handsome group of French and Yaqui Indian ancestry appeared delighted to have visitors and insisted we come ashore to
inspect their tropical home-setting. Although we found their
dialect was quite unlike the usual Peninsula language, we were
able (mainly through sign language) to understand the general

Coyote Island, between San Francisco and San Jose Islands, is
little more than a rockpile, but at least it is bug-free say the
natives who live and fish here.

trend of their conversation. Some of the women pointed with
pride to their handmade flower baskets decorating the eves of
their thatched roof porch. A variety of wild flowers and ferns
cascaded from suspended cans, adding a little touch of elegance
to this community so obviously proud of its rare Peninsula
luxury—proximity to fresh spring water.

Generally it is calm enough in Nopolo to lie quietly at anchor
and to land a dinghy on the beach—but there are times when
northeasterly winds will make it uncomfortable. If it is a strong
blow, the lee of San Jose Island six miles to the east, offers
good protection, particularly in Amortajada Bay on its southwestern end. From there shore parties can explore the mangrove-lined lagoon that is famous for clams. When the winds
drop, however, the gnats may make it miserable. An alternate
anchorage about 7 miles south of Nopolo is to the west of San
Evaristo Point. A small salt producing operation supports the
hundred or so Mexicans whose village is a short walk up the
road from the beach on which tons of sacked salt are frequently
stacked, waiting for the transient freighter to pick them up for
delivery to La Paz.

Before leaving this area we proceeded to San Francisco
Island, just south of San Jose Island, where there is a new-moon
shaped beach on three sides of the anchorage—ideal for those
needing a "run on the beach." Between these two islands are
Coyote Rocks on which a number of fishermen-families live.
When we first visited them by dinghy, we asked about their
selection of these isolated rocks for their homes. The eternal

bugs, they told us, were what had driven them from their former home on San Jose Island.

Fifteen miles south of San Francisco Island brought us to Isla Partida, where we were to rendezvous with a group who were heading north from La Paz. "Eclipse Bay" was the meeting point. Neither shown on charts nor described in *Sailing Directions*, this name has been aptly given the cove because it eclipses all others on Partida and the adjoining island of Espiritu Santo. It extends nearly one mile eastward into Partida, and is one of three such indentations north of the bay that separates the two islands.

Before entering La Paz Harbor we stayed a few more days to swim and snorkel at a number of other coves on lovely Espiritu Santo and La Partida Islands. In these blue-green waters puffer fish, bat rays, tiny electric-blue fish, red snapper and now and then a turtle would move in calm detachment before our face plates. On rocky outcroppings, armies of spindle-legged crabs paused to watch us fearfully with their hyper-thyroid eyes.

During many months, and over a span of many years in the Gulf, there was only one night of violent wind when we felt need of anchor watch. This was in an unnamed cove on the east side of Espiritu Santo Island where a magnificent arc of beach nestled at the base of a thousand-foot rocky cliff. Its very geographical setting should have warned us on that calm afternoon we beachcombed and swam around the shore. This was an area unsurpassed for snorkling. Massive schools of fish moved just under the surface, and only a few yards off the beach. We stared at them through our face plates while they in turn moved closer to stare back at us—completely unafraid. We thought, this must be the feeling of "raptures of the deep." Time passed unnoticed so absorbed we were with the changing spectrum about us—people and fishes mingling as if we were all of a species. It was nearly sunset when, reluctantly, we tore ourselves away from our afternoon's enchantment and returned aboard ship.

About ten that night a 50-knot wind came suddenly slamming down on us from over the cliffs, roaring like a cyclone along the granite walls. In all probability this cove was unnamed simply because it was unused by cautious natives. Our anchor held throughout the onslaught but by morning "no name" harbor had lost our interest. We weighed anchor and headed southwest for Prieta Point and the entrance channel to La Paz.

La Paz to Cape San Lucas

On a southwesterly course from Espiritu Santo Island headed for La Paz, we crossed San Lorenzo Channel in early afternoon. The sun-soaked Sea of Cortez glinted blue and gold in sparkling reflection from sky and shore. Abeam Diablo Point our heading bent southeasterly to leave Lobos Rock and Lobos Island close to port. From the southern end of San Juan Nepomezeino Island, marking the entrance to Pichilinque Harbor, we turned on our depth recorder. This is where shallower water commences, with depths varying from two to five fathoms. At Prieta Point, marking the La Paz channel entrance, we reduced speed and proceeded cautiously into the buoyed channel. In earlier days cement range markers on the hills were used to negotiate the channel. These are obsolete because the channel has moved considerably since the ranges were built many years ago. Now, buoys are anchored at intervals for more accurate guidance.

We passed the beautiful white mansion that La Paz citizens built for ex-President Aleman; then the bathing beach at El Coromuel and finally moved in to the anchorage at La Paz, the 455-year-old Capitol of Baja's Southern Territory. Along the harbor waterfront's malecon, buildings shone between palms and pina-blanca trees, and the fire colors of bougainvillea cascaded down faded plaster walls. Today La Paz has a population of over 40,000 people, many cars, good roads, and an airport serving jet flights. She is becoming a sophisticated little city and we are glad for her economic growth. But with some small pangs I missed the sight and sound of La Paz 25 years ago, when windmills clanged softly through drowsy afternoons, and the only traffic sounds on cobbled streets were horse-hooves clopping. In those days La Paz identified with her name—"peace."

Typical scene at La Paz commercial dock, where several boats await their turn to take on fresh water.

The most recent boon to tourist traffic at La Paz is the inauguration of passenger and car ferry services from Topolobampo on the mainland. For some years the Mazatlan-La Paz ferry has served both tourist- and Mexican-based traffic, and its value as a means of crossing the Gulf prompted addition of the second ferry. Both ferries are now being used by trailed-boat owners to bring their small craft from the mainland to the Peninsula. The Mazatlan ferry docks at Pichilinque, while the Topolobampo ferry docks in La Paz Harbor.

Whatever way one comes into La Paz, there are many comfortable and some very beautiful hotels and restaurants for his vacation comfort. Fast fishing boats are available for charter and the nearly surfless expanse of Coromuel Beach is inviting for sunning and swimming. La Paz Harbor is a protected anchorage but care should be used in anchoring to insure holding in the 2- to 6-knot currents occurring during tidal changes. During winter and early spring months there can be strong winds in the harbor at which times many boats move to Pichilinque's all-weather protection. Even though high winds and currents in La Paz Harbor may not be the reason to move to Pichilinque, many yachtsmen choose to do so to be out of the chaos that sometimes exists when upward of 75 boats from the States fill the harbor.

The older and original dinghy dock at La Paz is situated alongside the main commercial dock. A newer one is about a half mile to the north at the end of a pier, but it is not as convenient because it is further away from the central shopping district.

The morning following our evening arrival, we launched our dinghy for a trip ashore. It seemed good to walk again on freshly washed sidewalks, shade and sun dappled. A few blocks beyond the malecon is the cool, thick-walled office of our long-time friend, Senor Oscar Chacon Sandoval, who is now managing his late father's business as maritime agent. La Paz's other Agencia de Yates is Beatriz M. de Munoz. Each office has its own following among local and visiting yachtsmen; and each handles the voluminous paperwork necessary here for customs, clearances, fuel and water permits. Mail can be sent in their care, saving the boatowner or his crew endless trips to the post office; and a variety of other services that most visiting yachtsmen find indispensible. True, there are no laws demanding that an agent be hired, but those few who have tried the "do it yourself" route have heartily agreed, later, that it was not worth their efforts, nor did they save any money in the end. In short—don't try to buck the system. It simply won't work. We stress this because we have so often seen the newcomer to a foreign port attempt to bribe the lower echelon with money, liquor, or other; overlooking the fact that the bribee still has to answer to his superior, and bribor winds up in a stalemate, minus the bribe, his time, temper and, most important, has lost face with his native hosts.

After we had taken care of our business matters and visited a while with Oscar, we took a cab for grocery shopping. The old farm market has been moved into new and handsome quarters, though inside, its plentifully filled stalls are much the same as ever—eggs, fresh fruits and vegetables, staples, clothes, leather goods, stalks of sugar cane, live poultry or newly butchered cuts of pork or beef. Each commodity emits its own aroma. Food to eat and food for thought. The farm market has more color than the new supermarkets; except for foreign labels on their shelf goods, the super mercados are duplicates of our own at home—even to chromed shopping carts and turnstiles, and higher prices.

One day we took a taxi out of La Paz up to the old Triunfo gold and silver mines. A long day's journey into yesteryear—to El Triunfo and to San Antonio's mines which in 1862 were expected to bring unlimited riches to the territory. But transportation from mine to harbor proved too great a problem. Native workers were neither experienced nor dependable. Also during the first years of these mining ventures, all was turmoil in the Mexican Government.*

This combination of adversities has left El Triunfo and San Antonio virtually ghost towns, their empty, crumbling buildings rimmed 'round with green-gold torote, wild bougainvillea and red flowering octillo. Gaunt cattle roam the thickets for food, blobs of cactus on their sad faces. Overhead the vulture hovers, a black-winged cross against the blue.

But somehow a few families manage to wrest a livelihood from their tiny ranchos, their goat herds and poultry flocks. We lunched in one such casa in a small but tidy dining room surrounded on all sides with the latticed green of tropical foliage. Our host and his family appeared happy and content as we visited. They spoke no English and we only moderate Spanish. As is usual in these circumstances there is always the mistaken phrase, the fumbling for explanation, gesticulations and finally mutual laughter. Laughter at ourselves, humans with the same needs and desires, all with tongues for voice but, withall, this ridiculous lack of communication. We exit laughing.

It was dusk when we arrived back at the harbor from our day-long drive in the mountain mining country. And laughter again surrounded us while we loaded our dinghy to return to

*See *Exploration in Lower California,* 1868 by J. Ross Browne, Harper & Bros. Reprinted by Arizona Silhouettes, Tucson, Arizona

our anchored ship. I had gathered a load of rock specimens from the mine area—quartz, fools' gold, obsidian and any other stones I'd found that were colored or that sparkled. The native boat-boys were convulsed. "Look" they cried to one another. *"Mira!* This lady likes our *rocks!* She takes our old stones with her!" Indeed, how *loco* could one be?

A curious thing happened next day. Our son, Gordon, had been fishing and brought back several cabrilla. The fish lay there, dead, I assumed, in the bottom of the dinghy. When I started to pick one up it made one convulsive movement and bit my hand. It was only a small puncture and I thought little of it. But a few minutes later I felt completely drugged. For the next three hours I slept so soundly I had to be forcibly awakened. We have since wondered if this was a true cabrilla (which is not presumed to be poisonous) or perhaps some mutation or cross-breed, dressed in conventional cabrilla fins. Two big mugs of double strength coffee eventually cleared my sleepfogged brain, and there were no untoward after-effects. But I keep wondering about the chemical formula emitted by that biting fish. For insomniacs this extract might provide an excellent sleeping potion.

There are a variety of short trips one may take out of La Paz, by boat, plane or by taxi. It takes less than an hour by plane to reach Rancho Buena Vista, Bahia de Las Palmas or the several newer resort hotels at Cape San Lucas. For those with limited vacation time, the airplane has been a special boon here in Baja's Southern Territory. But reservations, especially during the winter season, are a necessity. Both Christmas and Easter holidays are particularly popular vacation intervals in these Cape resorts because of their fine weather and splendid fishing opportunities. For the sailor, however, blessed with boat and a little more time available, there is always the happy assurance of self-sufficiency, his bed and board forever with him.

Since La Paz is the last supply depot of any consequence for those circumnavigating the Peninsula, one stocks his boat at that harbor to last for the balance of his trip home. Both fuel and water are available here, but not without some problems of obtaining. If the quantity of gasoline or diesel fuel needed is nominal—up to 200 or 300 gallons—arrangements can be made to take it aboard at Abaroa's shipyard. Those requiring larger quantities of fuel, and those needing water, can count on the better part of a day being consumed for obtaining permits and

Boats may back into Don Jose Abaroa's shipyard at La Paz to take
on fuel pumped from drums delivered by truck. Strong cross-
-currents encountered during maneuvering stern-to the concrete
mole can be a hazard, as the area is usually crowded.

negotiations with the oil company—through a broker. Water is available from the municipal, commercial pier—when a temporary let-up in its usage by freighters permits getting alongside the dock. Fuel is taken at Prieta Point, at a new fueling terminal designed only for tankers and large ships, which can be rough on smaller craft when winds are blowing from the south.

The distance from La Paz to the Cape's extremity is approximately 150 miles, with no particular hazards along the route. Navigational lights on the most important points provide a higher degree of safety for night-time cruising not found in the upper reaches of the Gulf. But there are many pleasant anchorages to explore, enticing most boatmen to make this leg in easy daylight stages.

After heading southward from San Lorenzo Channel, the western shoreline of Ceralbo Island presents a number of anchorages. Four and a half miles from the northern end of the Island is El Limona, which has a sandy beach, as does the northern side of Punta Viejos where there is a lighthouse. Ten miles south of Viejos takes us around Point Arena de la Ventana to Muertos Bay on the Peninsula. Here is an excellent

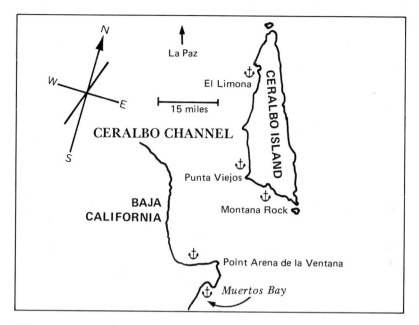

CERALBO CHANNEL can sometimes be extremely rough when winds are from the north or south, and against the strong tidal currents. On the west side of Ceralbo Island are three anchorage areas frequently used by sportfishermen wishing to remain in the area during strong winds; and to the west of Ventana Point there is protection from southerly winds; and at Muertos Bay there is good protection from all but south winds.

anchorage, protected from all but southerly winds. There are no facilities ashore, other than a few fishermen's huts and an abandoned shed built originally for storing salt for shipment. We anchored directly off the shed in three fathoms and enjoyed a refreshing swim in waters so clear we could see every sand ripple on the bottom.

Las Palmas Bay, a few hours' cruising time south, is another tiny green oasis sprouting from an otherwise barren vista of low rolling hills studded with cactus and thornbush. A fresh water spring at Las Palmas produces a small grove of palm trees and attracts the inevitable rancho, a few crops, and a resort hotel, with an airstrip for its flying clientele. The resort is a low rambling structure with thatched roof patios surrounding a swimming pool and out-of-doors bar. Las Palmas is noted for its Mexican chuckwagon-styled dinners with an atmosphere infor-

A school of small whales which has swum ashore near La Paz.
Scientists are unable to explain why the sea mammals do this.
Hundreds have been known to die in this seemingly senseless act.

mal and relaxed. Eight miles further south is the popular Buena
Vista resort with its fleet of sportfishing boats anchored off the
beach when not at sea with enthusiastic anglers.

After rounding Punta Arena there comes the unmistakable
feeling of approaching ocean swells, at first gradual, then an
increasing awareness of the open Pacific. Los Frailes Bay, south
of Punta Arena, is another good anchorage protected from
north and northwest winds, but offering no shoreside facilities.
It does possess a long white arc of empty beach and several
rocky outcroppings offering the skin or Scuba diver another
underwater paradise to explore or to hunt a fish for dinner.

A little way south of Los Frailes, the Cape's rocky contour
bends westward around Punta Gorda, southwest of which is a
navigational light marking the one-time commercial port of San
Jose del Cabo. This village, situated about two miles inland

Typical Mexican fishboat, of the type that plies the waters of Baja California.

from the open-roadstead port, was the Peninsula's major trading post from the 16th to the 19th century. But now few vessels attempt to lie at anchor there. Surge is constant, even in relatively windless weather. Breakers crash unceasingly against its uninviting shore. The town site is best approached by taxi, overland, from Cape San Lucas or from La Paz.

A newly built road connecting La Paz and Cape San Lucas passes through San Jose del Cabo. The route is rich with spectacular scenery as it winds over mountain passes or along the rugged shoreline. This is the valley of the San Jose River, nearly dry at times, although occasionally a raging torrent during a summer's rainy season. From a dry, cactus-ridden ridge overlooking the valley, the great swath of green below appears as unlikely as any mirage at sea. With the first trickle of water the wastelands explode into a veritable jungle—tone on tone of leafy green. Fruit trees, sugar cane, artichokes, bananas and all manner of tropical foodstuffs proliferate the length of this 30-mile valley which tumbles down toward the ocean. The Mission established in 1730 was first built high in the arroyo some 20 miles inland. Later it was moved to its present site at San Jose del Cabo where it still stands, little weathered by the years. It's a serene little community with strongly built structures and great wide streets, reminiscent of an earlier day large population when its exports of cheeses and panoche were avidly sought by ship crews from across the world.

Directly west of San Jose del Cabo, Palmilla Point extends a small arm of protection against the efforts of the pulsing surf. And in the apex of this more quiet cove, Palmilla Hotel tethers

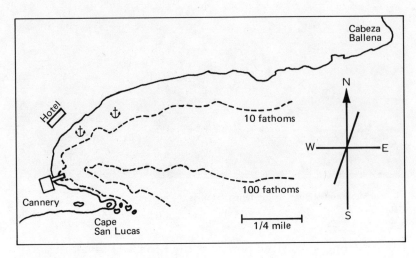

CAPE SAN LUCAS
22° 53' N lat; 109° 54' W long.

Approach to San Lucas Bay should be made in daylight because there is no light on Cape San Lucas, which forms the southeastern extremity of the Bay, nor can the light on the cannery dock be depended upon. There is deep water within 400 yards of the shoreline from Cape Falso to Cape San Lucas, and within San Lucas Bay the 50-fathom curve is within ¼ mile of the beach. When approaching from the northwest, round Cape San Lucas and take a heading of approximately 315 degrees magnetic toward the prominent hotel. There is a shelf with approximately 5 to 8 fathoms of water, hard sand bottom, that should be located; care should be taken to be well over the shelf to avoid having the anchor drag off into water that deepens rapidly to 50 fathoms or more. The beach at the northwest side of the dock affords relatively easy landing under most weather conditons. During the summer months of mid-August to mid-October the Bay is frequently unsafe, because no protection is afforded from easterly and southerly winds, which often reach gale force.

its little fleet of sport fishing boats. The hotel structure perches importantly above, on a rocky eminence. Its white arches along the verandas and red tiled roof might very well have been plucked from a Mediterranean shore. Elegant stone work points up a series of pools and terraces that descend gently to the rocky beach at water's edge.

Palmilla and the next four Cape hotels in line, Cabo San Lucas, Baja Colorado, Camino Real and Finisterra, have air strips carved to windward in the raw red land. The hotels are imposing structures, the more striking because of their wilder-

Fueling and taking on water at Cape San Lucas' cannery dock is a game of one-upmanship, with too many customers for too little space.

ness settings. In early afternoon, as if suddenly magnetized out of nowhere, the fleets of little charter boats come speeding in to their respective coves—white chargers flying aloft their battle pennants. Marlin and sailfish are transported ashore and for a while all is activity about the resort. Later, music drifts from shaded verandas. It's cocktail time, and sunburned happy fishermen talk of the day's catch. Shadows lengthen. Mares' tails in the sky change from cotton-white to rose and crimson, and the huge gold globe of sun is sucked beneath a darkening sea. Night comes quickly below the Tropic of Cancer.

The village at Cape San Lucas is set back a mile inland from the beach, the better to weather severe southerlies (chubascos) that strike with little warning in summer and early fall. This community grows each year, and newly opened *super-mercados* carry a fair supply of canned food and fresh vegetables. The Port Captain's office is in the center of the village, and it must be visited for clearance in and out of Cape San Lucas since this is a Port of Entry. If fuel and water are to be loaded aboard your boat from the cannery dock, a permit must first be obtained from the Customs Officer near the Port Captain's, or a broker must be engaged to handle the paper work.

What the fueling situation will be at the Cape is a question. The cannery where fuel is now dispensed was to be torn down at the end of 1973 according to their Port Captain. A small-boat

On the seaward side of Cabo San Lucas, sandstone is sculptured
into weird forms. Sea birds nest in some of the stone's apertures.

marina is promised at the western end of the old air strip, to be
ready for occupancy "sometime" in the future. No one
knows for sure when a new fueling depot will be a reality.

Beyond the massive gray monoliths ("The Friars"), the most
impressive sight here at the Cape used to be on the ocean side of
the point where prevailing winds and currents swept the sea into
giant breakers and had carved weird sculptures in ancient
sandstone cliffs. A narrow valley lay secluded above a line of
sand dunes. Shielded from scouring winds, wild flowers used to
grow beneath towering wild-fig trees. Boulders, house-size and
larger, were scattered at intervals amidst the native shrubbery,
offering little caves of weather sanctuary.

When we first visited this private hideaway 25 years ago, I
thought: "Here's where I would like to retire." Some years later
when I looked in again, I found an old man living there. He was
cooking a savory stew of fish and rice over a small campfire. On
a later trip to the Cape, "my" retirement plot was occupied by
a group of guitar-playing, bearded fellows with very dirty feet.

And what is there now? Just an enormous new hotel called
Finisterra.

Ever since its discovery by one of Cortez' skippers in 1537, Cape San Lucas has been a refuge cove and a watering place for boats from all points of the globe. These aspects have changed but little through the centuries. Only the boats themselves have been modernized. All else is pretty much the same, except perhaps not so many pirates nowadays. (Or maybe the same number, only better camouflaged.) In any event, "I'll meet you at the Cape" is a common phrase for those heading up or down coast. And after many days at sea there is always the welcome feeling of mingling again with those who have had identifiable experiences in their recent watery wanderings.

During the season, there are often as many as four dozen pleasure craft at anchor for varying spans of time at Cape San Lucas Bay. The anchorage marks some sort of dividing line. For those heading northwest up-coast, crews are busy fueling and watering, bringing warm jackets and foul-weather gear up from below decks. Many of these boat owners fly home from this port (if they have not already flown out of La Paz), leaving a crew to bring the boat back the long, uphill haul to the States. For the sailor headed around to the Gulf or across to Mazatlan and south along the Mexican mainland coast, he, too, is concerned with reorganization, readying his boat for warmer climes. He may be mending sails, replacing broken bats or scouring salt from himself and his craft. Whatever new heading is to be taken, a rendezvous at the Cape with its interval of friendly camaraderie, adds a pleasant and memorable interlude for all who sail near its port.

Of our many trips up the Pacific from Mexico, some were rough trips and others were reasonably smooth. No one can

Monsoon II bites into a big one, while running up the coast northwest of Cabo San Lucas.

foretell precisely what weather will bring. Time of year means a
lot, however, in such forecasting. Our roughest trips were in
January or February. Of the smoother cruises, one took place in
March and the others in late May or early June. From this and
from others' experiences, a possible weather guide may be
drawn.

Mexican fishing boat operators can be depended upon for
their wise judgement concerning weather forecasting and
suggested anchorage protection—logically enough, as most of
their lives are spent afloat in the area. Their lives and cargos
depend upon their proper assay of both fish and weather habits.
And it should go without saying that when the big purse-seiners
come steaming into the Cape harbor, minus full holds of fish,
this is a good indication that the winds outside are strong and
seas lumpy.

The radio "party line," active at 0800, 1200 and 1600 hours,
among U.S. boatowners cruising in Mexican waters, can also be
extremely helpful in learning weather conditions beyond one's
immediate area. In recent years it has become somewhat of an
unwritten rule to maintain a radio-watch at those hours on
2638 kHz.

If this sounds too precautionary, it is not meant to intimidate; rather, only to point out that from the Cape by direct line to the next harbor of refuge to the northwest, there is a span of about 165 miles. For those with fuel limitations, a radius-of-action problem might have to be taken into consideration, should one decide to return to the Cape because of inclement weather or mechanical difficulties.

There are only a few small and partially sheltered anchorages along this leg; namely, south of San Pedro Point where there is a small village (but rough-surf shore access) and below Marquis Point. Local fishing boats anchor in these small bights, on occasion, but they are not recommended for anyone without local knowledge. Normally one makes a direct run from abeam Cape Falso to Redondo Point, the entrance to Magdalena Bay. If head winds are too strong for comfort on this heading, somewhat smoother seas will generally be found close to shore following the 10-fathom curve until reaching the protection of Point Tasco. This point is on the southwestern end of Margarita Island which forms part of Magdalena Bay, and anchorage can be taken to the east of the point, if the skipper and crew are too exhausted to continue another 20 miles to Redondo Point. Some shoaling has been reported in this area, although commercial fishing boats frequently use the protection of the point to break their long trips up the coast. While the Canal de Rehusa appears inviting as a short cut to Magdalena Bay, it should not be used because it is shoal with continuously shifting sand bars.

On one of our recent cruises running northwest from the Cape we experienced another of our many reasons to bless our radar unit. It was shortly after midnight. Gordon and I were on watch and our position was about 50 miles northwest of Cape Falso. The night was clear with stars, but no moon. The vista ahead (and at first on the radarscope) was completely black. Every half hour or so, I changed the range down to the 10-mile, 4-mile, then 1-mile scale, for a closer inspection of any possible traffic near us. On one such range-switch, I suddenly saw a group of small targets ahead of us about 5 miles distant. We put the grid on them to plot their course, if any.

"That's odd," I remarked, "whatever the targets are, they're not moving. We're closing on them only at the rate of our own speed." (about 10½ knots). Gordon took the binoculars out on the foredeck to try to pick out visually some lights or other

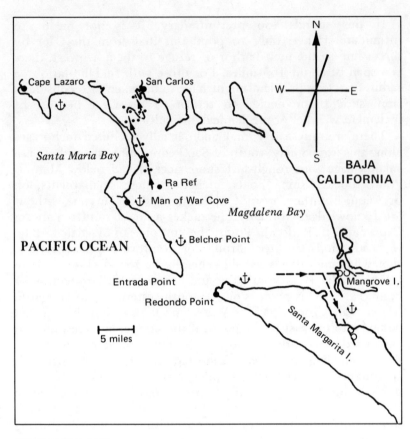

MAGDALENA BAY
24° 35′ N lat; 112° 00′ W long.

Once inside Magdalena Bay, anchorage can be taken many places
along the northern side of Santa Margarita Island or along the east
side of the peninsula extending from Man of War Cove to Entrada
Point. Within 1000 feet of the light at Man of War Cove there is
from 3 to 5 fathoms of water. The sea buoy marking the entrance
to the buoyed, 30-foot-deep channel to San Carlos is 3 miles
northeast of Man of War Cove light. Good anchorage is also
available just under Belcher Point. although the sounder should be
used when approaching it because it is relatively shallow. If Puerto
Cortez is the destination, the ranges on Mangrove Island and on
Margarita Island must be used to avoid the shallow waters on
either side of the ranged channels. The Mexican Navy maintains
a dock and air strip at Puerto Cortez, and a cannery is also
located there. During summer months, strong northeast winds
occasionally blow and none of the anchorages named are
comfortable; Santa Maria Bay will provide better protection.

Man of War Cove, lying about 8 miles inside Magdalena Bay, was formerly a Port of Entry into Mexican waters. Now the Clearance Port has been moved to San Carlos at the head of the Bay.

indication of what the blips might be, but nothing was visible except dark sky and blacker water. From the size of the blips, which were now positioned at only a mile ahead, we knew we could visually see navigational lights if any were there.

"Maybe they're sea monsters, Mom," Gordon joked. "Let's turn on the searchlight. Maybe it will give us a clue." The moment our light focused ahead, *voila,* seven fish boats burst into bloom—running lights, masthead lights and sternlights. It looked like a group of lighted Christmas trees bobbing on the swells. So these were our mysterious radar targets, Mexican fishing boats floating dead in the water, probably saving their current by dousing all lights.

As we altered course to avoid them we both wondered aloud if our searchlight awoke their crews to display their position, or would we have made big boats into little pieces had we not detected their presence on radar. As the natives say, "quien sabe?" Who knows?

There are several choices of good anchorages in the 80 square miles of Magdalena Bay. Until recently, Man of War Cove was the official port of entry, but it has been changed to San Carlos

San Carlos, about 20 miles inland, northwest from the entrance to
Magdalena Bay, provides commercial ships with fuel, water and
some repairs. Pleasure boats often experience a wait—a few hours
to days—for refueling. The L-shaped pier is on the eastern side of
the buoyed channel leading to it from Magdalena Bay.

which lies about 10 miles north of Man of War, and is reached
through a rather tricky but well-buoyed channel. In 1970 the
new fuel dock at San Carlos was a bright promise of a modern
and dependable fuel and water facility for those boats plying
the 800-plus-mile stretch of ocean passage from the U.S. border
to Cape San Lucas. Now, unfortunately, it is "maybe" or
"maybe not." Sometimes a truck loaded with barrels holding
the requested amount of fuel does appear, but the boatowner is
told he will have to rig his own hoses and pumps to get the fuel
from the barrels. Some of the boats awaiting fuel there, we

Inspecting giant clam shells found along lagoon shores which wind
for miles inland from Man of War Cove at Magdalena Bay.

found, had been tied to commercial shrimpers for several days
and nights before being serviced. At other and completely
unpredictable times, fuel will be delivered by tank truck with a
hose for gravity filling.

Puerto Cortez, in the southern part of Magdalena Bay, offers
the best protection from all winds, but one should run this
dog-leg course slowly and with careful attention to the ranges
which point up the devious channel. The courses are well
defined on Bahia Magdalena detailed chart No. 1636. There is a
cannery and Navy Base at Puerto Cortez, and occasionally one
may be able to buy a small amount of fuel from the Base or
from a commercial fishing boat, but it is nothing to be
depended upon.

Probing for clams in the mangrove-lined lagoons of Magdalena Bay
is now only seldom rewarding. Prior to the 1960s this area was
particularly noted for its giant clams, shells of which measured 6
to 8 inches across.

With time available we have always enjoyed a day or two of
gunk-holing by dinghy from Man Of War Cove, into the
mangrove-lined lagoons that wind for several miles into the
northern reaches of the Bay. Protected by sun-warmed rolling
hills and sand dunes that divide the Pacific from the Bay, such a
junket provides a rest and pleasant contrast from the ocean's
energetic bounce and blow.

On one of these occasions we loaded our tender to its
gunwales with picnic lunches, bags for shell gathering, fishing

At Belcher's Cove, Magdalena Bay, the rusted remains of an old
boiler now serve as a fisherman's shelter.

gear, snorkels, fins, ad infinitum. It was going to be an all-day
exploration. Having forgotten to take along our outboard motor
repair kit, however, it almost turned out to be a "forever" trip!
While returning from the lagoon to its point of entry into the
Bay, the motor stopped. Nothing could induce it to start. There
was no choice but to row. Once away from the estuary, we felt
the full force of a strong off-shore wind blowing against us,
pushing us away from the western shoreline. Also, the tide was
going out. Even with two strong men rowing, the combination
of wind and tide was drifting us further into the middle of the
17-mile-wide Bay.

One of our group tried to rig a sail using a large beach towel,
but the elements held their advantage. Fortunately, the receding
tide finally took us over a shoaling sand bar where the water
was only hip deep. Two of us jumped out to guide and push the
dinghy toward shore, leaving one couple aboard to continue
bending their backs at the oars. Then one oar broke; more
pushing, and wind still howling. But we were at least making
some progress toward safety. Every so often a small sting-ray
would dart to the surface near our legs, but this seemed a minor
danger compared with the possibility of having ourselves and
dinghy carried away from shore. After an hour's exertion we

had the small boat a few yards from the beach. I swam ashore and offered to haul the boat by its bow-line, back to Man of War Cove. "Oh no," said the men, "We're safe now. We can paddle and sail along here in the shore protection." Not me! I walked back on good old terra firma.

During spring months, whether entering or leaving Magdalena Bay, one is often accompanied on all sides by whales. And it is not a rare sight to see one of these huge grays leaping clear of the ocean with a quick writhing and twisting motion. It is said that this is a way the whale rids himself of annoying ramoras that attach themselves to his hide.

Moving on northwest out of the Bay, another good anchorage may be found in the northern arm of Santa Maria Bay where 868-foot Smart Peak and 1300-foot San Lazaro Peak, forming Hughes Point, shield the cove from prevailing northwest winds. This is a huge empty bay with white sand beaches curving its indentation to meet a constantly booming surf. Were it not for its isolation, Santa Maria Bay would be a surfer's heaven with its 15-mile arc of giant breakers and nothing but gulls and sandpipers ashore.

Out of the anchorage behind Hughes Point, weather conditions usually determine a course on up the coast. With mild winds and seas, most sailors take a direct heading for Turtle Bay or for Cedros Island. During winter months, however, there are apt to be northeasterly winds of varying intensity, making the going slower and inviting refuge coves more often. In such cases, one may prefer hugging the 10-fathom line offshore to seek partial protection at Pequena Bay, Ballenas, San Hipolito, Asuncion, San Roque and San Pablo Bays.

On our first cruise up-coast in this particular area we had our only occasion to find it advisable to turn and run to sea. It was early January and a northeast gale had made up in the matter of hours. With family and friends aboard *Monsoon I*, our 104-foot, triple-screw ship, we were on a direct heading from Cape Lazaro to Ballenas Bay—a target we never reached.

Ever since leaving the Cape, weather had been rough and was now worsening. I had been making innumerable trips to the engine room to throttle back and throttle back again, from our cruise speed of 12 knots, finally down to 6. As night worn on, winds increased to 40 and 50 knots with higher gusts. Our poor, belabored ship would spring off one huge roller and drop with a resounding thud into yet another trough.

"This is just getting too hard on her," Jack finally said. "We'll take her out to sea till the gale blows through." I timed our course-change in the log and went below again for bridge orders. With throttle full-ahead on the starboard engine and down to slow on the port, and with a series of sickening lurches, we pivoted around 120 degrees to a southwest heading—down wind. Although this was a less arduous course, it took extra strength for the helmsman to keep the ship from overly yawing. We spelled each other at half-hour intervals at the wheel.

My mother was with us on this trip. (Her first sea voyage, and one she thought would be her last!) Mom is not a sailor, despite the fact that Nathaniel Bowditch was one of her great, great, great uncles. I was concerned that she might become dehydrated as she had been seasick ever since we had left the Cape. For the last eight hours it had been too rough to cook. Those in their bunks weren't hungry, and the four of us on watch had fended for ourselves from the galley. I decided I would make some hot biscuits and brew a pot of tea for Mother, on the chance she would be able to retain some nourishment.

It was a real feat to prepare the food and at the same time to stay upright in our dancing galley. Finally I had my chore finished and felt proud of the accomplishment. I carried the meal in to Mother's stateroom in a small basket. A tray would have been useless. Then it was my turn at the wheel, after which, another trip to the engine room to top off lube oil in our three diesels. Eventually I was able to get back to Mother's stateroom to see how she was faring.

"Did you like your supper, Mom?" I asked expectantly.

"The tea was very nice," Mother answered, "but next time, Carolyn, I wish you would try to get more *salt* in your biscuits." (I guess my resulting laughter bordered on hysteria.)

After nine hours of running before the seas, the winds had somewhat abated, and we turned back on a course for Asuncion. By first light of the second day, land loomed ahead through our sea-smeared windows. Bone-weary, we dropped anchor in Asuncion Bay. Our bunks had never before felt so soft and inviting.

Asuncion, like Turtle Bay and Cedros Island village to the northwest, are all fish cannery settlements where a variety of products are processed. One of their richest harvests of the sea is abalone, some of which is canned and another portion frozen for export markets. The life of the abalone diver is a strenuous

Seals and seagulls are the principal inhabitants of Asuncion
Island. It is now off-limits to shore parties in an effort to protect
the wild life on the Island.

one. He arises at dawn and works an approximate 6-hour day, 6
days a week; diving often to a depth of 150 feet. During
abalone season, mid-March through October, the divers risk
moray eels, swift underwater currents and pressure dangers, to
bring up an average of 200 abalone per hour. Some of the divers
wear Scuba gear and others full diving dress with air lines from
the decks of their helpers' small boats.

"It's a good life," one young native told us. "We make up to
$40 per day while we're diving, and our helpers who handle our
air hoses and clean the ab's get $20. a day. Besides, we *like*
diving!" The boy went on to explain that the most obvious
danger of the deep, the shark, has never bothered them. Perhaps
the sharks are so well fed with other fish in these warm,
productive waters, they cannot be concerned with this new
predator descending with his bubbling airhose, his prying-irons
and baskets.

Turtle Bay, despite its safe anchorage and its economic
affluency, is not a picture postcard spa. All fresh water must be
brought by boat 20 miles across the ocean from Cedros Island,
or during canning season, sea-water is distilled from the

Although Turtle Bay is the best all-weather harbor along the western peninsula's shoreline, there can be considerable surge around the pier. For fueling, pleasure boats should back toward the pier with a bow anchor down, and use a short stern line to the pier to hold the boat in position.

processing boiler. Rainfall is practically unheard of in the area. With hardly a tree or shrub or blade of grass to relieve the vista of sear tans and browns, Turtle Bay's little huddle of dusty dwellings appears to have taken on the protective coloring of its environment, as if in lying there couchant, immobile, and feigning death, it might somehow escape extinction from the scouring wind and sun.

But its hospitable inhabitants are lively with good spirit. "We have no water to spare," they will say, "but would you like some fresh hot bread or rolls? Some lobster, perhaps? Maybe a few cans of abalone? We have much of that."

Less tangible, yet most important, the natives of Turtle Bay have contentment—very much of that. Certainly no foreign element eyes with greed their tiny hamlet. The only war they know is with the elements—the wind, the sun, the sea.

To some extent Turtle Bay is like Cape San Lucas, for those cruising up the coast. It is a good harbor to wait out weather; in fact, far better than San Lucas in that respect. Not infrequently there will be half a dozen boats or more at anchor waiting for a break in the winds that can make the run from here toward the north one of the roughest stretches to be sailed. Usually fuel may be had here, although there is often a considerable wait if the village supply is low or used up. Old "Gordo's" fuel barge has long since sunk. One now backs his boat to the dock, lays out a bow anchor—and waits, as patiently as possible.

Twelve miles south of Cedros Island, Point Eugenio marks the southern spur of the great bay of Sebastian Viscaino. Although the word "bay" is ordinarily considered an area of protected water, here such is not the case. All during cruising season, November to June, one may expect northerly winds in this region of anywhere from 10 to 40 knots. Sometimes these blows decrease with sunset, but just as often they continue in intensity for days and nights at a time. For this reason the several anchorages on the eastern side of Cedros Island are oft-sought refuge coves by both pleasure boats and the fishing fleet.

Dewey Channel, separating Point Eugenio and Natividad Island, is the favored course in approaching Cedros from the south. In negotiating this four-mile-wide channel, one should stay well to the eastern side to clear rocks and shoals surrounding the southeastern end of Natividad. When abeam Point Eugenio, a course of 330 degrees magnetic puts one on a direct heading for Cedros Village, the Island's principal settlement.

Not long after passing Point Eugenio, the white mountains of salt stacked near Point Redondo—the southeastern tip of Cedros Island—will come into view; and a little later, the bulk loading terminal that is used by ships to carry the salt to the four corners of the world. The salt is brought by towed barges from Scammon Lagoon, 50 miles to the east on the Peninsula, where one of the world's most extensive and modern salt producing facilities is situated.

Besides its advantages of shelter, early-day sailors were first attracted to Cedros Island because of the availability of its pure spring water. From the 16th century, sailing ships paused at Cedros' southeast shores to fill their water casks at the spring

The fueling pier at Cedros Island Village is often beset with high winds and rough water. The boat shown here is waiting at anchor until he is assured of fuel before putting a stern line to the dock in order to get close enough to take the hoses.

about two miles north of the village, and lighter them out to their vessels. Lightering of water and limited quantities of diesel fuel or gasoline, is still necessary when ground swells make it impossible to lay alongside the cannery dock; or if it is not possible to drop a bow anchor and back down close enough to the dock to take their hoses for fueling and watering. Shore going is accomplished by taking a tender to the pier, securing it to pilings and then climbing a vertical ladder.

The fish cannery at Cedros Village is its chief economy. Behind its plant and warehouses, a small group of homes climbs up a red slant of earth. At the top of the first rise is the church with its twin belfrey towers. The school and a few more tiny houses are sprinkled at intervals on higher reaches of the slope. Just to the north looms the nearly 4000-foot peak of Mt. Cedros, alternately displaying or hiding its green forested dome in a blue-black mass of cumulus nimbus. Rain is not infrequent on the island, which, combined with its several mountain springs, make livlihood possible for deer, goats and other wildlife.

On a recent visit to Cedros Village, we were amazed to see a half dozen television antennas sprouting from some of the

Looking down on the anchorage below Cedros Village, Cedros
Island.

rooftops. One of our friends invited us into his home to see his
TV and proudly turned the set on to show us the snowy outline
of an old movie originating in San Diego, over 300 miles and
several intervening mountain ranges distant. A freak in television transmission provides this isolated community with a fairly
regular series of pictures and sound, much to the delight of their
inhabitants.

East of Cedros Island, Scammon Lagoon reaches back into
the Peninsula nearly forty miles. This many-armed shallow bay
is notable as being the West Coast's greatest whale-calving
nursery. Each fall the great gray whales move south 6000 miles
from their summer home in Alaska's Bering Sea to produce
their young in the warm quiet waters of Scammon Lagoon.
Once threatened with extinction from early-day whalers, the
grays have been protected since 1937, by the International
Whaling Agreement. Now their count has risen to an estimated
10,000 head, or about an 11% increase each year. The
California gray whale is actually a black color underneath a
grayish mantle of parasites. He reaches a top weight of 50 tons,
and is reported to go without eating all the way down from
Alaska and Siberia to Baja California; likewise fasting through-

out his return trip to northern waters.

Not all of the gray whales calve inside the confines of Scammon Lagoon. Occasionally a birth occurs in the ocean. It was a rare sight one December day to see a great circle of porpoises swimming near the surface. In the center of their protective ring was a gray whale, about to give birth. Obviously the porpoises, mammals of the whale species, were guarding the laboring whale from any dangerous marauders—sharks, barracuda or humans. After the whale calf was born and safely protected by its mother, the porpoises bowed out of their self-imposed guard, broke ranks, and sped away.

Scammon Lagoon might look inviting on a chart as a refuge harbor, as might also Black Warrior Lagoon, 15 miles northeast. The facts, however, are that neither will be used by the more experienced cruising yachtsmen because of shoals off the entrances. Since 1968 Scammon Lagoon has been the shipping point for millions of tons of salt each year, which is barged to Cedros Island for reshipment to all points of the world aboard bulk carriers. A sea-buoy to the northwest of the Lagoon entrance is the starting point into the Lagoon, and the dog-legged channel is marked with steel dolphins with red or white quick-flashing lights atop them. In approaching the channel, the sea-buoy and the two red dolphins should be kept on the starboard side, with the white dolphins on the port side.

Once inside the Lagoon, deep water along the eastern side of the sandspit can be followed on a northeasterly heading until the large mooring buoys are reached. These buoys are used for mooring the salt barges by seagoing tugs that tow them to and from Cedros Island. A harbor tug then moves the barges an additional five miles to the salt loading docks at Chapparito. There are no facilities for fuel, water or supplies in Scammon Lagoon. It is strictly a commercial salt operation and signs are so posted, prohibiting craft from proceeding on to the terminal.

Tug and barge tows arrive and leave from Scammon Lagoon on an average of every 18 to 21 hours, 7 days a week. Those determined to go into the Lagoon generally wait for a tow from Cedros Island and then follow the tow through the channel and follow another tow that is outbound when leaving. On numerous occasions the dolphins have been demolished by heavy seas or by the barges swinging into them, which increases the hazard of entering and leaving the Lagoon.

Until 1968 Black Warrior Lagoon channel was continuously

dredged, and the channel buoys maintained to permit bulk carriers using the salt loading terminal within the Lagoon. Since the terminal's abandonment, in favor of the new facilities at Cedros Island, there has been no maintenance of the channel into Black Warrior—nor are there any facilities for fuel, water or supplies. During heavy weather conditions, the shoal water seaward of the entrances to both Lagoons is continuously breaking—and the more prudent yachtsmen take shelter if they must, to the northwest in the lees of headlands.

It was in this area that one of our friends, Milt Farney, was harbor-hopping around Baja California some years ago (when Black Warrior was a commercial port) in the *Searcher,* a boat incredibly small for these waters—an 18-foot outboard! He had called at Black Warrior for gasoline and supplies and was on his way out of the channel when a call came over his radio-phone from another boat: "We are low on fresh water," the other skipper advised. "Can any boat in this vicinity spare us some?" Milt checked his own meager water container, then replied: "Yes, I guess I could let you have about 3 quarts. I've a pretty good beer supply." There was a moment of (probably stunned) silence on the airwaves before the other voice came back: "That will hardly be enough," a short chuckle, "we are the _____ (a freighter). We need at least a couple hundred gallon."
gallons."

A half hour later, Milt's tiny outboard met the approaching freighter coming into harbor. Now that the respective skippers were alerted to each other's identity there were deep-throated hoots of recognition from the ship and responding tinny blasts from Milt's hand horn. When abeam, the freighter's Captain came out on his bridge and called down to Milt: "Well thanks anyway, *Searcher,* for your offer. You're sure you don't want something from *us*?"

Heading on northwesterly along the upper contours of Bahia Sebastian Viscaino, there are a fair number of small anchorages affording varying degrees of protection from prevailing winds: Lagoon Head, Santa Rosalia Bay, Bahia Maria, Blanca, Canoas, and San Carlos Bays on the mainland, and on the eastern side of Geronimo Island. They are adequately described in H.O. No. 153, none have facilities nor shore access except through the surf. From a safety standpoint, the span of coastline from Point Eugenio, the southwestern extremity of Bahia Sebastian Vizcaino, to Point Antonio, southeast of Geronimo Island,

Monsoon II lies at anchor at the south end of Guadalupe Island
where we were taken ashore in a native dory, the surge being too
great for our own dinghy. This "small-boat landing" scene was
taken in what the natives consider "calm weather."

should be cruised during daylight if it is planned to drop anchor
in the lee of some of the points named. Except for the
sometimes lighted buoys at the entrances to Scammon Lagoon
and Black Warrior, there are no navigational lights along the
coast, and at night it is difficult to make out the ill-defined
headlands.

unless on a direct course from the northern end of Cedros
Island to a point well seaward of Geronimo Island. The light on
Geronimo is not always visible its rated 19 miles, and at night it
is the only aid (other than shipboard radar or depth sounder) to
insure passing Sacramento Reef which lies south of the island.

At low tide and with reasonably calm seas, breaking water is
plainly visible across the more prominent pinnacles of this
vicious reef. Uncharted in 1872, this reef gained its name after
the 271-foot, side-wheel steamer *Sacramento* foundered on its
rocky shoals while coming up the coast from Panama. Within
minutes after striking the reef, the ship filled with water to its
freight deck. Its 80 passengers and crew were fortunate in
making their escape to nearby Geronimo Island and five days
later were rescued by the steamer *Montana*. The *Sacramento's*
268 tons of merchandise cargo and $1,500,000 of coins, bound

for San Francisco from Mazatlan, were salvaged but remains of the ship's hull still attract adventurous skin divers who frequent the waters around Sacramento Reef. Not so fortunate were those aboard the 136-foot schooner *Good Will* which grounded on Sacramento Reef in 1969. There were no survivors, nor was the yacht salvageable.

Guadalupe Island, lying 140 miles west and slightly south of Geronimo, is perhaps best known to fishermen and scientific survey parties. Rising to nearly 4300 feet at its northern end, the island is a long-quiescent volcano. One of Mexico's most rugged and unapproachable offshore possessions, it housed a prison camp at one time. It is so remote from normal steamer traffic that there is not even a lighthouse on it, nor a radio beacon. Even in calm weather, thunderous breakers crash unceasingly about its rocky shoreline where offshore ocean depths quickly drop to over a mile—straight down. But despite its isolation and inaccessability, a settlement of some 50 people make their homes at Guadalupe's southern end, where there is a Mexican Navy Guard and a weather reporting station.

Our last visit to Guadalupe Island was at Christmas-time in 1967. When some of the fishermen saw *Monsoon II* standing off their "small boat landing," they came out and offered to bring us ashore in their sturdy dory. When we had a closer look at the rocky indentation—"the landing"—we were convinced that the average pleasure boat dinghy would have a difficult time negotiating this rugged shore access. Even with skilled hands maneuvering the heavy fishing dory, it was a considerable feat to cope with shoreside surge. The Guadalupe islanders seemed happy to have visitors and eagerly took us on tour of their settlement. Besides the weather station where hourly radio reports are sent to Mexico City and to U.S. stations, we were shown their small water-desalting plant which produces about seven gallons of fresh water per hour. To fill out their needs, additional water is brought over in casks from Ensenada once a month, on a supply ship.

Our party from *Monsoon II* had brought along pinatas for their children's Christmas, and in turn, we were presented with a bountiful supply of fresh lobsters. So prolific is their lobster catch, the fishermen told us, they were able to take 10 to 15 tons from their traps every three weeks during the season— October to May.

On Christmas day we cruised the western perimeter of

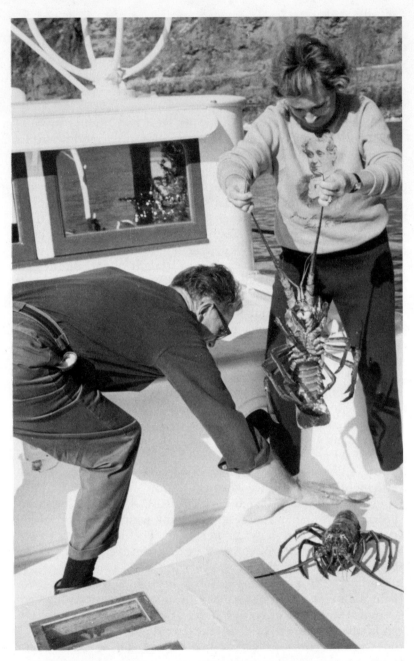

Lobsters instead of turkey were on our Christmas menu at Guadalupe Island.

Guadalupe, past the only other habitation at West Anchorage where a small fishing camp is situated. After rounding the island's northern end and passing an abandoned Army post, we reached a stretch of rocky beach where a large colony of sea-elephants make their home. The mature bull is reported to weigh more than a ton, with the sea-cow a close second in size. The bull's foot-long snout hangs as a foreshortened elephant's trunk. To signal his herd or just to join in the noise making, he tucks his proboscus into his open mouth and exhales in a ponderous blast. Once hunted almost to extinction for their oil, now the species is protected by Government regulations and is slowly making a comeback.

Returning to the Peninsula, San Quintin and Hassler Cove, the latter protected by San Martin Island, are the two more favored anchorages after passing Geronimo Island. San Quintin was once a seaport for the shipment of grain and other products grown or mined in the vicinity. But as is historical throughout Baja, the foreign interests (in this case, British) found their business methods incompatible with those of the natives and both mine and milling ventures dwindled to extinction. Now San Quintin is almost a ghost town except for the recent advent of several guest ranches available for touring hunters and fisherman. Two airstrips serve private or charter-plane pilots while others drive the 240 miles from San Diego on a paved highway.

Pismo clams, lobster and abalone abound along San Quintin's bayshore, beside the ever-present ocean fish. Ducks, geese and black sea-brandt frequent the coastal area from October until April. And for the minority group (those of us who hunt only with camera, or with hands for the inert stone, the shell, or piece of twisted driftwood) the Bay also presents a wealth of beach combings where tides roll in regularly to deposit their flotsam: glass net floats from Japan, fragile sea-fans from some southsea shore, gnarled fists of hardwood polished to a high red lustre—all are flung along the strand with their less exotic drift-mates, the bottle, the carton, the can. This polyglot tide of trinkets appears, for some geophysical quirk, to become pocketed here at San Quintin's nearly landlocked harbor as nowhere else along Baja's ocean coast. Even for the non-collector, it's an unusual show—pop-art of the sea.

Without local knowledge and shallow draft, boats should not be taken across the bar from San Quintin Bay to the inner

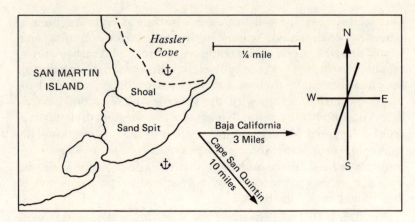

SAN MARTIN ISLAND
30° 29′ N lat; 116° 07′ W long

There are 10 fathoms of water within 1/2 miles of the Baja Calif-
fornia Peninsula to the east, and within 1/8 mile of the east
side of San Martin Island, and there are no obstructions along
either shore. Extending northeastward is a low sand spit with a
stone breakwater at the end. Anchorage in Hassler Cove affords
moderate protection from prevailing winds and seas, although
the south side of the sand spit affords better protection from
northwest winds. Some kelp extends from the lagoon along the
sand spit, which should be avoided when anchoring. Landing on
either side of the sand spit can usually be done with the average
dinghy during the early part of the day, before afternoon winds
commence blowing.

(former) harbor. Best anchorage area is in the northeast part of
the Bay, although there are plans now under development for a
protected small-boat harbor and marina facilities which may
replace the ghost-town face of this historic bayfront.

Roughly 12 miles northwest of San Quintin is San Martin
Island, a nearly 500-foot-high extinct volcano. The island has a
navigational light and two good anchorages. The best in
prevailing northwesterlies in Hassler Cove, on the east side; the
other is on the southwast shore in the lee of a low neck of
rocky outcroppings. (See chart). Due to the topography of
adjacent peninsula shores where mountain peaks rear abruptly
from sea level to 4 to 5000 feet and to extreme temperature
variations between inland desert heat and cool ocean waters,
winds along this particular section are apt to be erratic.
Sometimes they will switch 180 degrees in as many seconds.

One may be snugly anchored one moment and dragging all over the cove the next. We have experienced such abrupt wind changes, particularly at Colnett Bay, some 32 miles northwest of San Martin. Here the winds will freakishly switch to slam in on an anchored boat from the east or south, even though its direction is still strong from the northwest outside this semi-circular harbor.

There are two more coves of partial refuge up-coast from Cape Colnett before reaching Punta Banda, 10 miles west of Baja's last Pacific port of call at Ensenada. These are found at San Jose and Santo Tomas Bay. The former is heavily ridden with kelp and the latter anchorage proves an obstacle course for boats moving into ist small protection. Santo Tomas Bay is a shipping point for lobster, and traps used for holding them before shipment are scattered at random across the cove. But despite the many lacks in these and other Peninsula coastal refuge coves, when sanctuary is needed, any of them will appear heaven-sent to the weary skipper and his crew.

For those not intending to enter Ensenada's harbor, which requires clearance in and out with the Port Captain and Customs officials, there are a number of small anchorages on the eastern side of Todos Santos Islands. Uninhabited except for itinerant native fishing camps, the anchorages provide easy access to shore and their water-carved caves and arches are interesting to explore by dinghy. Dive if you will for lobster and abalone which line the rocky island shorelines, but in keeping with Mexican law, none of this shellfish may be taken across the U.S. border.

Ensenada is not typical of other Mexican communities to the south. A border town never is. But it does have its own charm and appeal, especially so during its several annual fiestas. The week before Christmas celebration of La Posada and the week-long Mardi Gras carnival preceding Lent, are two of the most festive celebrations with daily parades, dancing and, always, their own inimitable music.

Each year this port is host to and finish line for the colossus of all sailing races, the Cinco de Mayo (May fifth) contest which starts at Newport Beach, California and has for the last several years included well over 500 sailing entrants. Ensenada's ample harbor offers good anchorage within its breakwaters, but as afternoon northwest winds are often a brisk 15 to 20 knots, the wise skipper will be certain to pay out sufficient anchor chain

Mardi Gras parade and fiesta held annually at Ensenada.

before leaving his boat unattended. There are no slips for visiting boats, but water-taxi service is available. The visitor's own dinghy can sometimes be used and tied to floats used by the water taxis. Gasoline or diesel fuel is not easily obtained; if needed, arrangements must be made through a broker to have it delivered by tank-truck, and the boat maneuvered close enough to one of the water-taxi floats, or across the harbor to one of the commercial piers, to take the hose from the truck.

Ensenada's history since the 1880s has been a colorful series of contrasts. Once a gold rush center and a cross-roads for soldiers of fortune from Europe and the Orient, it thrived with a winery, a tannery, a soap factory and flour mill. In 1887 it became Mexico's territorial capital with its prosperity heightened by a British firm leasing 16 million acres of farmland from the Mexican government and investing huge sums in roads, a wharf and a spur railroad. By the early 1900's, however, the gold veins were depleted. The English Company, as the syndicate was known, failed in its grandiose undertakings and moved away. Ensenada dwindled to nothing—a ravished ghost-town—and the capital site was moved inland to Mexicali. For the next 20 years, the small remaining populace subsisted primarily by fishing.

Tourism commenced Ensenada's upswing toward prosperity when, in 1930, ex-boxing champion Jack Dempsey financed the construction of a lavish gambling casino, Hotel Playa, later known as El Riviera del Pacifico. Although gambling was declared illegal in Mexico only two short years after the Casino's opening, this was enough to start an ever-increasing tide of tourists to Ensenada. In 1958 a Mexican harbor improvement program was responsible for the completion of a 54-million peso breakwater protecting what had been strictly open roadstead. This, coupled with an upgrading of roads and irrigation in the fertile inland farmlands, has combined to strengthen the economy of Baja's largest ocean port where cotton export rates highest of its varied products.

Commercial ships and pleasure boats from all over the world may be seen at any time in Ensenada's duty-free port. And elsewhere in town and along the sunny beachfront there are many new hotels, restaurants and gift shops. Charter sport-fishing boats move in and out of harbor trailed by a wake of gulls. High on Chapultepec Hill, overlooking Todos Santos Bay, real estate subdividers are hard at work building more miles of residential streets and erecting scores of modern homes—vari-colored houses which rise as formal rows of flowers against this balding sun-baked hill.

So grows the long-touted "forgotten land" of Baja California. One by one the tiny village assumes first the outline of a city, then of a budding spa. Tourist and new-business seeker alike march into line, as an ant colony moving steadily into that long, strange finger of land we know as Lower California. Each is drawn to his own "discovery": the fish, the salubrious climate, the palm-shaded but short-lived hideaway.

Meanwhile, the high-humped mountain spine bisecting Baja's longitude broods over its hidden wealth of precious stones and minerals, once briefly sought and fought for. Along with tourist dollars now flowing in with pleasure boating, mining may yet provide Baja with its biggest boom.

The 60-mile run from Ensenada to the border and San Diego may be run fairly close to shore, the better to note the coast's significant signs of economic growth. Only a decade ago these shores were as devoid of habitation as is much of the Peninsula's lower region. Now clusters of motels, shopping centers and beach resorts appear to spring up overnight, insidiously merging to form a nearly unbroken line of facilities for passing motorists

The lighthouse is the only operating structure remaining on South Coronados Island today. Years ago a lavish restaurant-and-bar resort flourished (to left of anchored boat) but shoreside access proved too dificult. Now only the skelatal remains of the resort buildings stand at water's edge.

along the coastal highway extending from the U.S. to Tijuana and Ensenada.

In clear weather and when abeam Descanso Point, the group of four rock islands, Los Coronados, rise above the horizon ahead and are normally passed to port. Waters around their barren perimeters are favorite fishing grounds in this ocean segment but due to a lack of shore access, nothing but seals and birds live on the islands proper, except for the lighthouse keepers on South Coronados Island.

Ten miles beyond the Coronados sway the long line of red and black buoys marking San Diego's entrance channel, and boats from Mexican waters slow to a halt at the well-marked Harbor Master's dock on Shelter Island for Customs Clearance into the United States.

Appendix to Part One

Types of Boats Suitable for Mexico Cruising
Facilities and Supplies
Approximate Distances in Nautical Miles
Food Supplies for Mexican Cruising
Mexican Requirements for Clearance of Pleasure Boats
Security
Electric/Electronic Equipment
Spare Parts
Film
Imports — Merchandise, Liquor
Air Transportation
Ferry Service
Marine Weather Reports
Tropical Storms
Fueling and Watering
Fenders
Mechanical and Hull repairs
Books and Guides

TYPES OF BOATS SUITABLE FOR MEXICO CRUISING
 Although an 18-foot outboard cruiser has successfully cir-
cumnavigated the Peninsula, starting from Los Angeles and
ending the trip at San Felipe, it is not recommended. Similarly,
20- to 25-foot sailboats have made the trip down the coast,
proving that it can be done. In general, however, powered or
sailboats of up to 25-foot length should limit their cruising to
the upper reaches of the Gulf. Launching points would be from
San Felipe on the Peninsula, and Guaymas, San Carlos or Kino
on the mainland. Fuel, water, provisions and general comfort of
the crew are the limiting factors.

There are hundreds of charter sportfishing boats under 30-foot length operating from all the mainland ports and from Bahia Los Angeles, Chivato, Mulege, Loreto, La Paz and by the resort hotels near the Cape. The majority were either built locally, shipped down on the decks of freighters, or launched from trailers at the upper end of the Gulf. Their radius of action, however, is normally confined to 25 to 50 miles from their home ports.

Auxiliary-powered sailboats of 30-foot length, or more, and equipped with larger fuel and water tanks than normally provided, have only a few more problems than they would have in cruising stateside waters. The distances between provisioning stops, lack of ice for refrigeration and relatively long distances between harbors on the Pacific side of the Peninsula are the principal ones. Forty-foot, diesel-powered cruisers, with sufficient fuel for at least 350 miles of sustained cruising, are adequate for cruising the Gulf region, but need to pick their weather when going up the Pacific side of the Peninsula. Nor would they be too well suited for crossing the Gulf and continuing as far south as Acapulco.

Trailed-boat owners should recognize that most such hulls are critical to the amount of load they can safely carry. Emergency equipment, provisions, extra water and fuel required when cruising on the Gulf can materially reduce their normal speed and seaworthiness. The buddy-system of a number of boats cruising together is highly recommended, with at least one boat in the group equipped with a radiotelephone. Filing of a cruise plan with a responsible person at the point of departure and ultimate destination is an additional safety measure—since there is no Coast Guard in Mexico ready to rush out from a nearby harbor to effect a rescue in case of engine failure or adverse weather.

For those who plan to trail their boats south from Tijuana on Baja's newly completed highway, some words of caution: There is no opportunity to launch a boat in the Gulf until reaching Santa Rosalia, approximately half way down the Peninsula. At this point there is a dirt-and-sand ramp. Similar ramps exist at the five other launching areas to the south, namely: Mulege, Coyote Bay in Concepcion Bay, Loreto, Puerto Escondito and at La Paz. On the mainland side of the Gulf (reached on paved highway from Nogales), boats can be launched from concrete ramps at San Carlos, Guaymas, Kino, and San Felipe. San

Felipe is connected to Mexicali by paved highway.

Mexican regulations: Permits, valid for 180 days only, must be obtained from the Mexican customs office at the port of entry. Carry proof of ownership of your car, trailer and boat. If any of them are not fully paid for or are registered in another's name, obtain a notarized statement from the lienholder or owner authorizing use of the vehicle in Mexico for a specified period and present it at the border. U.S. automobile insurance is not valid in Mexico. Motorists should arrange for full coverage, property damage and public liability with a Mexican insurance company at port of entry.

FACILITIES AND SUPPLIES

Mainland Mexico:

Acapulco	a	b	d	g	h	m	r	s	t	w
Zihuatanejo	a	-	-	g**	h	-	r	s	t	w**
Manzanillo	a	b	d	g	h	m	r	s	t	w
Puerto Vallarta	a	b	d	g	h	m	r	s	t	w
Mazatlan	a	b	d	g	h	m	r	s	t	w
Topolobampo	-	-	d	g*	-	m	-	s	t	w
Guaymas (area)	a	b	d	g	h	m	r	s	t	w
Kino	-	-	-	g**	h	-	-	s	-	w**

Baja California:

San Felipe	a	-	-	g**	h	-	r	s	-	w**
Bahia Los Angeles	a	-	-	g*	h	-	-	s	-	w*
Santa Rosalia	a	b	d*	g*	h	m	r	s	t	w*
Mulege	a	-	-	g**	h	m	r	s	t	w**
Loreto	a	-	-	g**	h	-	r	s	t	w**
La Paz	a	b	d	g	h	m	r	s	t	w
Cabo San Lucas	a	b	d	g*	h	m	r	s	t	w
San Carlos (Magdalena Bay)	a	-	d	g	-	m	-	-	t	w
Asuncion	-	-	-	g**	-	-	-	s*	-	w**
Turtle Bay	a	-	d*	g*	-	-	-	s*	-	-
Cedros Island (village)	a	-	d*	g*	-	m	-	s	t	w
Ensenada	a	b	d	g	h	m	r	s	t	-

Key

a - air service, scheduled or charter
b - butane gas
d - diesel fuel
g - gasoline
h - hotel(s)
m - mechanical repairs

r - restaurant(s)
s - supplies
t - telegraph office
w - water
* - limited amounts
** - limited and lightered

APPROXIMATE DISTANCES IN NAUTICAL MILES

BETWEEN PRINCIPAL MAINLAND AND UPPER GULF POINTS:

1	2	Between col. 1 & col. 2	From Acapulco to col. 2 (cumulative)	From San Felipe to col. 1 (cumulative)
Acapulco	Popanoa	102	102	1385
Popanoa	Zihautanejo	33	135	1283
Zihautanejo	Isla Grande	10	145	1250
Isla Grande	Mangrove Pt.	32	177	1240
Mangrove Pt.	Bufadero	32	209	1208
Bufadero	Lizard	22	231	1176
Lizard	Maruata	14	245	1154
Maruata	Manzanillo	75	320	1140
Manzanillo	La Barre Navidad	30	350	1065
La Barre Navidad	Tenacatita	10	360	1035
Tenacatita	Chamela Bay	25	385	1025
Chamela Bay	Ypala	40	425	1000
Ypala	Cape Corrientes	12	437	960
Cape Corrientes	Yelapa	15	452	948
Yelapa	Puerto Vallarta	12	464	933
Puerto Vallarta	Punta Mita	17	481	921
Punta Mita	Jaltemba	15	496	904
Jaltemba	Ensenada de Chacala	20	516	889
Ensenada de Chacala	San Blas (Matenchen)	21	537	869
San Blas (Matenchen) (San Blas to Cape San Lucas 272.)	Isabel I.	42	579	848
Isabel I.	Mazatlan	84	663	806
Mazatlan. (Mazatlan to Cape San Lucas 240.)	Topolobampo	212	875	722
Topolobampo	Guaymas	190	1065	510
Guaymas	San Carlos	16	1081	320
San Carlos	San Pedro	14	1095	304
San Pedro	Tiburon I.*	70	1165	290
Tiburon I.*	La Guarda I.*	50	1215	220
La Guarda I.*	Refugio	45	1260	170
Refugio	San Felipe	125	1385	125

BETWEEN PRINCIPAL BAJA CALIFORNIA POINTS:

1	2	Between col. 1 & col. 2	From San Felipe to col. 2 (cumulative)	To San Diego from col. 1 (cumulative)
San Felipe	Puertocitos	40	40	1438
Puertocitos	Willard Bay	40	80	1398
Willard Bay	Refugio	45	125	1358
Refugio	Los Angeles Bay	40	165	1313
Los Angeles Bay	San Francisquito	46	211	1273
San Francisquito	Santa Rosalia	72	283	1227
Santa Rosalia	San Marcos I.	18	301	1155
San Marcos I.	Mulege	20	321	1137
Mulege	Loreto	66	387	1117

(Mulege to Guaymas 85,
Mulege to Kino 110.)

1	2	Between col. 1 & col. 2	From San Felipe to col. 2 (cumulative)	To San Diego from col. 1 (cumulative)
Loreto	Puerto Escondito	12	399	1051
Puerto Escondito	Agua Verde	25	424	1039
Agua Verde	Nopolo	35	459	1014
Nopolo	La Paz	62	521	979
La Paz	Muertos Bay	55	576	917

(La Paz to Pichilinque 7,
La Paz to Mazatlan 240,
La Paz to Esperitu Santo I. 24.)

1	2	Between col. 1 & col. 2	From San Felipe to col. 2 (cumulative)	To San Diego from col. 1 (cumulative)
Muertos Bay	Las Palmas	20	596	862
Las Palmas	Los Frailes	28	624	842
Los Frailes	Cape San Lucas	45	669	814
Cape San Lucas	Magdalena Bay**	160	829	769
Magdalena Bay**	Asuncion Bay	200	1029	609
Asuncion Bay	Turtle Bay	55	1084	429
Turtle Bay	Cedros I.***	32	1116	354
Cedros I.***	San Martin I.	155	1271	322
San Martin I.	Colnett Bay	32	1303	167
Colnett Bay	Ensenada	70	1373	135
Ensenada	San Diego	65	1438	65

*   South end of both Tiburon and La Guarda.
**   Entrance to Magdalena Bay.
***Village at Cedros Island.

FOOD SUPPLIES FOR MEXICAN CRUISING

Fish— Although sport-fishing for the so-called "game fish" continues unabated in Mexican waters, both turtles and shellfish are becoming scarce. In view of this decimation, the Mexican Government has established a total ban on turtle harvesting, and lobster-taking is restricted to certain months of the year. Certain varieties of clams and scallops, formerly found in abundance at low tide close to the Peninsula's shoreline, now can only be located in remote areas at depths of 60 feet offshore. Other clam beds, such as those in Concepcion Bay, are now almost barren. Because of this scarcity of lobster, shrimp, clams and abalone, their prices are proportionately higher if purchased, and entail far greater effort, if sought. As for the few butter-clams still remaining that one may happen onto, an easy method for determining if they are safe for consumption is to place a silver spoon or silver coin in the pot while the shellfish cooks. If the silver stays brilliant, the shellfish are safe to eat; if it turns dark, they are not safe.

Fresh Meat— Resort restaurants ordinarily have much of their food stuffs, including meats, flown in from Mexico City. This food is comparable to that in the U.S. and Canada. Locally raised beef and pork is usually not aged. Some sailors carry a meat-grinder aboard to render unhung meat chewable. More often, canned or frozen meats are carried aboard.

Mexican Home-Made Bread (*pan,* pronounced "pahn") may almost always be purchased anywhere half a dozen or more families make their homes, and it is delicious by anyone's standards. It does not keep fresh as long as our own commercial variety, so it's best not to overstock unless it can be frozen.

Eggs— In all but the very smallest communities the local citizens will have a few eggs to spare from their own flocks or from their market places. These are smaller than our U.S. hens' eggs, but this might be expected. Scratching is harder down there.

Beer, Wines and Liquor— Mexican Government cannery towns are not allowed by law to stock or sell alcoholic beverages. This also applies to the Mission settlement of Mulege. On Baja California the only sources are La Paz, Loreto, Santa Rosalia, San Jose del Cabo and Ensenada. On the mainland, supplies can be obtained at Acapulco, Manzanillo, Puerto Vallarta, Mazatlan and Guaymas. Resort hotels cater to bar customers but do not sell packaged goods.

Fruits, Vegetables and Staples— To answer the question "Is it safe to eat fruits and vegetables grown in Mexico?" it may be noted that much of the farm produce (tomatoes, lettuce, semitropical fruits, etc.) grown in the lower Peninsula area is exported to the southwestern United States. This could not be done if such exports did not meet U.S. Pure Food standards.

MEXICAN REQUIREMENTS FOR CLEARANCE OF PLEASURE BOATS

To enter Mexican waters the owner or captain is required to have a crew list and clearance from the United States, certified by the Mexican consul at Los Angeles or San Diego, for presentation to the Port Captain and Immigration officials at the first port of entry in Mexico. The form, in quadruplicate, shows name of boat, nationality, registration or documentation number, gross and net tonnage, port of departure and first Mexican port of entry; name, age, nationality and position aboard of each person on the boat. Cost of the Consular certification for clearance is $40, if the owner has access to the forms (which are not available from the consulates, but can be obtained from a broker); or somewhat more if a broker handles the entire transaction. In addition, the owner must have a declaration form to the effect that the yacht is not carrying cargo or engaged in any type of commercial work in Mexican waters. These forms can be completed by the owner if he has access to them, but again they are generally available only from a broker. If sport fishing is contemplated while in Mexico, both the boat and each person must have a permit, obtainable from the Mexican Fish Commission Offices in San Pedro or San Diego.

Tourist cards for each person aboard the boat must also be obtained prior to leaving, for presentation to the Port Captains and Immigration officials at ports visited, at the time the boat's and crew's clearance papers are tendered for entry or departure. They can be obtained from offices of the Mexican Tourist Bureau without charge, but only by the person named on the card.

There is little uniformity of port clearance procedures when going from one Mexican port to another, notwithstanding statements frequently published by Mexican officials. At some ports they are insisting additionally on a six-month permit for the boat, at varying amounts of money from $8.00 upwards. To obtain one they require the serial numbers of the engines and considerable other information. In some cases the Customs officials require an inspection by one of their men, at an additional charge, to verify the engine numbers. Another new wrinkle in obtaining departure papers at some ports is to assess a delayed departure fee, even though the boat may be leaving immediately. Normally a boat is allowed to depart within 24 hours after being cleared to leave, without being penalized. There is also wide variation from port to port on what hours the paper-work will be done by officials without charging overtime. When we handle our own papers we try to do so between 0900 and 1100 hours, but generally we use a broker and let him worry about the problem. There appears to be no recourse from these variances and a first-time visitor to Mexican ports should anticipate them; if he does not, they can spoil the trip.

Before re-entering U.S. waters from Mexico, it is necessary to obtain a departure clearance from the last port of call in Mexico. This can be done at La Paz if it is planned to omit Cape San Lucas or Ensenada as ports of call on the return trip; or at Cape San Lucas or at Ensenada if they are the last ports of call. Such clearance papers are not required by the U.S. Customs Service, but serve the purpose of officially removing the yacht and its crew from the list of those still cruising in Mexican waters. The cost varies between $4.00 and $15.00, depending on whether a broker is used to obtain the clearance or if done by the skipper.

Upon arrival at the first U.S. port, the skipper must immediately phone the nearest U.S. Customs Service office and report his arrival. At the option of the Customs Service, they may clear the boat over the phone, or send an Inspector to determine if there is dutiable merchandise, prohibited foreign fresh foods or liquor aboard. Until cleared by phone or by the Inspector, guests and crew must remain aboard. This service is provided without charge between 8 AM and 5 PM, except on holidays or Sundays when there is then imposed an overtime charge, and is available to numbered boats as well as those that are documented.

SECURITY

The increasing number of cases where tenders, outboards, gasoline tanks and other gear in dinghies have mysteriously disappeared, is appalling. Similarly, the reports of boats being broken into while owners and guests are ashore, and equipment stolen, are increasing. These situations are mainly at the major harbors, such as Acapulco, Mazatlan, Guaymas, La Paz and Ensenada, but have also occurred at such isolated anchorages as Hassler Cove, San Martin Island. It is unfortunately true that there is evidence that crew members from stateside boats are not without suspicion. Unless a tender is taken aboard at night it should be chained and padlocked, including the engine, to its mother-ship. Cushions, fenders, flashlights and gasoline cans should be removed and stowed in a safe place. There is no assurance that when ashore, and the tender theoretically is "being watched by a dock-boy," loose gear will not be found missing, even in broad daylight.

ELECTRIC/ELECTRONIC EQUIPMENT

With the exception of trailed boats, both power and sailboats will find an electric anchor-windlass a near necessity, because in all of Mexico's mainland and Baja California there are virtually no docks or slips for visiting boats. The best of ground tackle is extremely important, which means at least one spare anchor and extra chain. Of equal value are a depth sounder and radio telephone. Especially for the short-handed crew, an automatic pilot is of importance in reducing the work load for those on watch. Due to the limited number of broadcast stations and radio beacons in Mexico, direction finders are of only nominal value. Radar is useful for nighttime navigation and for use during the occasional periods of fog along the Pacific side of the Peninsula.

SPARE PARTS

Caution: Carry aboard as much spare equipment as possible. There seems to be no easy way to receive parts sent from the United States to a Mexican port.

FILM

Do *not* send exposed film back to the U.S. from Mexico. It rarely, if ever, is received in this country for processing.

IMPORTS

Merchandise— Each person clearing Customs back into the U.S. is allowed $100 worth of duty-free merchandise. Save your receipts for proof.

Liquor— California State law forbids entry of alcoholic liquor purchased in Mexico by a resident of California. If one or more passengers or crew on a private boat maintain their legal residences in some other state he *is* allowed to bring from Mexico an amount of alcoholic beverage up to one gallon, but must have proof of non-California residence to present to U.S. Customs authorities.

AIR TRANSPORTATION

Scheduled air service to both Baja California and Mexico's western mainland seaports brings the more popular areas to within a few hours of the States. Charter operators at La Paz serve the area between there and Cape San Lucas.

FERRY SERVICE

Combination passenger and car ferries operate between Guaymas and Santa Rosalia, and between Topolobampo and Mazatlan and La Paz on frequencies of three or four times each week. Trailed boats can also be transported on the ferries.

MARINE WEATHER REPORTS

For weather reports in Mexican waters, most skippers rely on radiotelephone communications with commercial fishing boats or other yachtsmen cruising the area. An informal "radio watch" schedule of 0800, 1200 and 1600 hours (La Paz time) has been the custom of yachtsmen, for exchange of weather information, on 2638 kHz. For those who understand rapid Spanish, Mazatlan Radio broadcasts a weather sequence on 2715 kHz at 0910, 1100 and on 2660 kHz at 1200 hours local time. Tropical storm advisories are broadcast by KOU (San Pedro) and KMI (Oakland, Calif.) Boats equipped with medium- or high-seas radiotelephones can monitor the broadcasts which are made two or more times daily.

TROPICAL STORMS

The months of June to October inclusive are when severe tropical storms, nearly one half of them rising to hurricane force (over 64 knots), can be expected over Mexico's waters. ESSA Weather Bureau records, as published in summarized form in their *Mariners Weather Log,* show that a few are reported as early as May in the area near Acapulco, and that the greatest number are generally in September. Plotted tracks of the cyclones (34 to 63 knots) show that the storms move further northward along the Baja California Peninsula during late summer, with some reaching Southern California.

Quoting from *Mariners Weather Log,* "The probability of tropical cyclone development continues to rise sharply in June approaching the late summer and early fall maximum. These storms are usually short-lived but can be dangerous to both shipping and coastal areas." Movement of these storms is generally from the southeast to the northwest—parallel with the Mexican mainland or Peninsula coasts.

H. O. No. 153 has a number of pages discussing tropical storms, but it should be noted that the most recent date of the data used was 1935—long before the use of weather satellites and frequent radio reports from vessels that now provide a great deal more data on the storms. The basic tracks of the storms reported in H. O. No. 153 appear to be approximately the same as tracks plotted in recent years from more complete data.

Below is a table from ESSA showing average monthly frequencies of storms for the 15-year period between 1947 and 1961—admittedly somewhat old data, but more recent than the material in H. O. No. 153.

Month	Total Number	Hurricane Force	Average Duration
May	4	none	4.8 days
June	18	6	4.1 days
July	23	9	4.8 days
August	14	5	5.1 days
September	30	15	4.6 days
October	20	11	3.6 days
November	3	2	2.7 days

FUELING AND WATERING

The only harbors at which diesel fuel and drinking water are available from docks are Acapulco, Manzanillo, Puerto Vallarta, Mazatlan, San Carlos, Guaymas, La Paz, Cape San Lucas, San Carlos in Magdalena Bay and Cedros Village on Cedros Island. At La Paz, diesel fuel is taken at Prieta Point, about four miles out from La Paz at the channel entrance, and water from the municipal pier in the harbor. At Ensenada, fuel must be brought to the harbor by a tank truck. Permits are generally required from the Customs Office for fuel, except at San Carlos in Magdalena Bay. For those needing only moderate amounts of diesel fuel and gasoline at La Paz, drums of fuel will be delivered to the Abaroa shipyard for pumping aboard the boat. This necessitates dropping a bow anchor, backing down toward a stone jetty, use of a stern line to the jetty, and either hand or electric pumps to transfer fuel to the boat.

Even though gasoline and diesel fuel are shown as available at certain harbors on the facilities and supplies tabulation, there are times when supplies are exhausted by local fishermen and it may be necessary to wait until the coastal supply ships arrive with new supplies. At all other harbors where limited and/or lightered amounts of gasoline and water are available, the visiting yacht must have the necessary hoses and pumps to transfer the fuel and water to boat tanks. For that reason, separate hoses and pumps should be carried aboard, to avoid contamination. When taking fuel oil or gasoline from drums, it is prudent to keep the suction line a few inches above the bottom of the drum to avoid pumping sediment and water condensation into the boat tanks—or else to filter the fuel through a fine mesh screen or chamois before it goes into the tanks.

Trailed boats launched in Gulf waters, powered with gasoline engines, can get fuel from hoses at a dock or float only at San Carlos Marina near Guaymas and at Bahia Los Angeles. At all other harbors it is necessary to take jerry cans ashore to a service station to have them filled.

FENDERS

Without exception, the skiffs and canoes of local fishermen or water taxis are heavy, rugged boats without gunwale guards. This necessitates many substantial fenders for hull protection. The most practical are automobile tires covered with sack-like canvas bags, to avoid black tire marks on hull sides. The average yacht-type fender, suitable for stateside usage, is far from adequate.

MECHANICAL AND HULL REPAIRS

There are a number of marine railways at Manzanillo, Mazatlan and Guaymas on the mainland side; those at Mazatlan and Guaymas are shipyards building wood and steel shrimpers for the Mexican fishing fleets. The railways at Santa Rosalia and La Paz are used mainly for hull repairs of local boats. All of them, however, may be tied up for days or weeks with craft undergoing extensive repairs. Ensenada has both a floating drydock for large craft and marine railways. There are machine shops associated with the shipyards, capable of handling general repairs.

Machine shops are also available for emergency repairs at each of the cannery harbors: Cape San Lucas, Puerto Cortez in Magdalena Bay, Asuncion, Turtle Bay, Cedros Village and Ensenada.

Since La Paz is a mid-point in cruising Mexican waters, it has become better equipped to repair and service such equipment as refrigeration, engines, radiotelephones and radar. Main problem may be the lack of a particular part needing replacement, but the availability of jetplane service between La Paz and the States helps in getting replacements—although Customs red-tape is frequently a serious problem.

We have found (all in La Paz) Electronica Arechiga, S.A. qualified to repair electronic equipment; Lorenzo Verdugo M., Madero & Bravo No. 206, highly experienced in repair of engines; Soldadura Y Maguinado En Metals, Av. Revolucion No. 195-B Sur, operated by Javier Sanchez A. (who speaks excellent English), thoroughly experienced in the repair of electric generators and alternators; and Embarcaciones Baja Californianas, operated by Mac Shroyer, qualified in wood and fiberglass fabrication. The latter firm also builds Uniflite sportsfishing boats under license; they can provide mooring buoys, water taxi service, guides and crew members, and they are engaged in powerboat chartering in the Baja Gulf. They maintain a radio watch on 2738 kHz, call sign YSM, which has proven of tremendous help to yachtsmen needing some special service or assistance.

BOOKS AND GUIDES

Sea Guide Baja, Leland R. Lewis and Peter E. Ebeling, Volume II, Sea Publications, Inc., Newport Beach, California.

Lower California Guide Book, Gerhard & Gulic, third revision, Arthur H. Clark Co., Glendale, California.

Cove Cruising Charts, Bahia Oculta to San Carlos and San Carlos to Guaymas, Gerry Cunningham, Blockits, Inc., Box 386, Boulder, Colorado.

Sea of Cortez, John Steinbeck, Viking Press: Compass paperback.

The Sea of Cortez, Ray Cannon and the *Sunset* Editors, Lane Magazine & Book Co., Menlo Park, California.

Many Mexicos, Lesley Byrd Simpson, University of California Press, Berkeley, California.

Kym's Guide No. 6, The Sea of Cortez and Baja California Peninsula, Ray Cannon, Triumph Press Inc., 320 E. Harvard St., Glendale, California.

Sailing Directions for the West Coast of Mexico and Central America, H.O. No. 153. Included are graphic indexes showing all charts, both small and large scale, that are available from the U.S. Naval Oceanographic Office.

West Coast North & South America Tide Tables has daily predictions for major harbors in Mexico and tidal difference tables for secondary harbors on the mainland and Baja California.

Tide Calender for the Northern Gulf of California, Department of Biological Sciences, The University of Arizona, Tuscon, Arizona.

Part Two

CALIFORNIA / OREGON / WASHINGTON

Topographically the California, Oregon and Washington coasts make a slow change from the dry, treeless shoreline of Baja California. The first 200 miles northward from the California-Mexican border only slowly become greener and timbered, and not until past San Francisco do winter rains and higher-moistured air give life to foliage.

The coasts of both Baja California and the United States have a common characteristic of a substantial mountain range close to the Pacific shoreline—sometimes rising 2000 to 3000 feet within a mile of the beach; other times further inland only as far as 5 to 10 miles.

Between San Diego and Eureka, California, a distance of about 630 miles, the coastal range and higher mountains of the Sierra Nevada range are separated by the vast Imperial and San Joaquin valleys. This has a distinct bearing on summer wind and fog conditions along this portion of the coast, with high heat in the valleys creating a strong draft of cool ocean air to flow into them as hot air rises from the valleys during the heat of day. This is followed by the warm air spreading out to the coast during the night and creating fog conditions that will persist until midday when the strong on-shore winds again take over.

Northward of the California-Oregon border, summer heat in the interior is not as great as in California, and there is less of a draft created. It is partially due to the more northerly latitude; more timbered mountains, which tend to hold down the interior temperatures; and smaller valleys, eastward of the coastal range. The result is less fog during July, August and September off such points as the Columbia River entrance in Oregon and Cape Flattery, Washington, than off such California points as Pt. Reyes and Pt. Sur. The *Coast Pilot* reports that during the three months of July, August and September the total fog-signal operation at San Diego averages 20 hours for the three months, at Los Angeles, 101 hours, at the entrance to San Francisco 331, at Eureka 517, at Columbia River Lightship 189, and at Cape Flattery 373. This is in contrast to roughly 60% fewer fog-hours during May and June when inland temperatures are considerably lower. Similarly, the amount of fog during the early fall is considerably less than during the three summer months, for the same reason.

When making a northbound coastal trip many purposely do so in either late spring or early fall, to avoid the consistently higher northwest winds and morning fogs that are common during summer months. Those who do cruise north during midsummer will frequently take departure from one harbor to the next in the very early hours of the morning—long before daylight—and pass by such headlands as Pt. Conception, Pt. Sur, Pt. Reyes, Pt. Arena and Cape Mendocino as early in the day as possible to avoid the midafternoon winds that whip around these points. Small commercial fishing boats often hug the shore on the theory that the hills and bluffs tend to lift the strong flow of air at a distance of ¼ to ½ mile from the beach—and thus reduce its velocity close to the shoreline.

Along the roughly 1200 miles of Pacific Coast that separate San Diego and Seattle, there are four major boating areas. The largest is between San Diego and Santa Barbara, which includes Newport, Long Beach and Los Angeles. Blessed with fair weather for most of the twelve months, this region of 175 miles length has more harbors than any other similar stretch of the Pacific Coast. Their development has been directly related to the density of population, which makes them economically feasible, although their year-around boat usage has contributed substantially to new harbor construction.

Second major boating center is in Puget Sound, Washington, with Seattle, Tacoma and Olympia the principal subcenters. While Southern California has as its main boating asset favorable weather conditions for open ocean sailing and cruising, the Puget Sound area's asset is its thousands of miles of protected waterways, hundreds of islands, and untold numbers of anchorages or mooring facilities.

The third boating center can be broadly described as in the triangle formed by San Francisco, Sacramento and Stockton, California. Here the many assets include some 1500 miles of rivers and connecting waterways of the Delta area, and the

Brisk afternoon winds are the rule in San Francisco Bay during
summer months. One tower of the Golden Gate Bridge is to the
westward of this sloop.

broad expanses of San Francisco and San Pablo Bays. These
areas enjoy favorable boating weather for the majority of the
year, and a larger number of small craft marinas and launching
sites has been constructed within this triangle during the past
five years than in any other area on the Pacific Coast.

Not to be overlooked is the boating activity on the Columbia

The abandoned lighthouse at Tillamook Rock is now privately owned. A lighted whistle buoy, ½-mile westward of the old lighthouse, has replaced this navigational aid.

River, which separates Oregon from Washington, and its tributaries. Starting near the mouth of the Columbia River at Astoria, these cruising and sailing waters extend eastward to the manmade lakes that have been created by the building of Bonneville Dam and others, on either the upper Columbia River or its tributaries. Some 500 miles of cruising waters are in this area.

Between San Diego and San Francisco, roughly 425 miles, there are harbors or sheltered anchorages that make it an easy trip. The longest stretch between them is only about 50 miles—between San Simeon anchorage and the lee of Pt. Sur. Many of the harbors are new within the last 10 years, man-made by dredging millions of cubic yards of earth from the shoreline and building jetties to form entrance channels. Most of the new harbor facilities along the California coast were constructed through long-term loans from the state's Department of Navigation and Ocean Development. During the past decade it has provided over $40 million for recreational craft harbor improvements.

North of Pt. Reyes, 25 miles northwest of the entrance to San Francisco, the distances between harbors or sheltered anchorages jump to between 75 and 150 miles. Going further north, along the Oregon and Washington coasts there are such harbors as Coos Bay, Waldport, Newport, Tillamook, Astoria (10 miles within the entrance to the Columbia River), Willapa Bay and Grays Harbor. Some of these are not more than 20 or 30 miles apart, but each is at or near the mouth of a river. Without exception there are bars to negotiate at the entrances. Under fair weather conditions there is no problem in crossing the bars, but they are tricky or downright dangerous if seas are running. Those who do go into the Oregon and Washington harbors along the coast should time their arrivals at the entrances to be in the mornings, and preferably during slack- or flood-tide conditions.

It has always been our choice to make a direct run between Port Orford and Cape Flattery. The distance is about 340 miles, but one completely avoids the problem of bars at the intermediate harbors. On one trip when we did not make a straight through-run, we found it necessary to enter Gray's Harbor, on the Washington coast. Although it was reasonably calm off the coast, the Coast Guard advised us to wait nearly six hours for the start of the flood tide into Gray's Harbor before crossing the bar.

Once around Cape Flattery, the northwesternmost point of Washington, it is a downhill ride through the Strait of Juan de Fuca to Puget Sound or the Strait of Georgia in British Columbia waters. The mountains of Washington and Vancouver Island are timbered down to the water's edge on either side of the 15-mile-wide Strait. Scores of coves, bays and harbors—such as Neah Bay just 8 miles inside Cape Flattery—offer excellent anchorage after the long and sometimes rough trip up the coast.

At a point roughly 75 miles eastward from Cape Flattery, the equally pleasant decision must be made whether to turn south into Puget Sound, or north toward the San Juan Islands. Thousands of miles of shoreline and hundreds of islands are in an area that measures only about 100 miles on its north-south axis and 50 miles in width. Here, the rigors of deep-sea cruising or sailing can be forgotten and exchanged for smooth sailing, great fishing and anchorages too numerous to count.

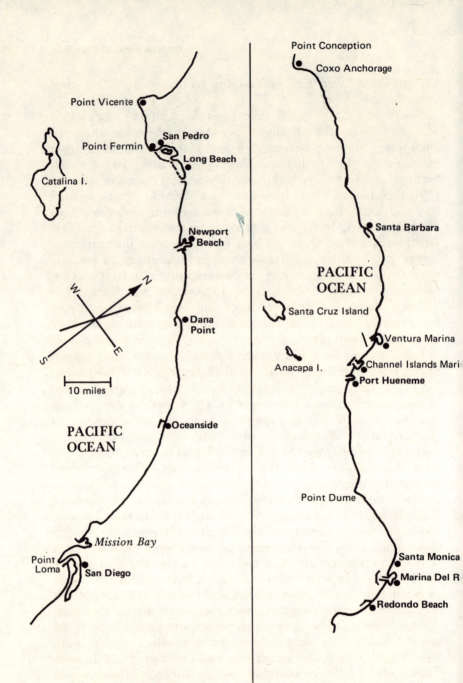

Point Conception
Coxo Anchorage

Point Vicente

San Pedro
Point Fermin
Long Beach

Catalina I.

Santa Barbara

PACIFIC
OCEAN

Newport
Beach

Santa Cruz Island

W   N

Dana
Point

Anacapa I.

Ventura Marina

Channel Islands Mari

S   E

Port Hueneme

10 miles

Oceanside

PACIFIC
OCEAN

Point Dume

Mission Bay

Santa Monica

Point
Loma

San Diego

Marina Del R

Redondo Beach

San Diego to Santa Barbara

In 1542 when Juan Rodriquez Cabrillo first sailed his ship into San Diego Bay there is no reason to believe he was particularly carried away with the sight before him of miles of tideland flats, water-acres of kelp and only the scrubbiest of brush ashore. But it was a natural harbor of sorts and a fairly protected anchorage under the headland of what is now Point Loma. Even after Junipero Serra founded his Mission at San Diego 227 years later, the harbor remained in its primitive condition for another hundred years. Actually most of its tremendous improvements have been made in this century, the most recent of which have favored the fishing fleet, a naval base and users of pleasure craft.

Today, San Diego's boot-shaped bay has been dredged and molded to allow for 25 square miles of navigable waters. Focal points for pleasure boats are the man-made peninsulas called Shelter Island and the newer Harbor Island. Shelter Island is studded with fine restaurants, hotels and docking facilities for 2400 of San Diego's pleasure boats. There is also a free launching ramp which has served over 1200 launchings in one six-hour period. Harbor Island, with its towering hotels, ultra-modern ship chandleries and attractive restaurants, provides 127 acres of usable water area for an ultimate total of 2000 slips. A London minibus makes frequent trips from Harbor Island to downtown San Diego, and is a complimentary service to visiting boatowners.

An unusual point of interest to yachtsmen visiting San Diego is the Maritime Museum near the foot of Broadway on the waterfront. There the restored bark *Star Of India,* built in 1863, the steam yacht *Medea* (both built at the turn of the century in England) and the San Francisco Bay ferryboat *Berkeley* are open to the public. When built in 1893, the *Berkeley* was the

San Diego's Shelter Island, looking northerly, with Customs and
Harbor Master's docks at southwest end of island. Southwestern
and San Diego Yacht Clubs are on west side of basin, Silver Gate
Yacht Club and a number of marinas on opposite side. A public
launching ramp is on the east side of the Island, on the main channel. Harbor Island Marina-restaurant-apartment complex is at center top of this aerial view. A number of new high-rise structures
have recently been completed.

first successful propeller-driven ferry on the west coast; it now
houses exhibits dedicated to maritime history.

San Diego's Unified Port District has looked wisely into the
future needs of pleasure craft in many ways. One aspect
important to the itinerant yachtsman who may not be a
yacht-club member is the availability of guest slips at the
marinas on Shelter or Harbor Islands.

Glorietta Bay, the southern segment of this vast San Diego
Harbor complex, serves the communities in and around Coronado—site of the venerable, circa 1884, Victorian-styled Coronado Hotel. Its picturesque boat house, close by the Coronado
Yacht Club, has recently been converted into a restaurant.

Five miles north of Point Loma lies Mission Bay, another
swamp-to-swank Aqua Park, encompassing 2500 water acres, a

Boathouse adjacent to the venerable Coronado Hotel on Glorietta Bay, San Diego, is now a restaurant.

number of free launching ramps and a half dozen luxury hotels overlooking the water. Because of its vast size and purposeful design, a full gamut of water activities may be engaged in, each in its own designated area—swimming from sandy beaches, water skiing, casual day sailing, fishing and speed-boat racing. Quivira Basin is designed as a large boat marina and, along with its complete facilities, fuel, service, restaurants and hotels, has easy access from its mooring area to the ocean. This basin will ultimately have 1200 slips available and at this time generally has guest slips for overnight visiting boats. Free anchorage is permitted in Quivira Basin for a period of up to 72 hours.

In one section of this huge Aqua Park at Mission Bay is the entertainment center of *Sea World,* patterned after the *Marineland* enterprises of Los Angeles and Florida. Whale and porpoise shows, Japanese pearl divers and other spectacles relating to marine life, highlight this popular exhibition.

The foregoing brief description of these San Diego situated marinas closely resembles that of the balance of southern California's sophisticated pleasure-boat facilities. Space does not permit an itemization of the wealth of accouterments offered boatowner and tourist at each of the subsequently noted

Oceanside Harbor is home port for some 800 yachts, has transient berths for visitors, a number of shore-side restaurants and a launching ramp. Use of the channel and basin to the northwest is forbidden to private craft, being part of a military training base.

harbors. For a list of book and chart sources containing such detail, see Appendix to Part 2.

Oceanside Marine, 30 miles up the coast from Mission Bay, is one of the southland's newest harbors with slips for over 600 boats, some of which are reserved for guest use. Oceanside's channel entrance is usable most of the year by average-draft boats, but silting has necessitated the use of dredges at fairly regular intervals to keep the channel open. During southerly blows, entrance and fairway waters are apt to be dangerous. Under these circumstances, one should check by radio with the Harbor Master before attempting entrance or exit. Under usual favorable conditions, however, Oceanside Marina is a comfortable harbor, well-endowed with both necessities and luxuries— from marine fuel, to coin-operated laundry machines, quaint shops and hostelry of a New England styled Fishing Village. Complimentary bus service for transportation between points in the harbor, and to downtown Oceanside, is also provided.

To interrupt the 33-mile span between Oceanside and Newport, a new harbor and marina at Dana Point is in its final stages of construction. Engineering eyes were particularly drawn

Dana Point Harbor's eastern basin is entered from the southeast portion of the breakwatered harbor, after passing the Harbormaster's building. When the facilities are completed in the west basin, over 2000 craft will be accommodated.

to developments at Dana Point as this was the first Pacific coastal harbor to be completely tested in scale model form, at. Vicksburg, Mississippi, *before* final breakwater plans were adopted. During the testing, several changes were found necessary in the breakwater design to insure quiet waters in the fairway of the facility. Such changes in model form were of course insignificant in cost and time compared to expenses of alterations on a completed breakwater. The investment of roughly $200,000 for testing the Dana Point design at Vicksburg was a lowly 2% of the $9-10 millions that were budgeted for breakwater construction; or 1% of the $22 million the entire development will represent. Without computing monies spent in duplicate and triplicate re-studies of, and in remedial construction work on other California harbors, Dana Point promises to be the most economical recreational harbor project on record. When completed there will be over 2000 slips, including guest docks, marine railway, hotel and restaurant facilities, launching ramp and hoist able to handle a thousand trailed boats per day.

Since 1934, the Newport Harbor/Balboa Bay boating mecca has expanded to make room for approximately 7000 boats. The area contains many of southern California's most distinguished yacht clubs, sport fishing clubs and a number of fine restaurants which provide dinghy dockage for their water-borne customers; in fact, if there is any enticement missing for the pleasure boat owner, either in Newport or in its southern counterparts, it might be only a little more sailing space within harbor confines. Unlike harbors to the south, there are virtually no facilities in Newport Harbor for visiting boats. At the south end of Lido Island is a small area designated for anchoring, and the visiting boat's own dinghy has to be used in lieu of a shoreboat or water taxi.

With so many boats congregated in a relatively small area, visitors may ask: "Where do they all go? What do they do?" True, there are not the multitude of quiet, forest-fringed coves of seclusion available for our southland-based boats, such as New England and the Northwest offer in abundance. But many choices remain for this southern fleet's water-borne entertainment. Trailed boats enjoy both ocean-going and smooth-water adventures in the State's inland lakes. Hot-boat speed races entice their aficionados to full summer and fall scheduled events. Predicted-log power-boat contests and sailing races are on the agenda throughout the year. Meanwhile, high on the list of fun afloat for almost all types of boats are the harbor-hopping holidays enjoyed between southern ports and out to the offshore islands of Catalina, Anacapa and Santa Cruz. Ocean fishing goes on all year with the anglers' greatest excitement culminating in late August at the start of the marlin run. Christmas lighted-boat parades, character-boat pageants, opening-day parades—scarcely a week of the year is without some special event being held for spectator or boating participant.

Fourteen miles northwest of Newport is Anaheim Bay which is the site of the U.S. Naval Weapons Station where ammunition and other explosives are handled by the Navy. Passage through the Bay to Huntington Harbour is restricted to boats under power; smoking aboard while in the Bay is prohibited; no radiotelephones or radars are allowed to be operated while enroute toward the highway bridge that marks the western end of the Harbour. The bridge has 25 feet of clearance at high water which effectively puts a limit on the types and sizes of boats that can use the Harbour. Once within it, the Sunset Aquatic Park Marina is on the north side of the channel, fuel docks on the south side, and then miles of man-made canals

Passage into Huntington Harbour is between abutments of the former
highway bridge and under a newly constructed one with a higher clearance.

with private docks backed by residences. Facilities for transient
boats are limited.

Barely a mile further northwest of Anaheim Bay is the
entrance between breakwaters to the City of Long Beach
Alamitos Bay Marina. It is a vast complex, accommodating
many thousands of boats. End-ties are generally available for
visiting boats, where for a moderate fee they can berth for up to
15 days in one month. Facilities within the Marina include fuel
docks, shipyard, chandlers and a number of fine restaurants. It
is also the site of the Long Beach Marine Stadium where
speedboat races and water skiing competitions are held
regularly and of the Long Beach and Alamitos Bay Yacht Clubs.

It is ironic that Los Angeles Harbor, the largest Pacific Coast
port, has no accommodations for transient pleasure boats. The
number of marinas has even been reduced in recent years by
replacement of a number of them with commercial terminals,

For many years the lighted boat parade at Christmastime in San Pedro harbor drew thousands of spectators and had scores of boats competing for prizes. The side-wheeler of the San Pedro Yacht Club was formerly their floating clubhouse.

and the remaining ones are crowded with permanent tenants, with waiting lists running into the thousands. After many years of urging from boating organizations, the City of Los Angeles Harbor Department did agree in 1970 to build its first marina at Fish Harbor on Terminal Island. Four years later, however, there were no signs of construction, despite repeated promises that it would be completed by 1973. Only Los Angeles Yacht Club could offer other club-members a possible moorage or end tie, space permitting, at their facilities on Terminal Island. This sad state of affairs is especially troublesome when the Trans-Pacific or other major sailing race is scheduled to depart from Los Angeles Harbor. Requests to marina operators for overnight tie-up start months before starting day for these races. Likewise, those vacationing on their boats must attempt to reserve a slip at points on their itinerary weeks in advance of departure from

Looking westward from Los Angeles Harbor to 20-mile-distant
Catalina Island, beyond which can be seen San Clemente Island.
Eighteen yacht and small-boat anchorages provide mooring for
approximately 3500 boats in this area comprised of San Pedro,
Wilmington and Terminal Island, lower left.

home port. Maybe they will be assured of a berth, but more
likely not, depending on how crowded the marinas are during
the vacation interval.

Looking up-coast from Los Angeles Harbor, there are four
more marinas in this 82-mile span before one reaches Santa
Barbara: King Harbor at Redondo Beach, Marina del Rey,
Channel Islands Harbor at Oxnard and Ventura Marina. Of
these, King Harbor does keep a few end-ties open for visiting
boats in the 25- to 35-foot class. Giant-sized Marina del Rey can
accommodate only three or four visiting boats at the Harbor
Administration floats or on moorings, although a visitor can
sometimes find space at the commercially operated marinas or
privately operated yacht clubs in temporarily vacated slips of
the harbor's 5750 tenants.

The Fisherman's Fiesta is an annual event of the commercial fishing fleet based at San Pedro, Los Angeles Harbor.

After leaving Marina del Rey, on a westerly heading up-coast, one passes the indenture of Santa Monica which 70 years ago was expected to become the State's greatest commercial port. Its open roadstead soon proved that breakwaters are entirely inadequate to stand against the continual hammering of wind and storm-built seas. This thundering surf is welcomed, however, by an increasing horde of surfers who frequent the several-mile stretch of sandy beach fronting Malibu, which adjoins Santa Monica to the west.

Before long the headland of Point Dume is visible to starboard, beyond which are more bright sand beaches. Paradise Cove lies two miles northeastward of the Point, with a series of similar coves spotted at intervals along this shoreline interval. These coves are ringed with kelp and are used primarily by small boats. They are not suggested as overnight anchorages.

Point Mugu, 15 miles west of Point Dume, is a large Navy missile-testing station. Consequently, the waters surrounding the area are frequently designated danger zones for boats traveling in the vicinity. Notice of missile firing schedules from Mugu are broadcast to mariners Mondays through Fridays at 0900 and 1200 hours on 2638 and 2738 kHz. When such firing is occurring, boats must follow alternate courses as advised by the Navy.

A mile before reaching Oxnard's Channel Islands Harbor is Port Hueneme (Y-nee-mee), an important naval base and semi-commercial port. If in distress, a pleasure boat would be allowed refuge in this harbor, but otherwise yachtsmen are requested to use either of the adjacent harbors at Oxnard or Ventura, which lie only eight miles apart to the northwest. Channel Islands Harbor is noted as a sport-fishing center, offering charter or rental boats, a launching ramp and the usual array of marina facilities. Visiting craft can generally find slip space without difficulty, with good restaurants and supply stores nearby.

Ventura Marina has had its share of silt insidiously building up at its channel entrance ever since its breakwaters and jetties were completed in 1963. The silt situation is indeed one of the many problems besetting Pacific Coast harbor designers and engineers. But until the solution for eliminating this incubus has been found, dredges keep busy and boats continue to fill the harbors they keep open. During a severe storm in 1969, the entire harbor was wiped out by a break in the Santa Clara River levee. It poured millions of yards of silt into it—and for nearly two years it was useless as a harbor. Since building a new, detached breakwater, and dredging out of the inner harbor, many of Ventura's slip tenants are coming from as far as 50 to 80 miles away to enjoy Ventura's new marina facilities, plus its advantage of proximity to the offshore islands of Anacapa and Santa Cruz.

While cruising the 13-mile coastal span from Ventura to Santa Barbara, shoreside scenery takes on a subtle change—now with intermittent patches of green relieving the bluffs and mountainsides. And a half-mile off Punta Gorda a new island appears to have suddenly risen from the sea. Its tall stand of palm trees sways in the wind—its aspect that of a south sea atoll. This is Rincon Island, man-made by offshore oil well drilling interests, camouflaged in respect to its surrounding beauty, but in no way resembling the natural offshore islands dimly discernible to sea.

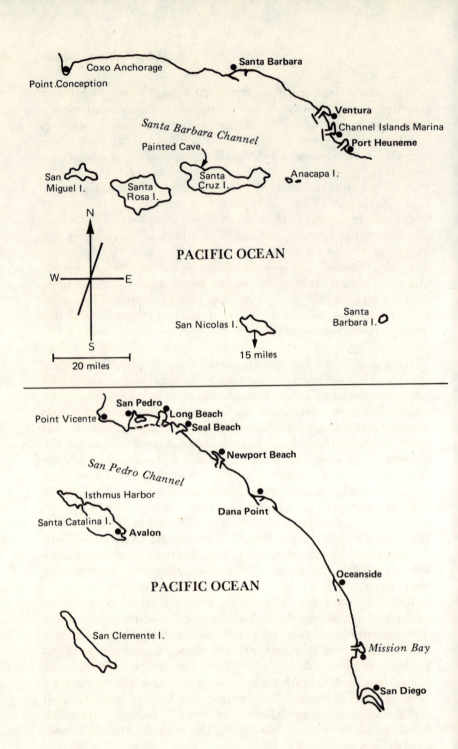

California's Offshore Islands and Painted Cave

Despite weather statistics compiled in *Coast Pilot* concerning numbers of "fog hours" per month and related data, residents of southern California will agree that since 1962, each spring and early summer month has had successively less and less sunshine. The months of May and June have always been notorious for overcast and little wind, but this same static condition is now extending well into July and August. It is therefore suggested that late August, September and October are best months of the year to enjoy cruising these southern ocean waters. At this time water temperature averages 60-plus degrees, and weather settles down to a fairly dependable forecast of "light variable winds in morning hours, becoming northwest, 10 to 20 knots in afternoons." For boats afloat in the Catalina or Santa Barbara channels, this means smooth water cruising early in the day and good sailing winds for afternoons, plus an all-day opportunity to upgrade the suntan.

Scattered from 11 to 53 miles offshore between Los Angeles Harbor and a point beyond Santa Barbara are eight islands which if combined, would comprise an area approximately a third the size of Rhode Island. Locally termed "the Channel Islands," they are best known to the sailboat fraternity and to United States Navy and Air Force personnel who man the various island bases as part of our Early Warning System.

Scarcely a month of the year passes without a major sailing race scheduled from the mainland shores out to and around one or more of these lonely yet historic islands. Prevailing channel winds present the greatest of challenges for those with stout boats and crews to use these natural pylons as outer markers for their often beyond-hull-speed contests. These are the races that separate novice from experienced. There's little chance of becalmed periods out there where winds can reach gale-force peaks at any time of year.

Winds of lesser velocity may be found around others of these islands situated more closely to the mainland, but times are rare when the sailing vacationer is not assured of a brisk run to Catalina, Anacapa and Santa Cruz Island.

Historically, islands have always been known to "beckon" the sailor, but of these eight offshore chunks of land, only Santa Catalina Island may be visited ashore without permission from either private ownership or the government—and even Catalina owners now require a small landing fee for shoregoing at any cove except its one commercial community of Avalon. As the number of pleasure boats increase in the state, so rise the number of people visiting the three remaining accessible islands—if not for shoregoing at least to lie at anchor in some of our last remaining peaceful quiet coves.

Geologists and archeologists inform us that in the Wisconsin Ice Age, some 45,000 years ago, all of these islands were probably a part of the mainland, when an estimated 20,000 Canalino Indians made the coastal section their home. Perhaps that tribe had its own type of Early Warning System to protect it from warring enemies' spear missiles and from the roving mammoths, bones of which are still being discovered on these windy island shores. Other artifacts unearthed in kitchen middens and at burial sites have disclosed the Canalinos had a highly developed culture before they were assimilated with mainland Indian tribes of lesser intelligence, and before the era of the missions, which followed Cabrillo's arrival in 1542. Jesuit padres brought the Canalinos to the mainland to "educate" them and this marked the beginning of the tribe's end. Now only hawks, ravens and pinnipeds (sea lions and sea elephants) carry on an island lineage commenced so long ago.

Most recent settlers to all but Catalina, Santa Barbara and Anacapa Islands are the military. The geographical sites of these outposts make them ideal for such missile firing practices and radar tracking projects as are necessary for linking our western defense chain. Thus, San Clemente Island is now off limits for the pleasure boat owner. Before its restrictions in the late '40's, we recall many pleasant cruises to this 18-mile-long island, where giant pink abalone show themselves at low tide and where fox and wildcats used to scurry from our children's shoreside camp sites. Once they used a hand foghorn to scare the wildlife from their campfire. Now Navy aircraft boom a

Catalina Harbor, on ocean side, is typical of most other coves at the island. There is very limited anchoring room because of the beach-to-beach carpeting with boats on mooring buoys. California and Del Rey Yacht Clubs each have out-stations at Cat Harbor.

grim admonition to a more menacing adversary.

Twenty miles southwest of Los Angeles Harbor lies Catalina Island. Although its summer season is becoming more crowded yearly, it remains the most popular of the island group primarily because of its proximity to the State's highest-density pleasure boat area. Occasionally there are winter storms over these channel waters, and there may be sudden Santanas (dry east or northeasterly winds) in spring or fall, but most of the year this ocean span is benign. At Avalon and the Isthmus harbors there are restaurants, fuel and such shoreside entertainments as are appealing to (or necessary for, as the case may be) its many seekers. Catalina Harbor, nearly landlocked, also provides calm-water anchorage for boats taking the longer run around to the windward side of the island. Almost every major Catalina Island cove is the site of a yacht club mooring facility, filled with buoys owned or leased by their members; some have dining and play areas ashore for their seasonal use. Unfortunately, as each year goes by there are less and less protected anchoring areas for boats that may be cruising up or down the coast. Public transportation, both air and water, carries thousands of summer visitors to famed Catalina—the one island of the offshore group which may be termed a "spa."

Westward of Catalina some 28 miles is the chain's smallest island, Santa Barbara, a black, rocky hump rising to a 600-foot summit. Except for two unattended navigational lights, the island appears nearly barren during most of the year. Due to heavy kelp ringing its perimeter, a landing is virtually impossible. Most of the commercial fishing boats frequenting this area rely on their kelpcutters for negotiating these exceptionally rich fishing grounds; and they in turn are of the privileged few who see Santa Barbara at its glorious best during springtime. In early April the giant coreopsis burst into bloom, sending their golden sunflower-like blossoms up 6 to 8 feet high, a brilliant mass of color often visible 10 miles distant. And it's in order to perpetuate this singular flower and other waning species of flora and fauna that the Channel Islands National Monument was created in 1938. Thus these unusual plants, as well as birds and sea-mammals previously headed for extinction, are now under National Park protection for their perpetuation.

Further westward another 24 miles is San Nicolas Island, completely off-limits to all but the military. Despite this outpost's violent winds and blinding sandstorms (or perhaps *because* of the elements' hostile nature) one of the world's largest concentrations of sea elephants and sea lions congregate and propagate. Sharing these desolate shores, lobster and all classes of abalone—pinks, blues and blacks—cling to their eroded rock homes; rocks so hole-ridden they appear to be hard gray sponges. Although skin-diving is not allowed, the government personnel manning their San Nicolas station are welcome to this bountiful shellfish so long as it is taken only at lowest tide level. "They call this the poor man's Catalina," one of the officers laughed, "but I'll take our grub anyday rather than a snow-cone or hot dog!"

The last two of the Navy and Air Force base islands of Santa Rosa and San Miguel lie well to the northwest of Santa Barbara on the mainland. Both islands share a unique historical possession of dwarf-mammoth bones unearthed by archeologists. It is assumed that when these original pieces of mainland fell away to become islands, the mammoth colonies became inbred and eventually stunted. Neither island has much to attract pleasure boatmen.

Santa Rosa, the chain's second largest, does have several anchorages that may be used by yachtsmen, providing missile firing or other exercises are not in progress at their base. A huge crane near the government dock provides a cage-lift for service men and cargo to be hoisted some 70 feet from their boats to the station high on the rocky hill above, indicating the nearly inaccessible nature of this island's shoreline.

Turning back toward the mainland, the Anacapa Islands lie offshore 11 to 16 miles southwest of Port Hueneme and the two previously described marinas at Oxnard and Ventura. Usually referred to as one island, the Anacapas are actually a narrow line of mountain peaks forming three separate islands as they rise abruptly from the ocean floor. Here the sea has honeycombed the shoreline into arches and caves where at intervals surge builds up astronomical pressure beneath surface rocks, only to spout a resounding geyser of spume from recessed blowholes. Anacapa's habitations consist solely of a one-man maintained Forestry Service camp on the northern island, whose duties are concerned with the National Parks wildlife program. The access beach to the Forestry camp lies on the easterly shore and during prevailing winds its anchorage is protected and has good holding in three to five fathoms. The Coast Guard lighthouse and radio beacon station on the southeastern island is now fully automated and unattended.

From atop the narrow island's center, a view down the razorback ledge is an awesome sight. Breakers slam unceasingly against windward cliffs, relentlessly disintegrating its lava base, forming new arches, eroding older formations. Historians say the Canalino Indians called the island "Eneeapah", meaning "changing" or "deception" and pronunciation's evolution brings us "Anacapa".

One of our most memorable visits to Anacapa and Santa Cruz Islands was a group cruise with six other boats joining us, the primary purpose of which was to inspect and photograph the

Near the northeastern end of Anacapa Island is a National Parks service facility at Frenchy's Cove. Rangers are on duty during summer months. Anchorage close by on the eastern beach affords easy access for shoregoing.

Prisoners' Harbor, about 8 miles northwest of San Pedro Point on
Santa Cruz Island, has good protection from prevailing summer
winds.

interior of the Painted Cave on Santa Cruz Island. We had
aboard with us our friend, Milt Farney, who was making a
television movie of the channel islands and it is to him we are
indebted for these accompanying illustrations of the two islands
and inner cave.

Although Santa Cruz island is privately owned, one wishing
to visit ashore may do so from Prisoners' Harbor westward,
providing he secures a permit from the owner. (see Appendix to
Part 2). Such permission prohibits the boatowner from taking
firearms or pets ashore, and its purpose is understandable from
a view of preserving island wildlife and the remaining stands of
evergreen trees, oaks and succulent undergrowth. From Pris-

Pelican Bay is a favored anchorage on the northeast side of Santa
Cruz Island.

oners' Harbor east, there is a Navy radar tracking station and
other government operations which bar it from the general
public.

Surge is the dominant obstacle in the Painted Cave area so
our little expedition force felt extremely fortunate for a rare
calm morning and flat sea for our venture into this cavern. Due
to extreme water depths which discourage anchoring near the
cave entrance, we left our vessels anchored in Cueva Valdez
cove which lies only a few miles east of Profile Point and
Painted Cave, and proceeded west in our dinghies. Milt brought
all manner of lighting equipment—Frezzo-lites, magnesium
flares and torches—without which it would have been impossible to even partially illuminate the stygian blackness of the
cave's inner recesses.

At its 150-foot-high entrance, the grotto appears to be spattered with varicolored paints. Iron, zinc and copper strata mingle their corroded colors with brighter tints of sea-lichen, and cave-nesting birds add their daubs of white to complete this natural mural. Colors dimmed as we ventured further underground where the ceiling slants down to an eventual infinity—300 feet back at the cave's bitter end. We shut off our outboards and paddled, trying to glide along as quietly as possible in order not to scare the seal colony which we knew inhabited the dead-end beach. After the faint shaft of entrance light had been cut off by a bend in our watery corridor we were in a darkness impenetrable beyond belief. From the dank rocky overhead came a drip, drip of moisture while eerie noises emerged from unseen blowholes. Our voices echoed hollowly. A seal's sudden bark startled us all, tensed as we were for the unexpected.

Milt was especially hoping to photograph an albino seal who, with his dark-haired family, had appeared briefly with the first flash of his Frezzo-lite. But before we could focus our cameras there was a tremendous snorting and splashing and at the next beam of light, only one tiny seal was left in view. Apparently too young to fear us, he blinked, bewildered, but clung to his rock. Meanwhile the adult mammals were swiftly making for the outer ocean, no doubt terrified at the sight of 7 boats, 25 people, and what was probably the first bright light ever to illuminate their home.

Despite smoothest of seas that day, surge inside the cave measured up to 3 feet in rise and fall, giving us little head room at the end of the cavern. Tide was on the rise and smoke from our torches commenced to thicken the air. "One more picture, *please*," Milt pleaded, "then you can get out."

Eventually out in clear air and open ocean, we turned our motors up to full speed and raced back to our ships for a long overdue breakfast and a chance to stretch our legs ashore. Later in the afternoon one of our little fleet's skippers hauled in his fishing line to find attached a 10-foot killer shark! Needless to say, our swimming after that was confined closely to shore.

Later in the week we leisurely cruised the island's perimeter with overnight anchorages at such harbors as Pelican Bay, Smugglers' Cove, Chinese and Fry's Harbor. At Lady Harbor we hiked up to its natural "bathtubs" where spring water gurgles through fern and moss, rushes over boulders in tiny waterfalls,

Exploring the Painted Cave, Santa Cruz Island, by small boat. From the entrance, shown here, the cave tunnels back approximately 300 feet into utter darkness.

finally to fill to brimming three stone basins each the exact shape of a bathtub.

Whether climbing the island's bluffs or contemplating this panorama from the sea, always some indications remain of early island days: a vineyard's skeletal remains, or the silver-gray order of a one-time fig orchard, now dead and bleaching on a windy slope. From Indian to European, to bird and animal kingdom—so the island's rulings were transferred. Now another era has commenced with most of the channel islands lending their vantage points to our national defense. Perhaps the day is imminent when these offshore outposts will either be closed in their entirety to pleasure boating, or more likely, turned into massive resort projects. Whatever may be their future, those of us who have taken our boats to their primitive shores and can still do so today, are indeed thankful that we could heed these islands' beckoning.

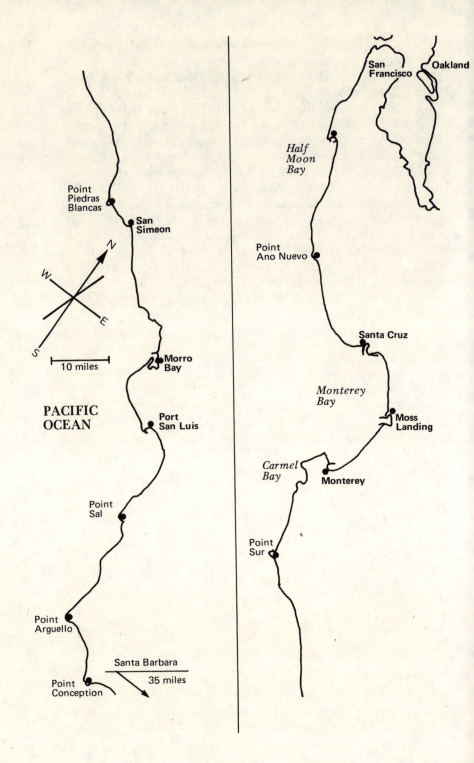

San Francisco

Oakland

Half
Moon
Bay

Point
Piedras
Blancas

San
Simeon

Point
Ano Nuevo

N

W

E

S

Santa Cruz

10 miles

Morro
Bay

Monterey
Bay

Moss
Landing

PACIFIC
OCEAN

Port
San Luis

Carmel
Bay

Monterey

Point
Sal

Point
Sur

Point
Arguello

Santa Barbara

35 miles

Point
Conception

Santa Barbara's harbor is important to the north-bound yachtsman in several respects. For those with limited cruising range it serves as a last fuel and supply depot before commencing the sometimes arduous, 90-mile run up coast to Port San Luis. Its proximity to Santa Cruz Island, 20 miles offshore, presents a fine sail or power cruise for either day trips or extended vacationing. And perhaps most important, Santa Barbara is a gay and festive community with shoreside enticements reminiscent of its historical background during Spanish and Mexican rule.

Two of the most notable festivals held annually here are *Semana Nautica*, with its scores of sailing races, regattas and all manner of marine contests and exhibitions, during the week preceding Fourth of July; and the *Old Spanish Days Fiesta*, enjoyed during the full moon week of August. The latter event tells in parade and pageantry of Santa Barbara's changing years since its discovery by Cabrillo in 1542, its official christening by Vizcaino in 1602, on through its tenure as Presidio and Mission Center, to present days. Probably no other coastal city has cast its allegiance to as many flags as has Santa Barbara; the flag of the Spanish Empire of Carlos V was first to wave in 1769; the Spanish National Ensign, from 1785; flag of the Mexican Empire of Iturbide, from 1822, and of the Mexican Republic, from 1824; the California State Bear Flag, superseded by the 28-star American Flag, was raised in July 1846, and finally its Official City Flag and the Star Spangled Banner with its present field of 50 stars.

Although much of Santa Barbara's former vast ranch holdings have since been divided many times, much of her former heritage remains in evidence in architecture and, to a lesser extent, in custom. It is actually one of the West Coast's few

Part of the Santa Barbara small craft harbor, looking northwest
toward Stearns Wharf. The entrance channel requires continuous
dredging to keep it open. Entry into the harbor at night should be
avoided if possible due to the confusion of lights ashore and the
navigational lights marking the channel.

cities which, in a figurative sense, appears to have no visible
means of support. Rather than a backdrop of smokestacks,
factories and highrise business structures, only the rich green
heights of Santa Inez Mountains tower behind harbor and town,
as if to isolate it from the grubby mechanics of industry. This is
primarily a summer place, a wintering spa, a sanctuary for
retirement, higher education, scientific research, and the arts.
Thus bemused, no great effort has been spent on harbor
maintenance, although a small dredge is operated most of the
year to clear the entrance channel of its continuous silting. But

once inside the breakwater a visiting boat and crew receive the most gracious attention. In all but southerly storms the harbor provides good protection for its 700 boat-slip tenants and visiting craft. Early summer weather is for the most part overcast during morning hours with gradual clearing by afternoons. Generally, day-long sunshine commences in late August or September and prevails through fall and early winter.

Of our many cruises into Santa Barbara and on up the coast to San Francisco, all have been quite different with respect to weather, sea conditions and facilities encountered at shoreside. For this reason it would be difficult to call any one of such cruises "typical." Rather, we will recount a group cruise in which we participated, to point up the fact that boats in the 30-foot class can cover this span, often with aplomb equal to that of their larger cruising companions.

A dozen boats joined forces in July to cruise together from San Diego to San Francisco with overnight stops planned at intervening harbors. By a direct course the distance is 426 miles, but our more devious harbor-hopping route took us 500 nautical miles. We were a heterogeneous fleet, reading from small to large: a 35-foot diesel-powered Monterey, a 38-foot Chris-Roamer, a 40-foot Huckins sport fisher, a 40-foot ketch-rigged motor sailer, several cruisers of from 48 to 63 feet and our own 72-foot *Monsoon II*. As this will indicate, no two boats were alike in design or in speed, and over half the group had not taken their boats this far northwest before. But we were well organized as to plans and equipment and all had radiotelephones for intercommunication at frequent intervals. Slower boats—those cruising 7 to 9 knots—planned their starting times earlier than those with faster cruising speeds and radar-equipped boats acted as leaders for those without the seeing eye. Because dense fog was the order of the day for the first three days, such radar leadership proved a definite asset for all concerned. But with the fog came a cessation of wind, resulting in just about the smoothest seas we had ever experienced offshore along this coast.

By our fourth day out, sunshine finally broke through. Only two boats of our fleet had had to return to their home bases—due to a time element rather than to mechanicals; crews had become well acquainted and all were getting their sea legs. Most days saw us gathered in ports long before sundown, visiting aboard each others' boats and later joining for dinner at

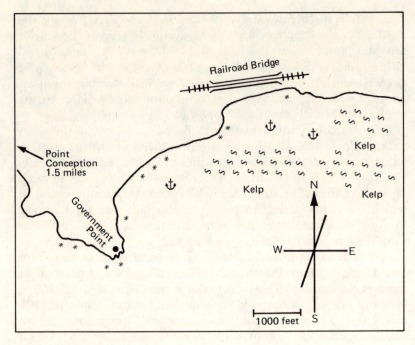

COXO ANCHORAGE
34º 27' N lat; 120º 27' W long.

Anchorage at Coxo is in relatively shallow water, from 2 to 5 fathoms, and preferably between the heavy growths of kelp and the northerly shore. The bottom is hard sand. Some parts of the kelp are so thick that caution should be exercised to find open paths through it. These openings change position from season to season, but are generally discernable as routes through smoother water where kelp is thickest. Prevailing summer winds from the northwest whip across Point Conception and Government Point, generally from noon until sunset, and more than the usual amount of scope should be paid out after setting anchor. When winds are from the northeast to southwest, there is no protection from them in this anchorage. There are no facilities ashore at Coxo and the amount of surge normally precludes access to the beach. Breakwaters close by Government Point are planned for this anchorage, as a part of a harbor-of-refuge program. They will give protection during all wind conditions.

yacht club or marina restaurants. (It is worth comment here, in reference to earlier statements concerning a lack of guest slips at various of the southland marinas, it was a part of our planning to arrange in advance for both slip and dinner reservations at those harbors on our itinerary.)

Boats of our fleet having lesser fuel capacities stopped at Santa Barbara to top off their tanks, and our fourth night's rendezvous brought us to Coxo (or Cojo) Cove, just to the northeast of Point Conception. This small bight protected to some extent from north and west winds, has been used for many years by pleasure and fishing boats as a harbor of refuge but it is utterly untenable in south or easterly winds. Point Conception has long been known as the "Cape Horn of the Pacific" and those who have seen the elements rage around this 200-foot-high eminence, agree the name applies. We felt fortunate in finding calm weather when our flotilla moved into Coxo's protection that evening. Ashore there is nothing but tawny lion-colored bluffs, empty of tree or habitation except for a train which runs at intervals along the lower shoreline. The sound of its passing strikes a strange discordant note against the mumbling background sound of surge and surf. For some time an actual harbor with breakwaters has been planned, but it is still years away. And until that becomes reality, we can sit at anchor on this calm night, contentedly watching the sunlight fade across the dark-gold hills, listening to the surf and to the train, hooting off in darkness around the bend of "Cape Horn".

Our fleet weighed anchor early the following morning, anxious to put as many miles as possible behind us before early afternoon winds arose. Ocean swells were big but not breaking as we rounded Point Arguello, 12 miles beyond Point Conception. Regular seafarers along this route have also called Arguello by other than its true name. One of its (less-offensive) appellations is "Graveyard of the Pacific," since this has often been the scene of destruction for ships plying the steamer lanes in earlier days. The most tragic loss occurred in 1923 when seven U.S. destroyers followed one another to their destruction on these fearsome rocks off Point Arguello.

During this fifth day's run, some of our group stopped at Morro Bay for fuel, while others ran straight through to our second "anchorage only" stop of the trip, at San Simeon Bay. Our own ship was scheduled to stop briefly at San Luis Obispo Bay to pick up a friend. When we did so, their kindly Harbor Master and his wife presented us with a beautiful, freshly caught salmon and two loaves of homemade bread. Such is the kindliness and generosity so often manifested at many of these less-populated ports.

Port San Luis, and its adjoining city of Avila, has been

Hearst Castle, a unit of the California State Park System, San
Simeon, Calif.

through the years primarily a fuel depot for tankers, as well as a
haven for the fishing fleet. Now, after long and diligent work by
San Luis Harbor Commissioners and with necessary local, State
and Federal backing, this port is being greatly enhanced. Its
erstwhile dilapidated pier has been rehabilitated and paved; a
4-acre land fill has been created northwest of the pier, with such
facilities as a monorail boat launching unit, fueling stations, dry

boat storage area, rest rooms and free public parking areas. Other facilities at the pier include a marine elevator, ways, fuel barge, commercial fish buyers, a retail fish market, and a restaurant. Additional breakwaters, and slips for 380 boats north of the pier, are the next steps in Port San Luis' development plan.

Morro Bay's harbor, 21 miles beyond Port San Luis, offers its small craft patrons many of the accouterments associated with the large marina. Its primary deficiency is its narrow entrance channel which scarcely allows more than a single-file entry or exit into the nearly landlocked harbor. The Coast Guard maintains a station here; fuel and top-quality restaurants are handily adjacent to the limited slip and anchorage area. Caution should be used in anchoring due to the 4- to 5-knot tidal currents caused by the constriction of ocean flow in and out of Morro's narrow channel. Once securely moored, Morro Bay offers a variety of diversions, including golf on its stately tree studded grounds overlooking the harbor, and ocean fishing or clam digging along its several sand islands. Because of Morro Bay's geographical position and certain attending meteorological conditions, winter months are warm and generally sunny, but from June to September, overcast skies and fog are the rule. None of this bothers the ardent fisherman and both commercial and sport-fishing craft use the harbor to good advantage all year.

Our little armada consisted of eight boats when we moved into San Simeon Bay to anchor for the night. High on the hilltop overlooking the Bay, famed Hearst Castle stands a lonely sentry, guarding its Midas-wealth of art treasures. The Castle's western windows glitter in late afternoon sunlight; its high twin towers thrust upward against a deep blue sky. A tour to and through this baronial treasure house is certainly a rich experi-ence, as evidenced by the thousands of visitors who have been guided through its grounds and museum-like buildings. But this safari is one to be made from a point on land—from the small crossroads of San Simeon or from 18-mile-distant Morro Bay to the south. The only shore acess at San Simeon Bay is up a high vertical ladder attached to a fishing pier. Only rarely will surge permit any sort of a shore landing in the average dinghy carried by pleasure boats.

The five of us aboard *Monsoon II* had, we are certain, the finest dinner of our entire trip that evening while anchored in

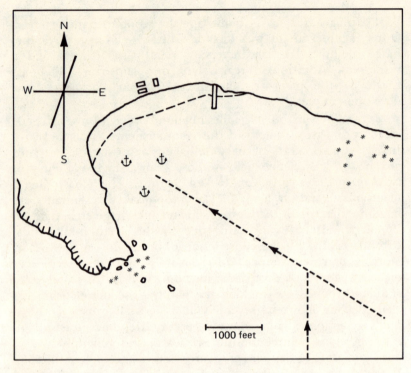

SAN SIMEON BAY
35° 38′ N lat; 121° 11′ W long.

This bay provides good protecion from prevailing northwest winds
and sea, although a moderate surge is almost always present. A
lighted buoy is to the southeast of the point and should be kept to
port when entering the bay, due to the reef and kelp which extends from the point toward the buoy. Best anchorage is close
under the wooded bluff in the western portion of the bay, in 3 to
6 fathoms of water. No fuel or water is available at the pier. A
breakwater extending northeastward from the point is planned,
along with other developments that will ultimately include full
facilities for local and visiting craft.

San Simeon Bay. We baked our gift salmon in foil where it
poached in its own juices to a mouth-watering perfection. We
logged that interval "night of the salmon" and felt a little guilty
that our other fellow cruising companions could not share our
feast.

As weather and seas build their own mosaics of contrast, we
had all felt uneasily that our sea-lanes had been quiet unusually
long. So it was with no surprise that, at next early dawn, we

Typical of the rugged shoreside scenery around Carmel and Monterey Peninsula is this view of Cypress Cove, Lobos State Park, Calif.

headed out of the Bay into increasingly turbulent seas. On the hour we called and talked with each of our fellow skippers, and their answers of "All's well!" were reassuring. Our admiration grew, particularly for the Tuttles in their 35-foot Monterey—such a small boat for those huge swells building up around Point Sur. In contrast to California's more southerly points, this bold headland is thickly forested down its many perpendicular valleys. The community of Big Sur is home to a growing art colony and other settlers who seek this picturesque privacy that lies betwixt towering evergreens and the breaker-bangled sea.

By early afternoon we were abeam Carmel and Pebble Beach's ocean-fronting golf course; rolling past the lovely shoreside vista of Cypress Point, Spanish Bay and Point Joe—all

Monterey's small-craft harbor is protected by a bulkhead and is entered through a narrow passage between the western end of the bulkhead and the pier on which there are a number of restaurants and marine supply stores. Moorings in the outer harbor are used mainly by the commercial fishing fleet.

scenic and historical landmarks on Monterey's notable Seventeen-Mile Drive which winds overland from Carmel to Monterey Bay.

Discovered in 1602 by Vizcaino, the same year he landed on Santa Barbara's beach, Monterey was once California's capital when the territory was under Mexican rule, and like Santa Barbara it retains much of its early-day flavor. Many of its old adobe buildings have been restored and are open to public viewing. One of the most venerable is the area's first Customs House, originally built in 1814. Within walking distance of the Customs House is Colton Hall, built in 1849; it is here that the Constitution for California was written prior to its admission as a State in 1850.

Alerted to our arrival, Monterey's Harbor Master came out to the breakwater to meet each of our fleet to guide them to an inner harbor slip. And from that moment on, we were treated as guests-royal by the friendly people of Monterey. We were invited to a succulent sea-food dinner that evening by members of Monterey Yacht Club, and those who wished to see the city were invited to tour some of the historical sites and buildings now rejuvenated through the efforts of Monterey's Historical Society.

Twenty-seven-ton Quadrapods are used in breakwater construction at Santa Cruz Harbor. Of French derivation and first successfully used in the Mediterranean, they were later manufactured in this country, and as Tetrapods were employed at the breakwater in Crescent City, Calif. Advantages of the pods include elimination of slippage due to their legs' interlocking action, and an increased porosity of the breakwater structure.

Our next day's cruise was a short one, across 22-mile-wide Monterey Bay to its north shore harbor of Santa Cruz. This is more of a resort town than is Monterey but it shares much of the same turbulent history under foreign rule. Interspersed with the new are scores of homes and commercial buildings built in the early 1800's. Protected as it is from prevailing northwest winds, Santa Cruz enjoys a warm summer climate. Its long stretch of sandy beachfront and scores of summer cottages are welcomed by visitors throughout the season.

We had an exciting roller-coaster ride into this channel. Poised momentarily atop a huge rolling sea, we then plunged downward while the undertow swept out behind us, pouring on the power to maneuver around the narrow dog-leg—some fast maneuvering to avoid Sunday's sailing sabots—finally to steerage

Recently expanded Santa Cruz Harbor, looking northeasterly. At lower right is dredge used to remove accumulated sand in harbor

entrance channel. Such silting sometimes makes it impossible for craft to enter or leave the harbor.

way and quiet waters, not to mention reduced pulse!

Once again the welcome mat was extended us by Santa Cruz Yacht Club members and others of their Harbor Commission. Ideally situated in a bower of great old trees and facing the harbor marina, the yacht club was the site of a delightful dinner held for our fleet from the southland. Later, cars were put at our disposal by local friends—an especial boon to those having boat shopping and laundry to take care of.

It may be well to point out here that this particular cruise was undertaken shortly after Santa Cruz Harbor was completed. A year or two later, shoaling commenced to fill the fairway, to the extent that a dredge was put to use several months each year in order to maintain even a minimum channel depth. Winter storms of 1969 and early 1970 finally washed so much sand across the jetty entrance that the harbor was completely unusable. Tenants who had their boats away at the time had to seek moorage elsewhere, and those at their slips were locked into Santa Cruz Harbor. This situation existed for nearly half a year, until funds were finally obtained to dredge from the harbor the thousands of tons of sand accumulated. Obviously this will be a recurring situation until further engineering work is done at Santa Cruz. Despite these entrance problems, an additional 455 berths were completed in 1973 when the upper harbor expansion program was completed.

Moderate fog prevailed during our 46-mile run up the coast from Santa Cruz to Half Moon Bay, sometimes referred to as Pillar Point Harbor, our last anchorage before our arrival at San Francisco. Only a few years ago, Half Moon had millions of dollars expended on breakwaters to protect its harbor; slips and mid-basin fueling stations were constructed, all with the expectations that it would provide a safe and functional marina for its fishing fleet and for pleasure craft. But before the first year was out, winter storms slammed in and over the new breakwaters, destroying slips, docks, and sinking seven of the boats that were moored inside. As with a number of other harbors to the south (such as Ventura, Marina del Rey, King Harbor and Oceanside) remedial steps were necessary to make Half Moon a safe harbor. An extension to the westerly breakwater was constructed to overlap the original entrance. Since then no further problems have been experienced.

After a good night's rest we were all up early to run our last 24-mile lap to San Francisco. Departures were planned so that

Pillar Point Harbor, or Half Moon Bay as it is better known, before
start of marina facilities construction, which are expected to be
completed in 1975. Fuel is available near corner of "L" shaped
pier; at shore end is Harbormaster's office and restaurants. The
launching ramp and dinghy float are to east of pier. At top of picture, to the north, is part of the airport runway.

each boat would meet promptly at 1000 hours under the
Golden Gate to pass through in formation. At 0955 hours, as
Monsoon II neared the bridge, we found ourselves a little ahead
of the rest of the fleet. In order to drop back into line, we
started a wide 360-degree turn, but no sooner were we well into
our turn, to our great amusement we saw all the other boats in
our group also doing little circles of their own! "Well" they told
us later, "we were just following our leader."

We have since wondered what other ship's crews thought of
us while we were making circles right in the center of San
Francisco's busy channel. Perhaps it's better that we never
know.

As we passed under the Golden Gate Bridge, it brought to
mind that existance of the entrance into San Francisco Bay was
not discovered until 173 years after Spanish explorer Vizcaino
had discovered Monterey Bay, where he landed in 1602. One
explanation given by historians is that no such channel existed
until the late 1700's, when an earthquake created a gap in the
mountain range that extends from Monterey northward for
hundreds of miles. The first recorded entry into the bay was in

A cruising fleet from southern California passes under the Golden
Gate Bridge, its upper towers shrouded in fog.

1775, and within a year the Spanish built a fort at what is now
Fort Point—directly below the San Francisco end of the Golden
Gate Bridge. The abandoned remains of the fort completed in
1861 still guard the entrance to the bay with two of its original
cannons.

One of San Francisco's municipal marinas now occupies an
area on which the Spanish built their Presidio, about 2 miles
eastward of the Bridge, at the western end of which is St.
Francis Yacht Club. Expanded considerably in recent years,
only a few slips are available for visitors and frequently it is
impossible to get a berth. In Richardson Bay on the north,
between Sausalito and Tiburon Peninsula, there are a number of
marinas, as well as to the east of San Francisco Bay in Berkeley,
Oakland, Alameda, San Leandro, or in the southern part of the
Bay at Oyster Point where there is a municipal marina, or
further south to Coyote Point and beyond toward Redwood
City.

The *Balclutha,* built in 1886 in Scotland, being towed to Pier 43 at
Fisherman's Wharf, San Francisco, where she is open to the public.
Steel hulled, 256.5' in length, the *Balclutha* carried wheat out of
San Francisco during the 1880s and 90s, and was the last ship to
fly the Hawaiian flag, from 1899 to 1901. For 28 years she was in
the Alaska salmon trade, most of the time named *Star of Alaska.*
In 1954 she was bought by the San Francisco Maritime Museum,
restored, and renamed *Balclutha.*

Those fortunate enough to find space at the Presidio will be
within minutes of downtown San Francisco and the many
attractions near Fisherman's Wharf. The Maritime Museum at
nearby Aquatic Park is open to the public, as well as a number
of restored ships built in the late 1800's.

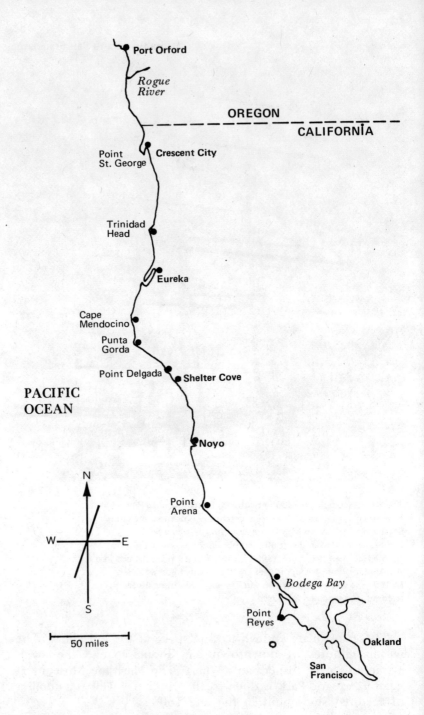

Port Orford

Rogue River

OREGON
CALIFORNIA

Point
St. George

Crescent City

Trinidad
Head

Eureka

Cape
Mendocino

Punta
Gorda

Point Delgada

Shelter Cove

**PACIFIC
OCEAN**

Noyo

N

W — E

S

50 miles

Point
Arena

Bodega Bay

Point
Reyes

Oakland

San
Francisco

Now we're headed out of San Francisco Bay, under the Golden Gate, usually into a noisy uproar: diaphone groaning, bell buoys clanging, whistles shrieking, each sound sending its individual warning to guide the skipper into his lane, outbound through what is locally known as the "potato patch." This section of choppy water extends roughly three miles beyond the bridge where shallow waters are more easily disturbed by wind and tidal change.

With usual summer fog, the radar-equipped boat progresses contentedly, noting each buoy and ship within its vicinity, and accurately gauging his distance offshore. To me, one of the most fascinating sights on the radar screen is that of approaching and passing under a bridge. At first there's the scanner's straight white line across our path—the bridge. Just as we reach this apparent barrier, an opening appears, like a little door in the white line's center. Then the door closes after we have passed under the bridge. Behind us once more is that unbroken line connecting the two shores. (This of course applies to bridges *only*. A breakwater, for instance, would also appear on radarscope as a horizontal white line, if we were headed directly toward it. A barrier that would *not* have a "little door" open for a boat heading into it!)

Once through the potato patch, on a westerly heading, Point Reyes lies ahead to starboard, the first of the many headlands to round before reaching the northern boundary of California. After leaving San Francisco there are a number of small coves and harbors one can use as rest or refuge anchorages before covering the 234-nautical miles to Humboldt Bay and Eureka. However only a few of them have fuel available and only two offer safe anchorage if winds are from the south. For this reason the wise skipper commences his northwest voyage with his

Looking down on Bodega Bay, lower left, and the small-boat harbor, upper right, at end of 100-foot-wide and 9- to 12-foot-deep
entrance channel. Bodega Harbor has a marine railway for boats
up to 40 feet long with 4-foot draft or less.

vessel as fully founded as possible.

Named for Sir Francis Drake who first landed here in 1579,
Drakes Bay is protected by Point Reyes and is the first of these
possible anchorages after leaving the Golden Gate. In northwesterlies it provides good holding in hard sand, at 5 to 6 fathoms.
Fuel and water are available ashore. A Coast Guard station is
maintained just inside the easterly end of the Point, which
protection is chiefly used by the fishing fleet.

Twenty three miles beyond Point Reyes, Bodega Bay offers a
good anchorage in its northern extremity; or one can proceed
through the 2-mile dredged channel leading from the Bay to the
head of Bodega Harbor where fuel and supplies may be had. On

the southern part of Bodega Bay is Tomales Bay. It appears inviting on the chart, but should definitely be avoided. A bar at its mouth has taken the lives of as many as 13 persons in one season, who were caught by "sneaker waves" that frequently occur during low tide or when Bay waters are ebbing at up to 6 knots.

Bodega was first settled in 1812 by a group of Russians who were hunting sea-otters which then proliferated these shores. Other Russian migrants settled at nearby Fort Ross and along the Russian River. Fort Ross is now a State Historical Monument and preserves several homes and a church of Russian architecture, built in the early 1800's. Long after most of the Russians and all of the fur-bearing otters were gone, Bodega Bay's small harbor became headquarters, during Prohibition, for rum-runners who were supplying such demands in San Francisco. The story is told of the coroner who drove almost daily from a dark night's rendezvous with boats in Bodega Bay to San Francisco and back, his hearse gurgling as it careened along the highway. "Yup" quoth the coroner, "we're having quite a serious plague over Bodega Way!"

From this point on up the coast, the mountainous shoreline becomes increasingly forested and a certain amount of debris may be found afloat. Logs or parts of trees are swept down the many rivers which empty into the Pacific. A helmsman should keep a watchful eye ahead.

From Bodega Bay there is no cove or harbor of any sort to the northwest until after rounding Point Arena, 30 miles beyond which is Noyo anchorage, adjacent to Fort Bragg, a distance of roughly (in both senses of the word) 80 miles. Noyo is the principal fishing boat center for this area, with some north and south protection in its small outer bay and a landlocked inner harbor for small craft.

On one of our trips up the coast a few years ago, we were experiencing strong head winds and extremely heavy seas with weather deteriorating after we had rounded Point Arena. It was a case of throttling back and back until we seemed to be making more miles up and down than forward. On marine radio fishermen were talking about the lumpy seas, saying that they were "all blowed in" to their nearest points of protection. We decided it would be well for us to do the same. A check of our charts showed the closest anchorage would be at Shelter Cove in the lee of Point Delgada. We had not been into that cove before,

Noyo Harbor looking seaward. In foreground is new 265-boat
marina. Supplies of all types, marine railway and repair facilities
are available in this snug harbor.

so Jack called on radio to one of the fishboat skippers, telling
him we were taking quite a beating, and asked some detail
about this anchorage and if it would be adequate for our boat's
7-foot draft.

"Sure, Cap'n" the skipper answered, "but there's a bunch of
rocks and shoals in there. You want me to tell you the best way
to go in?" Jack had just commenced replying to our unseen
benefactor when we took an unusually big sea, part of which
went down an engineroom ventilator, shorting out the motor-
generator that powered our radio. The set was dead and no way
to finish our conversation with the fishing boat. Darkness was
then falling and neither of us were interested in tackling a

strange cove at night without knowing more about it. So we changed course a few degrees to port to clear Cape Mendocino and trudged on to Eureka. We have since wondered if the friendly skipper we'd been talking to thought we had foundered in the blow when our transmission was so abruptly chopped.

Twenty miles beyond Cape Mendocino and outlying Blunt's Reef is the riverbar entrance to Humbolt Bay and the city of Eureka. From Humbolt's river mouth on to the northwestern boundary of the United States, there is only one major coastal harbor that does not have a river-formed bar to cross; this is at Crescent City, near the northern boundary of California. So this is the time to dust off the tide tables and keep them handy for navigational reference well in advance of one's entry into Humbolt Bay and all Oregon and Washington coastal harbors to follow. The best time to cross any of these bars is during the last of flood tide. During the ebb, and with afternoon winds strong from the northwest, all of those bar entrances are seething cauldrons of tormented waves and often impassible even for large ships.

Eureka's Yacht Harbor lies 2 miles inside Humbolt Bay, and the city proper, another mile inland. All supplies and facilities that might be needed can be found here. Slips and docks are well maintained, and nearby are several picturesque wooded islands. In particular, an interesting dinghy tour can be taken around Gunther Island which was the scene of a large-scale Indian massacre as recently as 1911. Indian arrowheads and other kitchen midden artifacts can be turned up almost anywhere around Gunther's grounds. We were fortunate in exploring the island when the Old Gunther House, a landmark since the turn of the century, was still standing. Not long afterward it was purposely destroyed by fire because, according to local citizenry, it had become an attractive nuisance. It was the typical "haunted house", long neglected, and with 3 levels of once-luxurious rooms to investigate. Gunther House was but one of the many historical structures on this coast with window glass, fixtures, and fine hardwood panelings brought from the Atlantic Coast on sailing ships in the 19th century—around Cape Horn and up the Pacific Coast. In contrast to the many rugged ocean miles that were covered in that era, and the hardships encountered during the establishment of new homes on this primitive coast, today's pleasure boat cruises along these waters appear tame as Sunday sailing.

The original oil-burning light, used on Trinidad Head until 1948, is
now a memorial overlooking the anchorage to the south of it.

A new light is on the southwest bluff of the Head. This cove is popular sport-fishing center during the summer salmon season.

Crescent City's harbor looking northeasterly across the western breakwater. Berthing facilities are under development to the west (left) of Fishboat Harbor, center right, where there is only limited dockage. The basin is generally crowded with local boats on moorings or at anchor.

Trinidad Head, 18 miles up the coast from Humbolt Bay, is the next cove with good anchorage and protection from the northwest. During the summer salmon run this small cove in the lee of the Head is awhirl with activity, with fishing boats, skiffs and outboards dashing about in quest of their silvery catches. Charter fishing boats and hourly rental boats are available on a first-come-first-served basis.

Crescent City's harbor lies another 40 miles beyond Trinidad. This is mainly a commercial harbor for the export of lumber. There is good anchorage within its breakwaters with protection from both northwest and southerly winds. Fuel and supplies are available at this bay-fronting town. A harbor improvement program scheduled for completion in 1974 will provide slips for about 250 boats. Temporary moorage facilities for coastal-cruising craft are a part of the development. Crescent City was first in the United States to use the Tetrapod in its breakwater construction. (Santa Cruz Harbor has since used them in their jetties.) Tetrapods are concrete forms molded in the approximate shape of huge jackstones weighing 25 tons each, and standing 11 feet high. When in use on the seaward breakwater slopes, their irregular masses become firmly interlocked with each successive surge of a stormdriven sea, and provide far more security than would the same weight in stone.

Entrance to Rogue River, Oregon appears docile in this view, but can be extremely dangerous during an ebb tide and a northwest wind. The deepest water is close by the north (left when entering) jetty. Shoal water extends along the south jetty from seaward to the bridge.

Although Crescent City suffered major damage from seismic floods resulting from the 1964 Alaska earthquake, such destruction as occurred here was estimated to be far less than it would have been without these unusually strong breakwaters.

St. George Reef, extending 6½ miles northwest of Point George, is well-marked on its most seaward rock with a navigational light and a diaphone. When abeam this light, a more northerly course can be taken up the coast to Port Orford, Oregon, a span of some 55 miles. Well-protected from the northwest by Cape Blanco, Port Orford provides good anchorage from all but southerly winds. Fuel and supplies are available at their village. This community is an export source of famed Port Orford yellow cedar, and great stands of these giant evergreens line the mountain slopes surrounding the anchorage, adding their spicy aroma to the cold salt air of the sea.

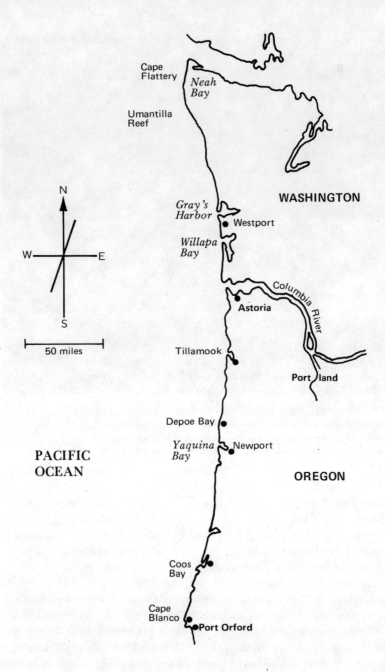

Cape
Flattery

*Neah
Bay*

Umantilla
Reef

N

W — E

S

50 miles

WASHINGTON

*Gray's
Harbor*
● Westport

*Willapa
Bay*

Columbia River

● Astoria

Tillamook
●

Port land

Depoe Bay ●

*Yaquina
Bay*
● Newport

PACIFIC
OCEAN

OREGON

Coos
Bay
●

Cape
Blanco ●
●**Port Orford**

Port Orford to Cape Flattery

Along the Oregon and Washington coasts there are a dozen major rivers pouring billions of gallons of pure mountain water into the Pacific. Though some of this water is wasted insofar as its primary purpose is concerned, the river mouths are welcomed by fishermen all up and down the shoreline. Fishing skiffs and small outboards use most of these exits to the ocean in all but stormy weather. They have been doing so since Indian times and most likely will continue to for years to come. But just because they *are* used at one time or another by a certain type of boat, it does not mean they should all be considered harbors of refuge for the ocean cruising vessel. For this reason we are mentioning in this chapter only those ports which are better endowed with protection and have easy access for the offshore cruiser who may not have "local knowledge," a phrase used wisely in *Pacific Coast Pilot* and other marine guide books. For those who *do* plan to negotiate any of the river bars of Oregon and Washington, they should arm themselves with Coast Guard harbor bar charts, and study them carefully before attempting a crossing.

From Cape Blanco it is only 35 miles north to Coos Bay, the major deep-water harbor between San Francisco and the Columbia River. Coos Bay is home port to a variety of enterprises, lumber rating foremost and sport and commercial fishing running a close second. Charleston pleasure-boat basin is situated just inside the southern jetty where all manner of marina facilities and charter fishing boats await such users. Salmon, striped bass, tuna and shad are some of the more prolific ocean fish in the area. Oysters, clams and crabs are also to be had in abundance along Coos Bay's shoreline.

Inland, within the Port area, State parks and picnic grounds are plentiful for those who would tarry ashore to explore the

Looking seaward over breakwatered entrance to Coos Bay, Oregon. Charleston Small Boat Basin has recently been enlarged to accommodoate the growing fleet of sport and commercial fishing boats. Coos Bay is noted for sportfishing with salmon, striped bass and shad runs predominating in the ocean, and clams, Dungeness crab and oysters closer to shore.

scenic hinterland of wild fern, huckleberry, azaleas and rhododendrons. This is a land of rain and sudden sunshine, which, teamed with the area's mild year-round climate, extracts the ultimate of richness in nature's verdure. One of the rare hardwoods indigenous to this coastal region is the golden, multi-whorled myrtlewood, from which novelties, furniture and gun-stocks are fashioned and polished to mirror finish.

Cruising further north and after passing the river mouths of the Umpqua, Suislaw and the Alsea, we arrive at Yaquina Bay and Newport, Oregon. After the usual proper timing of a bar entrance into Yaquina Bay, the visiting boat will find good facilities for either overnight or an extended stay at Newport. This is another fisherman's heaven, with its ocean fishing augmented here by trout and steelhead angling along the Yaquina River which is navigable up to 20 miles inland from the Bay. As elsewhere on the Oregon coast, State parks and camping sites are plentiful within a short range of the Bay. Some of these are situated along the forested river banks and others lie adjacent to the long expanses of duned, sand beaches on the ocean front. For the beachcomber-hiker, a rewarding stroll may be taken along the strand from Newport, 3 miles north to Agate Beach and Yaquina Head. When one returns heavily laden with agates, seashells, clams and crabs, or with merely a driftwood walking stick, his vitality will be enhanced from the exercise and his spirit eased by such a peaceful sojourn.

Moving on north, past aptly named Cape Foulweather, to a point about 8 miles beyond Yaquina Head, is a narrow corridor through the coastline's cliffs which leads into tiny Depoe Bay. The whole aspect is that of a doll-sized "sometimes" harbor. Despite its miniscule size, the presence of this little cove has engendered giant-sized arguments as to the advisability of its use by offshore cruising vessels. On the pro side of the question, it may be said that it can be negotiated by boats of up to 60 to 70 feet in length and less than 6 feet draft, *provided* these vessels can safely clear Depoe bridge which spans its entrance. The bridge has a clearance of 50 feet from mean high water and is flood-lighted at night. There is much more that might be said *against* the use of Depoe as a harbor of refuge, but we prefer to let the matter rest with other published guides, such as Morris & Heath's *Coastal Harbors of Oregon and Washington*, the *Pacific Coast Pilot*, or those skippers who have negotiated controversial Depoe Bay more often than we have. Certainly the type of boat under consideration, the proficiency of its pilot and weather situation at time of a projected entry will have much to do with such a decision. There are supplies and fuel available inside "the hole" as it is referred to by local users of Depoe Bay.

The next major harbor to the north is Tillamook Bay, 5 miles northward of Cape Meares Light. The channel entrance to this harbor averages 20 feet deep at the bar and therefore is little used by deep-sea vessels. Log rafts are towed or barged out of Tillamook Bay but primarily it is used by commercial fishing fleets and pleasure boats. Supplies and fuel are available at the

Controversial Depoe Bay on the Oregon coast offers inner sanctuary to the daring coastal cruisers who may choose to negotiate its
challenging entrance. Recently a short rock groin has been constructed on the north side of the channel (left when entering), but
it adds little to making this harbor an inviting one for those going
up or down the coast.

small boat basin in Garibaldi which lies on the north shore of
Tillamook Bay. Visitors are welcome to tour Tillamook's
famous cheese factories and there are canneries which will
process a fish catch should the angler care to have his salmon or
other marine-take canned.

From this point north to the Columbia River, shoreside
scenery is one of scenic contrasts. Densely wooded heads or
capes extend to seaward, curving down to meet white beaches
with their row on row of tumbling breakers. Windswept
evergreens crown the heights of sand dunes 'til the dunes give
way to more jagged rocky points—scalloped off to infinity. This
section of the coastline from Tillamook Bay to a point some 30
miles north, comprises the recreational beach area of the
Oregon coast. From Rockaway Beach at the southern end up to

A new spur breakwater, shown in upper center, has been constructed at Tillamook Bay. Weather reports and water conditions
existing at the bar are given by Radio Station KTIL, 1590 Khz
twice daily and when conditions change, or Coast Guard Tillamook can be called by 2-way radio if there is doubt about
conditions.

Seaside and Gearhart Beach beyond Tillamook Head—all are focal points for summer visitors.

There is probably no other major port on the Pacific Coast that is so well charted and detailed as is the Columbia River's entrance. The bar can become too rough to cross at times, but with clear, mild weather and at flood tide, even the smallest craft should have no difficulty in negotiating its corridor of well-marked buoys and navigational aids. From Astoria and Warrenton, the first cities inside the river mouth, the Columbia continues inland for many hundreds of miles. Together with its many tributaries to the east, north and south, the extent of opportunities for pleasure boatsmen to enjoy their craft in protected waters is far too vast to attempt description here. From a point near Astoria, both fresh water and ocean fishing is readily available. Further inland, along the Columbia and its main tributary, the Willamette, water pleasures turn to swimming, water skiing, fast boat racing or simply scenic cruising or sailing. Months on end could be spent in these waterways where one river joins another to create a water path reaching beyond the State of Oregon and into Washington and Idaho. Nearly all river marinas have launching ramps and small boats for charter or hourly hire, and picnicking and camping sites are only a few miles apart.

Cape Disappointment marks the northerly point of land at Columbia River's entrance. The River itself is a border division between Oregon and Washington. Twenty-five miles beyond Cape Disappointment is the first of Washington's two coastal harbors. This is Willapa Bay, previously known as Shoalwater Bay, because it is just that. The usual ocean fishing is engaged in outside the harbor while inside, emphasis is on the succulent Willapa oyster, Dungeness crabs and clams. Willapa's entrance bar is continually shifting and special care must be used in negotiating the fluctuating depths of this channel. Tokeland, 8 miles in from the bar, is the center of sport fishing activity where supplies, motels and charter fishing boats await their many customers.

As we have mentioned earlier, many of our trips along the coast have been made either non-stop between Los Angeles and Cape Flattery, or with relatively few overnight stops at harbors along the northern part of the coast. With our ship's ample fuel supply this could be done with relative ease and it avoided our having to cross the bar entrances to Oregon and Washington

Beacon Rock, on the north bank of the Columbia River, is an
ancient monolith, the core of a volcano. A Washington State Park
with 4025 acres is located directly north of this 872-foot rock. A
winding stairway takes you to the top. A boat moorage is in the
Columbia River directly below.

harbors. An exception to this pattern happened a few years ago
when we found ourselves with little choice but to cross the bar
into Gray's Harbor, approximately 25 miles northward of
Willapa Bay—worse yet, having to cross in the maelstrom of an
ebbing tide.

It was in the middle of a night when we were about 30 miles
offshore and some 40 miles northwest of Gray's Harbor, that
our ship took one particularly hard roll which dislodged the
lead tray containing our 2000 pounds of batteries. One end of
the tray was canted at a precarious angle resting against an

Gray's Harbor, Washington, is home to one of the State's largest fishing fleets. Salmon is the major catch during all but winter months, at which time crab fishers bring in thousands of pounds of the Pacific's finest shellfish, the Dungeness Crab.

engine and the other was caught temporarily on a CO^2 tank. The major threat was loss of power for radio, radar, pumps and other auxiliaries should the batteries tip further and lose their acid.

Small craft warnings were displayed north to Cape Flattery and our present heading of 350 degrees kept us in a mean quartering sea. Our best solution appeared to turn downwind and head for Gray's Harbor for repairs. As we yawed along in the early morning hours, we discussed the cause of our battery shift. There had been, we knew, about a quarter of an inch of space between the batteries and their containing tray. Inertia from our heavy roll had started the movement which generated enough force to tear loose the wooden bulkhead supports.

Dawn came, raw and gray, all the more unpleasant for us with our lack of sleep and tension of the preceding hours. Earlier we had called Coast Guard explaining our predicament and asking them to lead us through the devious channel to Westport. When we met them outside the harbor, it was apparant that they would have preferred we stay outside another six hours, until change of tide, but we felt our temporary shoring in the engineroom would probably not withstand such an interval of waiting and circling outside the bar.

"We'll go in now." Jack told their skipper. "All right" he replied tersely. "Follow me in, but if you lose your radio, strike your colors." Tired as we were, we laughed at that last message. If we lost our radio it would likely mean we had lost everything aboard ship in one big roll. Just who, I asked, is going to dash aft 60 feet to haul down Old Glory?

Although the Coast Guard cutter was a 125-foot ship, and she stayed about 300 yards ahead of us on our wild ride across the bar, its mast often disappeared completely from our sight in those tremendous seas. Seas that came up from everywhere and smashed against themselves in indescribable fury! It was no wonder to us that more people and ships have been lost at Gray's Harbor than have been at any other Pacific coastal port. Part of the time the channel buoys were out of sight behind towering seas. We were doubly glad to have a leader.

A carpenter in Westport spent most of the day helping us put our engineroom back in order. And when we headed out of Gray's Harbor channel on the following morning, their bar was smooth as a lake. It was hard to realize this was the same bar that for us had almost turned out to be the one in the well-known hymn.

Another 80 miles northwest of Gray's Harbor north jetty light is Umatilla Reef Lighted Horn Buoy 2UR. This replaces the old red-hulled Umatilla Lightship, which until 1972 had been in service for 74 years. 2UR is anchored about a half mile east of the lightship station and one-and-a-half miles west of the rocks and reefs which it warns against. This we keep to starboard and, on a more northerly heading, point toward Cape Flattery, 16 miles beyond.

Cape Flattery marks the end of the line for Washington's rugged coastline, and fittingly sums up the State's whole coastal aspect in one great exclamation point. High on Waatch Hill stands one of the Pacific's largest radar Early Warning installations. Below, along the wild and rocky shoreline, the sea thunders its eternal rage against a lonely beach where drift logs lie like scattered monstrous matchsticks, and sea birds fly screaming down the wind-torn sky.

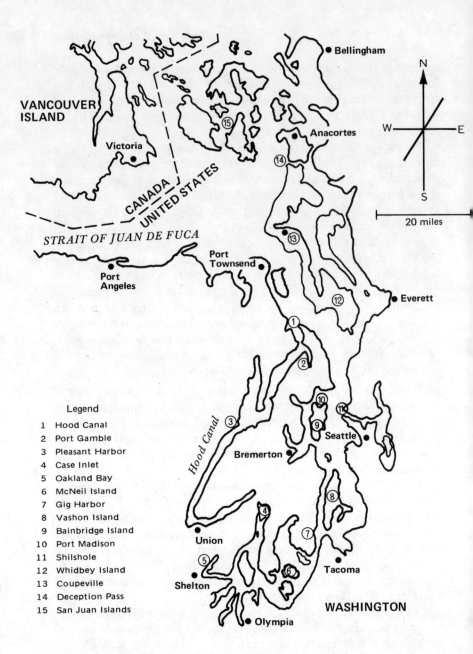

Bellingham

VANCOUVER
ISLAND

Victoria

⑮

Anacortes

N

W—————E

S

20 miles

CANADA
UNITED STATES

⑭

STRAIT OF JUAN DE FUCA

⑬

Port
Townsend

Port
Angeles

⑫

Everett

①

②

Legend

1   Hood Canal
2   Port Gamble
3   Pleasant Harbor
4   Case Inlet
5   Oakland Bay
6   McNeil Island
7   Gig Harbor
8   Vashon Island
9   Bainbridge Island
10 Port Madison
11 Shilshole
12 Whidbey Island
13 Coupeville
14 Deception Pass
15 San Juan Islands

⑩

⑪

③

⑨

Seattle

Hood Canal

Bremerton

⑧

Union

⑦

⑤

Shelton

④

⑥

Tacoma

WASHINGTON

Olympia

The Inland Sea of Puget Sound

Little did Senor Juan de Fuca realize, back in 1590, that his orders from the Viceroy of Spanish Mexico to find the Northwest Passage would someday be recounted in a cruising guide to the Pacific Coast. But no guide to the Inland Sea of Puget Sound would be complete without a brief review of the claims and counterclaims of the discovery of the Northwest Passage, which was reported by Juan de Fuca to have had its western terminus in the Strait that now bears his name.

The Spanish, English and Dutch sent expedition after expedition to find the mythical Northwest Passage that would shorten their trade routes to the Orient by giving passage from the Atlantic Coast to the Pacific. It was in 1592 that Juan de Fuca reported he sailed 20 days eastward from Cape Flattery, although it was not so named until 180 years later, and that he had reached the Atlantic ocean through the new passage.

Despite Juan de Fuca's positive statements, even naming the approximate latitude of the entrance to the passage, Capt. James Cook from England in 1772 stated in his log "It is in this very latitude where we now are that geographers have placed the pretended Strait of Juan de Fuca. But we saw nothing like it, nor is there the least probability that any such thing existed." Cook even sailed past the entrance to the Strait and the theoretical entrance to the Northwest Passage, without observing it. He did name the bluff at its entrance "Cape Flattery."

It was not until 1792 that Capt. George Vancouver, also from England, with two small ships, the *Discovery* and the *Chatham*, finally put world geographers straight on the Northwest Passage. Among the 145 officers and men making up the crews of the two ships were Capt. Joseph Whidbey and Lt. Peter Puget. Their names and others of the British Admiralty were appropriately given to discoveries made by Capt. Vancouver. They entered the Strait of Juan de Fuca in April of that year, and in six months charted the waters of Puget Sound and the Strait of Georgia. They also proved that Vancouver Island, later named after Capt. Vancouver, was not a part of the mainland. Every possible inlet reaching eastward was explored and Vancouver rightfully concluded that the Northwest Passage was a myth that had existed for nearly 200 years.

In early June of 1792 Capt. Vancouver wrote the first account of northwest boat racing activities by reporting the canoe races of the Indians. In an area now named Coupeville, on the eastern shores of Whidbey Island, his survey party came on friendly tribes of Indians who tested the strength of their youth in racing hand-carved, cedar-log canoes—not small dug-outs, but heavy 45- to 50-foot canoes with crews of eight handling brightly painted paddles. Until a few years ago those same Indian canoe races were annually staged and drew hundreds of yachtsmen to watch them, from all parts of the Sound.

Notwithstanding the high northerly latitude of this area, it is blessed with a mild climate. Average winter temperature is 41 degrees and the summer 63 degrees, thanks to the Japanese current which brings warmth to an area that would otherwise be as cold as the northeastern tip of the States.

A single statement summing up the magnitude of the Puget Sound cruising region is: "Here a boatowner could cruise for a hundred years and never anchor twice in the same cove." There is an estimated 20,000 miles of shoreline, with good anchorages never more than a few miles apart. With few exceptions, provisions and fuel are obtainable without going more than 25 miles. In recent years the State of Washington has taken an active and commendable step in building small boat mooring facilities at scores of water-recreational areas, including over-night camping sites ashore for those who are cruising in open boats. It is the farsightedness of the State, Counties and communities of Washington that has helped spur the tremendous increase in use of the 2000 square miles of inland waters.

From the standpoint of what type craft is suitable for Northwest cruising, the answer is literally "anything that floats and is seaworthy." Outboard runabouts and cruisers are proving increasingly popular and, because of the many overnight shoreside facilities, extended trips in outboard powered boats are routine. On the other hand, deep-draft sail and power boats

Puget Sound is not always smooth, as is obvious here during
annual Heavyweather Race.

have no problem because the entire area from lower Puget
Sound to Alaska is "deep water." While the weather from June
to October is mild, there are times when foul weather gear is
desirable. For this reason, there are fewer flying-bridge type
cruisers in the Northwest than in other areas of the Pacific
Coast. It is a reason, too, that wood or oil burning galley ranges
are popular to provide year-around warmth on many sail and
power boats.

Fishing, crabbing, oyster plucking and clam digging are more
popular extra-curricular activities than swimming or water
skiing. Average water temperatures are in the mid-fifties or low
sixties, except in isolated or protected areas.

While there are hundreds of sailing enthusiasts in Northwest
waters, the area is better suited to power boats. A glance at one

Three of a fleet of ten steam launches prepare for a Sunday parade
at Port Townsend, Puget Sound, Washington.

of the accompanying charts shows the reason: there are not too
many long reaches of open water. Other deterrents to a larger
sailing fleet are the tides and resulting currents, reaching three
to seven knots in some of the most picturesque passages, such as
Admiralty Inlet, lying between Whidbey Island and the mainland to the west, or in Saratoga Passage between Whidbey Island
and the mainland to the east. The result is an increasing number
of motor-sailers finding popularity in these waters, as contrasted
to the deep-water sailing types.

There are two main cruising areas between Port Townsend at
the entrance to Puget Sound and the southern extremity of the
inland sea. The easternmost of the two has on its shores the
State Capitol of Olympia, Tacoma, Seattle, Bremerton, Everett,
Anacortes and Bellingham; the western area in Hood Canal,
with its opening near Port Townsend. Misnamed a "canal" by
Capt. Vancouver, the name has stuck with this 55-mile-long
fiord which cuts deeply into the Olympic Peninsula. There are
no communities of size on the Canal, although scores of
summer resorts and a number of lumber mill villages are along
the shores to remind those cruising that they are not a million
miles from civilization.

Starting down the Canal on a southwesterly heading from Foulweather Bluff, the first stop is usually at Hood Point for a sack of oysters which abound the rocky beach during low tide. Two miles farther on the left is the 100-yard-wide entrance to Port Gamble where supplies of all kinds can be obtained from the lumber-mill-operated fuel docks and store. A landlocked harbor, it is a frequent haven for those not wanting to make the run to the Canal's southern end. Just past the entrance to Port Gamble is the world's longest floating bridge spanning a salt-water channel. Between Port Gamble and the south end of the Canal are harbors or coves that can easily go unnoticed because of their small openings along the Canal. Aptly named Pleasant Harbor is one of them, with a narrow mouth that opens into a forest-lined cove of serenity. At low tide, boats drawing more than four feet should not enter the harbor, although once inside there is plenty of water. Twenty miles farther south, where the Canal takes a sharp turn to the northeast, is one of the larger Indian Reservations and nearby, the village of Union, where fuel and supplies are available.

Less than two miles of land separate Lynch Cove at the end of the Canal from Case Inlet on the Olympia side of Puget Sound. No doubt Capt. Vancouver failed to reach this point in his early surveys and assumed the two bodies of water were connected.

Within a 15-mile radius of Olympia are a half dozen arms, inlets or passages that are a deterrent to sailing enthusiasts, but a cruising paradise to the powerboat owners. Typical is Hammersley Inlet which terminates in Oakland Bay. In a distance of 10 miles through this forest-lined waterway there are at least 14 changes of direction as the Inlet unwinds on its way past the lumbertown of Shelton. And to cover the 22 miles as the seagulls fly, between Olympia and Tacoma, there are a dozen different routes that can be taken around scores of small islands. The best-known island along this part of the Sound is McNeil, better known as the "resort" because of its Federal Prison, which commands a millionaire's view of the Sound and the majestic Olympic and Cascade mountain ranges.

Tacoma is approached from the lower Sound through The Narrows—well named because of towering cliffs close on each side. Here currents reach velocities up to six knots as they are compressed through the channel. Over The Narrows is one of the largest suspension bridges in the country, built after the

Hale Passage, between Tacoma and Olympia, Washington, in
southern Puget Sound.

original one was blown down during a terrific winter storm.
Tacoma Yacht Club is located two miles southeast of Point
Defiance—the northern extremity of The Narrows—in a landlocked harbor, only a few minutes drive from Tacoma's
residential area. Fortunate are these residents in that they can
cruise either to the north toward Seattle or toward Olympia to
the south—with hundreds of miles of shoreline and scores of
coves in which to anchor between their club and the two cities.

The north end of The Narrows has on its west bank the
well-known community of Gig Harbor, made famous by the
commercial fishing boats that ply Pacific waters, a distinctive
type of which are built here. Populated mainly by families of
Scandanavian and Spanish descent, Gig Harbor is a colorful and
hospitable rendezvous for northwest cruising enthusiasts.

Gig Harbor, looking eastward across The Narrows toward Tacoma.

Between Tacoma and Seattle is 10-mile-long Vashon Island, which is connected by a sandpit to Maury Island. Portage Spit was, for many years, the scene of historic Indian Clam Bakes. While the procedure seems simple, it took native Indians to get the right touch, in digging an immense basin in the sand, lining it with rocks, building the driftwood fire which would burn for a day to heat the rocks, then filling of the basin with alternate layers of seaweed, clams, chicken and salmon, topped by a blanket of seaweed. Nearby five gallon cans of clams steamed in a broth unequaled even by the French Bordelaise. In the bay were anchored all types of boats from all parts of the Sound, and around beach fires the owners and their guests gathered for an Indian feast that was unsurpassed except by previous ones.

Ten miles to the north of Portage Spit is Seattle to the east,

The smaller of the two locks that connect Shilshole Bay on Puget
Sound with the Lake Washington Ship Canal. Thousands of boats
pass through the locks each year enroute from Lake Washington,
Portage Bay, Lake Union or Salmon Bay to the Sound.

and the entrance channels to Bremerton to the west. Winding between the south end of Bainbridge Island and the mainland is the channel which leads to Sinclair Inlet on which Bremerton is situated and where the Puget Sound Navy Yard is the principal activity.

Another of Puget Sound's favorite clam digging areas is Hidden Harbor behind Bremerton, reached through Washington Narrows which connects Dyes Inlet and Sinclair Inlet. Completely landlocked, Hidden Harbor is a bowl of water garnished with towering evergreen trees that come down to the sand beach, and at low tide yield never-ending supplies of butter clams.

Cruising toward the northern end of Bainbridge Island brings one to Port Madison. It has become a year-around residential area for many who have in their front yards a pier or float for their boats, which they use to commute to Seattle. This is also the site of Seattle Yacht Club's "Fo'castle," a facility which many yacht clubs would be proud to call their headquarters. Floats are provided for visiting boats and a roaring cordwood fire is usually burning in a massive fireplace in the lounge. Although only a quarter-mile wide by a mile in length, Port Madison will frequently have 40 to 50 boats anchored in it on weekends, since it is only an hour's cruise from Shilshole Bay and the Locks at Seattle.

It is through these Locks that thousands of pleasure and commercial boats pass each season, from Lakes Union and Washington, around which Seattle is built. During peak traffic hours, the main lock (the largest on the North American continent) will have scores of small boats in it on their way to or from the Sound. A breakwatered harbor and slip facilities for 1400 boats are at Shilshole Bay on the Sound side. This is directly to the north of the entrance to the Locks, and is a boon to Seattle boat owners who prefer not to face the weekend bottle-neck at the Locks. Excellent restaurants are here, as well as supplies and fuel. It is operated by the Seattle Port Commission, and is an outstanding example of a port-authority-operated marina.

Before leaving Seattle, it should be noted that during mid-winter and spring, while Pacific Coast boatsmen are cruising, racing and sailing, a group of its civic leaders spend week after week planning and working on their annual Seafair celebration. Founded some years ago, it has become a water

Shilshole Bay marina is on Puget Sound, just outside the Locks
that connect the Sound with the Lake Washington Ship Canal.

All Seattle boats dress in their best for Opening Day parades. Here
the fleet lines up to move from Portage Bay through Montlake Cut
into Lake Washington.

carnival, an aquatic festival, a period of worship (by boat
owners to King Neptune). Spanning from ten days to two weeks
during August, the Seattle Seafair has had on its program the
outboard championship races, the Gold Cup unlimited hydro-
plane races, national water skiing competitions, Pacific Coast
championship inboard races for all classes, and sailing events.

Cruising northward from Seattle invariably takes one to the
San Juan Islands, either up the east or westward sides of
Whidbey Island. The westward side through Admiralty Inlet is
the main steamer lane, passing the entrance to Hood Canal and
finally past Port Townsend. The only hazards are the thousands
of weekend fishermen in the waters during the salmon fishing
season.

Going toward the San Juans via Saratoga Passage on the
eastern side of Whidbey Island is by far the most scenic route.
There are innumerable harbors or anchoring spots along the

Looking west through Deception Pass, during slack water.

island, excellent clam digging beaches and the historic Indian village of Coupeville. The climax of this route is Deception Pass through which tides will pour or empty at velocities up to 8 knots. Just east of the Pass and on Whidbey Island, is Coronet Bay, a development of the State Parks and Recreation Commission, with docks, floats, camping grounds, showers and barbecue pits. It is a favorite lay-over harbor for those waiting for slack water. A similar facility is at the western entrance to the Pass.

After passing through Deception Pass, heading westerly, the San Juan Archipelago of some 172 islands come into view, all spaced within a rectangular area measuring 15 miles by 20 miles.

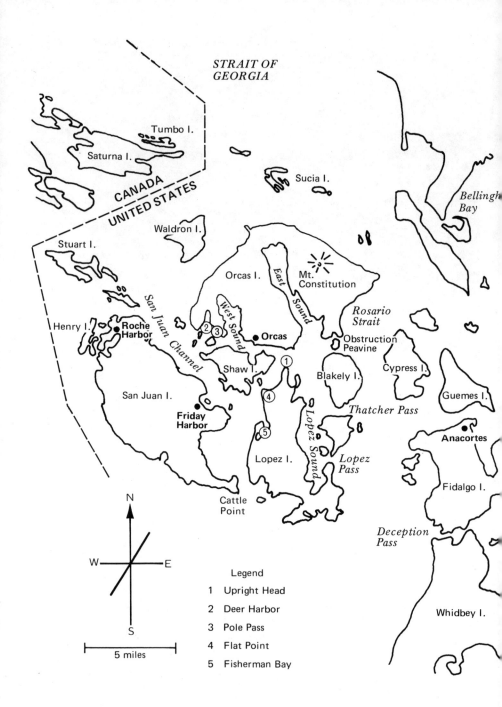

STRAIT OF GEORGIA

Tumbo I.

Saturna I.

CANADA

UNITED STATES

Sucia I.

Bellingham Bay

Waldron I.

Stuart I.

Orcas I.

East Sound

Mt. Constitution

Rosario Strait

Henry I.

Roche Harbor

San Juan Channel

West Sound

②③

● Orcas

Obstruction Peavine

Shaw I.

①

Blakely I.

Cypress I.

San Juan I.

Friday Harbor

④

Guemes I.

⑤

Thatcher Pass

Anacortes

Lopez I.

Lopez Sound

Lopez Pass

Fidalgo I.

Cattle Point

Deception Pass

N

W——E

S

5 miles

Legend

1 Upright Head

2 Deer Harbor

3 Pole Pass

4 Flat Point

5 Fisherman Bay

Whidbey I.

The San Juan Archipelago

Leaving Deception Pass on our cruise among the San Juan Islands, we have the choice of six passages into the lake-smooth waters of the archipelago. Four of these are from Rosario Strait on the eastern side of the Islands. They are most generally used when approaching the Islands from Deception Pass (or Anacortes and Bellingham, which are to the north of the Pass) because the distances are shorter.

If we approach the Islands from the Strait of Juan de Fuca or Puget Sound we would use Middle Channel, past Cattle Point on the southern tip of San Juan Island; or if returning southbound from British Columbia, we would use the northwestern portion of San Juan Channel.

Even though the *Coast Pilot* makes the statement that Lopez Pass, between Lopez and Decatur Islands, "is little used...and very narrow" it must be remembered that it is written primarily for the benefit of ocean-going vessel masters, and not for the average small-boat owner. With 9 to 12 fathoms of water through the passage, and deep water up to the steep shores of the Islands, Lopez Pass is free of hazards and the closest one from Deception Pass. In fact, the eight mile passage across Rosario Strait from Deception can provide far more excitement if it is made during ebb tide with a strong afternoon breeze from the west.

Alternate access to the 15-mile-long Lopez and East Sounds, from Rosario Strait, is through the half-mile-wide Thatcher Pass which is about three miles to the north of Lopez Pass; or through either Obstruction or Peavine Passes, another five miles north of Thatcher. All lead to the land-locked, island-studded waters of Lopez Sound and East Sound, formed by Lopez, Decatur, Blakely and Orcas Islands. These are oft referred to as the eastern part of the San Juans, as contrasted to San Juan,

Westward to Lopez Pass in San Juan Islands. Ram Island, left
center.

Henry, Stuart and Waldron Islands which make up the western
part of the archipelago. Standing to the north of Orcas Island
are the jewel-like Sucia Islands, with their deep indentations and
protected anchorages.

Once within the Lopez and East Sounds, roughly from
½-mile to 2-miles wide and 15 miles north-south, there are
virtually countless anchoring areas. Largest of the islands that
give protection to these waters is Orcas, with its 2454-foot-high
Mt. Constitution dominating the scene. For those with long legs
and a constitution to climb Mt. Constitution, it is a rewarding
outing because it provides a bird's eye view of the entire group
of islands, the mainland of Washington to the east, Vancouver
Island to the west, the Canadian Strait of Georgia to the north,
and Puget Sound to the south.

A number of small communities are on these two Sounds,
and cruising supplies are readily available. Most have docks for
the ferries that are the principal links with the mainland to the
east, and to the other communities in the San Juan group. Olga,
Rosario and Eastsound have particularly good facilities for
visiting boats, with floats, supplies, and at Eastsound an airstrip

Rosario resort and marina on Orcas Island's East Sound has been expanded, with more slips for visiting yachtsmen, and the harbor has been dredged for easier maneuvering.

for plane-commuting back to the mainland or to the other airstrips on nearby islands.

Heading westward between Upright Head on the northwestern tip of Lopez Island and the southern tip of a portion of Orcas Island, we have the choice of passing Shaw Island through the northerly passages, or turning southwest for the more direct route to Friday Harbor on San Juan Island.

Staying on the northerly of the two passages takes us past the community of Orcas and into West Sound which is a three mile long indentation into Orcas Island. Good dockage is available at the small community of Westsound, and anchorage can be taken practically anywhere within the Sound. Going toward Deer Harbor from West Sound can sometimes present a thrill while in Pole Pass. It is 75-yards wide at its narrowest point, and passage through it should be timed for slack or near-slack water to avoid currents that can reach 8 knots at the height of their ebb or flood. Deer Harbor is the westernmost of the secluded coves on

Orcas Island, and only about seven miles from the archipelago's metropolis of Friday Harbor.

Had we turned southwest from Upright Head on Lopez Island, we would have passed Flat Point, one of the area's greatest salmon fishing spots, enroute to the land-locked Fisherman Bay. Frequently it is overlooked or passed by without realizing that the S-shaped channel leads into the resort community of Lopez. Completely protected from all winds, Fisherman Bay has an excellent holding bottom or dockage for visiting boats, supplies and a restaurant at the shore end of the pier with a view towards the west and San Juan Island that is breath-taking.

Only about four miles westerly of Lopez is the county seat of Friday Harbor on the easterly shores of San Juan Island. Separating Lopez and San Juan Islands is the San Juan Channel, which is one of the three principal passages between Puget Sound and British Columbia waters to the north—the other two being on the eastern and western sides of the archipelago. The channel is about 13-miles long and varies in width from a half mile to three miles, through which the ebb and flood tides set up currents that reach as high as five knots as they pass Cattle Point on the Puget Sound end of the Channel. Sailing through this Channel without the help of an auxiliary engine is frustrating and unless one is going with the current it can be slow and exasperating.

Friday Harbor is a quaint mixture of a fishing village, summer resort, cannery town and shopping center. It is linked to the mainland with good ferry service the year around, and both charter and scheduled small-plane service. On the northern part of the Harbor is a University of Washington oceanographic facility. It is the center of a prosperous agricultural district and the headquarters for a sizable fishing fleet. In contrast to the new and modern motel facilities, until recently one of the older hotels was still using knotted ropes from the second-story windows for fire escapes.

In the middle of the roughly one-mile, semi-circular Harbor is heavily wooded Brown Island, with channels leading to Friday Harbor docks on either side of the island. Waters here, as throughout the entire archipelago, are deep to within a few hundred yards of the shorelines. Anchorage in the harbor in 5 to 8 fathoms is sometimes necessary when the city-maintained floats are filled with visiting craft. Friday Harbor is also a port

Beachcombing on Jones Island, about 5 miles north of Friday
Harbor, is a relaxing weekend activity. This is one of the rare
island beaches. Usually trees grow right to water's edge, with
ample anchorage depths close to shore.

of entry for those returning from Canadian waters, and during
the summer months the yacht clubs in Puget Sound underwrite
the over-time charges that would otherwise be assessed for
customs clearance during holidays and Sundays.

On the northwestern end of the roughly 15-mile-long San
Juan Island is a popular boating destination—Roche Harbor. We
had previously gone past it many times enroute to Canadian
waters, until Frank Morris, co-author of the *Marine Atlas of the
Northwest,* urged us to visit his summer home a short distance
from it. We are glad that he did, because we found at Roche
Harbor floats to accommodate a large fleet of summer-resident
boats, and still ample room for visiting craft. Ashore there are

Historic Roche Harbor, San Juan Islands.

supply stores; the same small hotel with restaurant that once catered to the visiting businessmen and sailing ship captains who came to the harbor in the early 1900's; and a giant-size barbecue pit that can provide barbecued salmon and meat for hundreds of guests at one time.

A short walk through a tree and shrub-lined trail is a stark reminder of Roche Harbor's early days. In the center of a forest clearing stands a circle of Grecian columns surrounding an enormous cement table and cement chairs around the table. It is said that under the seat of each chair are the ashes of the family members. A close look at the total picture shows one chair is missing, and the upper part of one column is unfinished. It is local lore that the elimination of the chair and part of the column represented the one black sheep of the family who was not entitled to join his family even after death.

At the turn of the century Roche Harbor was a bustling community, producing millions of tons of high-quality lime that was shipped to the four corners of the world. Now all that remains of the lime quarries and mill are graying skeletons of buildings and boarded-up entrances to mining shafts. On the pier that once saw sailing vessels of many nations tied to it while loading their cargoes, there are now facilities for visiting

Stuart Island, in the U.S. San Juan Islands group, borders British
Columbia territory.

boat owners, the Roche Harbor Yacht Club, and U.S. Customs
Office.

Within a few minutes' outboarding in a dinghy, to the west of
Roche Harbor, is Henry Island with its picturesque King's
Ransome Cove where, it is said, smugglers frequently took
refuge from pursuers. Now the Seattle Yacht Club has one of its
out-stations on the Island. Hardly a mile farther through
Mosquito Passage is the entrance to Westcott Bay, completely
land locked and with sand beaches around its perimeter. On a
bight off Westcott Bay is the site of the old English Camp and
blockhouse, remindful of the days of dispute between the
English and United States over the boundary between the two
countries.

Four miles northerly from Roche Harbor is Stuart Island,
with its two fine harbors that provide quiet seclusion and
perfect weather protection. Reid Harbor is on the south side of

Prevost Harbor, on the northern shore of Stuart Island in the San Juans, is a completely protected anchorage, and small boats can use the State Parks and Recreation Commission float. At Reid Harbor on the south shore of the Island, there is another small-boat float as well as a shoreside facility of barbecue pits and tables.

the island, about a mile in length and ending at a broad, sloping beach that is ideal for clam digging. On the north side is Prevost Harbor, where there is a dock and supplies can be obtained. Although less than a quarter-mile-wide neck of land separates Reid and Prevost Harbors, to cruise from one to the other is a 4-mile trip through the narrow, but perfectly safe, Johns Pass.

In contrast to the three, four or five miles of cruising between such anchorages as Rosario, Olga, West Sound, Fisherman Cove, Friday Harbor, Roche Harbor, Reid and Prevost, each of which offers days of exploring their immediate vicinity, the 12-mile run from Stuart Island to Sucia Islands becomes a distinct contrast. Enroute on a northeasterly heading is Waldron Island, and like all the others in the San Juans, it is timbered nearly to the hightide line. On its western shore is the community of Waldron, with a dock, supplies and shoreside facilities. If the weather is warm, the sand beaches by Waldron invite the swimming enthusiast. On its easterly shore is a small bight that provides good anchorage and ashore are a few summer homes.

Anchored in Reid Harbor, Stuart Island, in the San Juans of
northern Puget Sound (a Washington State Marine Park).

Our Sucia Islands destination is probably one of the most
pleasant in the San Juan Island group. The State of Washington
has provided floats, shoreside barbecue pits and camping
facilities, and there is ample room on both the east and west
sides of the main, horseshoe-shaped island to anchor without
fear of swinging into another anchored boat. Echo Bay on the
eastern side is a mile-deep cut into the island, with two narrow,
wooded islets splitting the southernmost part of the Bay at its
entrance. Deep water is on either side of the larger of them.
Fossil Bay is on the south side of the islands, and although
smaller in area than Echo Bay, often has as many as 50 boats at
the State floats or at anchor.

July, August and September are the prime months for San
Juan Island cruising, both from a weather standpoint and for
good salmon fishing, oyster plucking, clam digging or crab
trapping. The season is purported to last five months, rather
than three, but after a great many cruises into this territory
aboard our *Monsoon* or *Monsoon II*, we remain staunch
supporters of the three summer months.

The ardent fisherman may not mind rain, provided he comes
in with his catch, and of that he may be assured regardless of
weather. Of the many types of salmon caught in these waters,
the King and Silvers are the main take for sportsfishermen, July

Boats moor in the quiet of Sucia Island, which lies directly north
of Orcas Island, largest of the San Juan Archipelago in north Puget
Sound.

and August being the best fishing months. The Blackmouth, a
two-year immature King, is caught almost all year around. The
Humpback, another fighter, is normally caught in the odd-
numbered years and his run is short. Regardless of one's fishing
luck, however, there is always a small harbor store within a few
miles' cruising distance where one may buy his seafood, fresh
from the water and awaiting the barbecue or frypan.

In the San Juan group of islands a decided change in weather
and temperature is noticeable. It is warmer and dryer than the
areas both north and south, the annual rainfall is less than half
that of Seattle or Vancouver, B.C., which has led the area to be
known as the "sunshine group" of islands, and by others as the
"banana belt" of the northwest.

Appendix to Part Two

Types of Boats Suitable for Coastal Cruising
Facilities and Supplies
Approximate Distances in Nautical Miles
Permits for Offshore Islands
Electric/Electronic Equipment
Books and Charts

TYPES OF BOATS SUITABLE FOR COASTAL CRUISING

There are times when a canoe could be sailed or paddled from the coastal harbors, across their bars and out into the Pacific—but those times are few and far between; and it is quite unlikely that the Pacific would remain placid enough for the voyager to go from one harbor to the next without running into trouble. Boats little larger than canoes, but designed and built for ocean service and manned by adventurous people, have made long trips up and down the coast, and to the Hawaiian Islands—but again, they are few and far between.

Under favorable weather conditions, and crewed by persons with sea-going experience, well-designed and staunchly built power or sail boats of 30 feet in length can safely be used for coastal cruising. There may be times that they will have to lie at anchor behind a protective headland, or in a harbor, waiting for improved weather conditions; or make a retreat to a sheltered cove if a blow comes up and the going gets rough. There are also times that the heaviest hundred-footer will do the same. Fast, planing type cruisers have made the trip up the coast, but generally do so in short legs and during early morning hours before normal mid-day and afternoon winds create a chop or sea condition that forces them to reduce speed.

Power boats should have a minimum cruising range of 150 miles for cruising between San Diego and San Francisco; a minimum of 200 miles when going between San Francisco and Port Orford; and no less than 400 miles range for the Oregon-Washington sector of the coast.

Passenger ferries are operated by the State of Washington across Puget Sound from Seattle and Everett, and from Anacortes through the San Juan Islands to Sidney on Vancouver Island. They also carry cars and trailers, and are frequently used by those with trailed boats to reach areas in the Hood Canal or the San Juan Islands, where there are scores of launching ramps or lifts; or to reach the Canadian Gulf Islands without traversing the Strait of Juan de Fuca and the Strait of Georgia.

FACILITIES AND SUPPLIES

There are few harbors along the Pacific Coast that are not well able to serve the cruising boatsman's needs of fuel, water, ice, mechanical and electronic supplies or repairs, stores and provisions. The few that do not are the anchorages under the lees of headlands, which are yet to be developed as breakwatered anchorages. Typical of the latter are Coxo anchorage, the harbors on the islands to seaward of Santa Barbara, San Simeon and Shelter Cove along the California coastline.

The thousands of commercial fishing vessels, and the growing number of pleasure craft that operate along the coast have created the demand for supplies and services that leaves little to be desired.

Ship-to-shore communications, through the public correspondence stations, permit almost continuous contact with those ashore. Such stations are located at San Pedro, San Francisco, Eureka, Astoria and Seattle, and the majority of them have two or more channels to handle traffic. Weather reports are broadcast by these stations, as well as by the Coast Guard. Continuous ESSA VHF reports are broadcast in the Los Angeles, San Francisco and Puget Sound areas.

APPROXIMATE DISTANCES IN NAUTICAL MILES

BETWEEN PRINCIPAL CALIFORNIA, OREGON AND WASHINGTON POINTS:

1	2	Between col. 1 & col. 2	From San Diego to col. 2 (cumulative)	To Olympia from col. 1 (cumulative)
San Diego.........	Oceanside.............	35.........	35.........	1363
Oceanside.........	Newport Beach........	33.........	68.........	1328
Newport Beach.....	Los Angeles..........	20.........	88.........	1295
Los Angeles.......	Santa Barbara.........	82........	170.........	1275
Santa Barbara......	Coxo Anchorage.......	35........	205.........	1193
Coxo Anchorage....	Port San Luis.........	51........	256.........	1158
Port San Luis......	Morro Bay............	21........	277.........	1107
Morro Bay........	Monterey............	102........	379.........	1086
Monterey........	Half Moon Bay........	62........	441..........	984
Half Moon Bay.....	San Francisco*........	24........	465..........	922
San Francisco*.....	Pt. Reyes............	28........	493..........	898
Pt. Reyes.........	Bodega Bay...........	23........	516..........	870
Bodega Bay.......	Shelter Cove.........	117........	633..........	847
Shelter Cove.......	Eureka...............	54........	687..........	730
Eureka...........	Crescent City.........	60........	747..........	676
Crescent City.....	Port Orford..........	65........	812..........	616
Port Orford.......	Coos Bay............	51........	863..........	551
Coos Bay.........	Newport.............	77........	940..........	500
Newport.........	Tillamook............	55........	995..........	423
Tillamook........	Columbia River**......	40.......	1035..........	368
Columbia River**...	Grays Harbor.........	44.......	1079..........	328
Grays Harbor......	Cape Flattery.........	96.......	1175..........	284
Cape Flattery......	Port Townsend........	86.......	1261..........	188
Port Townsend.....	Seattle...............	40.......	1301..........	102
Seattle...........	Tacoma..............	25.......	1326..........	62
Tacoma..........	Olympia..............	37.......	1363..........	37

* San Francisco marina.
**Columbia River Lightship.

The direct steamer courses between San Diego, California, and Olympia, Washington, cover a distance of 1278 miles, but harbor-shopping as done in this table of distances increases the route to 1363 miles.

PERMITS FOR OFFSHORE ISLANDS

Permits to go ashore on the western end of Santa Cruz Island may be obtained by mail: Santa Cruz Island Co., 615 S. Flower St., Los Angeles, Calif. Price: $20 per year, or $5.00 for any 30 consecutive days. A shoregoing permit for this island's eastern portion (from Coche Point on the north, around the eastern end to Sandstone Point, including Potato Bay, Scorpion, Smugglers' and Yellowbanks Coves) may be obtained by writing: Mr. Pier Gherini, 230 La Arcada Blvd., Santa Barbara, or Mr. Francis Gherini, 162 South "A" St., Oxnard, Calif. This permit is without charge. Pyramid Cove, on San Clemente Island's southeastern end may be used for anchoring when Naval exercises are not being conducted. No shoregoing is permissible in this restricted area.

ELECTRIC/ELECTRONIC EQUIPMENT

There are many cruising areas on the Pacific Coast where the ability to anchor (instead of tying to a dock or slip, or mooring on a buoy) adds greatly to the pleasure of the cruise. This encourages the use of an electric-power anchor windlass and ample chain. Radio navigation aids are closely spaced along the entire coast, and between the marine beacons, airways beacons and broadcast stations, there is seldom a time that a radio direction finder is out of range of at least two or more stations. The advent of very-high-frequency VOR airways omni-ranges and companion receivers for use on boats, opens an additional means of radio navigation to augment the conventional low-frequency beacons and medium-frequency broadcast stations. Other electronic equipment should include a depth sounder, radiotelephone, automatic pilot and, if the ultimate in safety is desired, radar should be aboard. It should also be stressed that the navigator possess complete operational knowledge of all of his navigational devices. Unfortunately, too many boat owners buy the best of equipment without learning all they should know of its use.

Two-way radiotelephones in the medium-frequency band (2-4 mHz) make possible receipt of weather broadcasts from the public correspondence and Coast Guard stations. In addition, they provide the safety of being able to communicate with the Coast Guard on 2182 kHz.

VHF equipment can take advantage of the continuous broadcasts from Weather Bureau stations that now provide coverage in all of Southern California, parts of Central California and most of Puget Sound, Washington. Also, many Harbor Masters along the California coast monitor VHF channel 16 and can communicate on channel 12, to provide boatmen with information on sea conditions at their harbor entrances, where to dock or obtain fuel. Coast Guard VHF coverage on channels 16 and 22 now covers most all of the Pacific Coast seaward for at least 20 miles.

BOOKS AND CHARTS

Coast Pilot, U.S. Coast & Geodetic Survey; Volume 7 covers California, Oregon, Washington and Hawaii.

How to Fish the Pacific Coast, Raymond Cannon, Lane Publishing Co., Menlo Park, California.

Boating in Coastal Waters (of Oregon), State Marine Board, State of Oregon, Salem, Oregon.

Marine Atlas, Volume 1, Frank Morris and Willis R. Heath, P.B.I. Co., Box 54, Seattle, Washington.

Northern California Boating Atlas, Sunset Magazine, Lane Publishing Co., Menlo Park, California.

River Bar Guides, Oregon and Washington, Auxiliary Director U.S.C.G., 13th District, 618 Second Ave., Seattle, Washington, for the Rogue River, Depoe Bay, Coquille River, Yaquina Bay, Coos Bay, Nehalem River, Umpqua River, Chetco River, Willapa Bay, Columbia River, Siuslaw River, Tillamook Bay, Quillayute River, and Grays Harbor.

Sea Boating Almanacs, 3 volumes, covering Southern California, Northern California, and the Pacific Northwest, Sea Publications, Inc., Book Division, 1499 Monrovia Ave., Newport Beach, California 92663.

Cruising the California Delta, Robert E. Walters, Sea Publications, Inc., Book Division, 1499 Monrovia Ave., Newport Beach, California 92663.

Sea Marine Atlas, Capt. William P. Crawford, Sea Publications, Inc., Book Division, 1499 Monrovia Ave., Newport Beach, California 92663.

Sea Guide/Southern California, Leland R. Lewis and Peter E. Ebling, Sea Publications, Inc., Book Division, 1499 Monrovia Ave., Newport Beach, California 92663.

Northwest Passages, Volumes I and II, Bruce Calhoun, Sea Publications, Inc., Book Division, 1499 Monrovia Ave., Newport Beach, California 92663.

Cruising The San Juan Islands, Bruce Calhoun, Sea Publications, Inc., Book Division, 1499 Monrovia Ave., Newport Beach, California 92663.

Charts published by the U.S. Coast & Geodetic Survey are available through local agents in practically every harbor. Recently C. & G.S. have developed *Small Craft Charts* for such areas as Los Angeles to Long Beach, San Francisco to Antioch, and parts of Puget Sound. These have a great amount of detailed information on them, including tabulations of local facilities that are available, courses and distances. In addition, the major oil companies have cruising charts for the more popular areas, with varying amounts of local information to augment the charts. Besides the maritime charts, a complete set of aeronautical charts are helpful because they show the locations and frequencies of many low-frequency beacons, broadcast stations and VOR ranges that are not shown on all maritime charts.

Part Three

BRITISH COLUMBIA / ALASKA

Introduction to Part Three

Of all the areas on the Pacific Coast, this region is the most complex and difficult to paint in words. The Inside Passage spans a distance of about 1100 miles, between Victoria, B.C., and Skagway, Alaska. It encompasses thousands of islands, fiords that extend into snow-capped canyons with glaciers at their ends, the contrasting capitol cities of British Columbia and Alaska, and salt-water channels so narrow in places that they can be navigated only during a very few minutes of high or low slack water.

Once north of Vancouver, B.C., the economy of the area is almost solely dependent on nature—fishing, lumbering, wood processing and mining. Transportation is only by boat or airplane, with few miles of roads radiating but short distances from such cities or towns as Pender Harbor, Powell River, Queen Charlotte, Ketchikan, Wrangell, Petersburg, Juneau and Skagway. Between these isolated communities stand mountain ranges, glaciers, inlets, rivers and bays that make utterly impossible their connection by highways. On Vancouver Island, only slightly more than half of the mainland side of the island is linked by good roads, connecting such towns or cities as Victoria, Nanaimo, Port Alberni, Campbell River, and Kelsey Bay.

With the exception of Vancouver and Prince Rupert, B.C., every other city, town and fishing village is dependent on water transportation of its major supplies. The machinery and materials to construct buildings and what few miles of roads there are; fuel and lubricants for boats, planes and vehicles; most foods, household furniture and appliances; all are freighted by water from such mainland terminals as Seattle, Vancouver and Prince Rupert. Return cargoes are canned fish, pulp and paper, some finished lumber and aluminum ingots. In no other region of the North American continent is the economy of the people so dependent on water transportation, augmented by private planes and air carriers.

Entirely new transportation systems have been developed to serve the needs of British Columbia and Alaska. Train-barges towed by Herculean-powered tugs carry loaded freight cars and containers to as far west as Seward, Alaska, where they join the Alaska Railroad system; the Yukon territory is served by special steamers operating from Vancouver to Skagway, where their cargoes are transferred to the narrow-gauge White Pass and Yukon Railroad; float planes and amphibians carry freight and passengers to areas not served by regular scheduled surface or aircraft.

There are a number of ways to see the wondrous beauty of British Columbia and Alaska. The most pleasurable, of course, is aboard one's own boat. To make the round trip from Victoria, B.C. to Skagway, Alaska requires time—a minimum of one month, and preferably two. Even the longer cruise would leave unexplored the vast majority of the region. By the most direct route, the distance is about 1050 miles each way; to cruise to the headwaters of only one inlet, such as Princess Louisa, would add 150 miles to the trip, and for each Princess Louisa Inlet there are scores of others that await exploring.

For those with less time than can be spared for cruising their own boats, an alternate means of seeing these waters is from passenger ships which sail on regular schedules from Vancouver, B.C., and Seattle, Washington to as far north as Skagway, roughly 100 miles beyond Juneau. Depending upon the steamship line, stops are made at Prince Rupert, Ketchikan, Wrangell, Petersburg and Juneau. The long summer days, with daylight for an average of 17 hours, leave only a small part of each 24 hours when darkness shuts out the scenery.

A third alternate is to fly aboard modern jetliners from Seattle to Ketchikan and Juneau. From these cities local airlines provide frequent flying boat service to intermediate points and as far west as Sitka on Baranof Island. In many ways the air trip reveals more of the deep indentations and long inlets than does a trip by boat. Many have made their first trips to Alaska by steamer and returned by air, to get two views of the Inside Passage.

Still another means of cruising parts of British Columbia and Alaska is to use the car-ferry service of the Alaska Marine

Minstrel Island in Knight Inlet has an excellent facility for cruising
boats, with fuel, supplies at a well stocked general store, a laundry,
restaurant and bakery.

Dodd Narrows, about 5 miles southeast of Nanaimo on Vancouver Island, is aptly named. During maximum flow of tides through the narrow channel, velocities as high as 10 knots can be encountered. The current flows north on the flood and south on the ebb tide.

Highway System. These ultra-modern vessels run between Prince Rupert, which is the western terminus of the Canadian Pacific Railroad and the Trans-Canada Highway, and Ketchikan, Wrangell, Petersburg, Juneau, Haines and Skagway. On certain schedules the ferries include Sitka, on the Pacific side of Baranof Island, which was first settled by the Russians in 1799. It was here that the official transfer of Alaska was made from the Russians in 1867. There is also car-ferry service from Kelsey Bay on Vancouver Island to Prince Rupert, B.C., for those who do not have the time to go into Alaskan waters.

There are three well-defined cruising areas between Victoria, B.C. and Skagway, Alaska. The first is in the protection of 250-mile-long Vancouver Island between Victoria—Vancouver and Cape Caution. The Strait of Georgia extends from the southeastern end of the island to approximately its mid-length, with Vancouver on the mainland side of the Strait across from

A fisherman's floating home and means of livelihood are tied to the banks of landlocked Allison Harbor, British Columbia.

Nanaimo on the island side. The Strait is a large body of water, ranging in width from a few miles to as much as 30 miles. At its northwestern extremity, Quadra and Cortez Islands start an entirely different type of cruising waters that continue northwest to the end of Vancouver Island, across from Cape Caution. To cover this remaining portion of 120 miles, as the seagulls fly, could involve cruising thousands of miles if the many long inlets and bays are visited.

The second major area is between the northwest end of Vancouver Island and Ketchikan, Alaska. To the west are Queen Charlotte Sound and Hecate Strait, with Graham and Moresby Islands from 30 to 60 miles seaward. This portion of a trip can be either the wildest for rough water through the Sound and Strait, or the most placid by taking the back channels in the lee of the islands that fringe the mountainous mainland coastline. No matter how rough it may be outside, the inner Inside Passage is generally lake-smooth.

Cruising between Ketchikan and Juneau, the third area of the route, is comparable to cruising on the east side of Vancouver Island in that major islands are seaward, such as Prince of Wales, Kupreanof, Admiralty and Baranof, giving protection to the

Mendenhall Glacier at Juneau, Alaska.

winding channels that lie to the east of those islands. After leaving Juneau for Glacier Bay to the west, the channels are protected either by islands or by the mainland of Alaska; and between Glacier Bay and Skagway, by more islands or the snow-capped mountains that border Lynn Canal.

Lest the phrase "winding channels" or "back channels" be misunderstood as ones that are buoyed and dredged waterways, it should be recognized that the Inside Passage waters of British Columbia and Alaska are deep, extremely so, to within frighteningly close distances to the shores. The biggest problem in navigating these waters is to recognize a point or islet, and to take the correct heading to the next landmark. The options of routes to take between any two anchorages are so many that cruising these waters is a team operation of helmsman and navigator to avoid becoming almost hopelessly lost among the myriad of islands, coves and inlets. True, the principal and shorter routes are well marked with lighted structures on points and shores of islands, each of which is numbered and referenced on the charts but the many miles of back channels (generally the more picturesque ones) are only well-charted.

Fuel and supplies are readily available along the entire Victoria to Skagway route. In British Columbia waters, the

Canadian Government has built scores of small docks and floats, mainly for their commercial fishermen, but at which pleasure boats can generally tie for the night or even a few days. At some of the most remote island harbors where there is only a small store for supplies, an oil dock and a few fishermen who maintain their homes in the harbor, there will be a post office and radio communication to Vancouver or Prince Rupert. Much of their shore-based radio communication is by very high frequency equipment which is basically line-of-sight in its range—but there are repeater stations on the mountain tops that result in a network of radio communication that is used by all who need contact with the outside world.

From Petersburg north, even in mid-summer, the presence of glaciers at the heads of inlets is evidenced by icebergs in the bays and straits—often many miles away from where they broke off. This need not imply that the weather is cold; to the contrary, summer temperatures range in the 60's and this warmth is the cause of the break-offs from the glaciers.

Once docked at Juneau, the sportsman can be fishing for 40-pound salmon in Gastineau Channel, on the side of which the capitol city is built; or fly by helicopter to the Alpine-like ski areas atop the Juneau Icecap; or do both within an hour if he chooses. And from the small boat basin at Skagway, it is only a short walk to the narrow-gauge train that winds its way to Whitehorse, in the Yukon Territory. It follows the historic Klondike trail that was trudged by thousands during the gold rush days. Few other cities of the world can offer these contrasts, at conclusion of a 5000-mile coastal cruise.

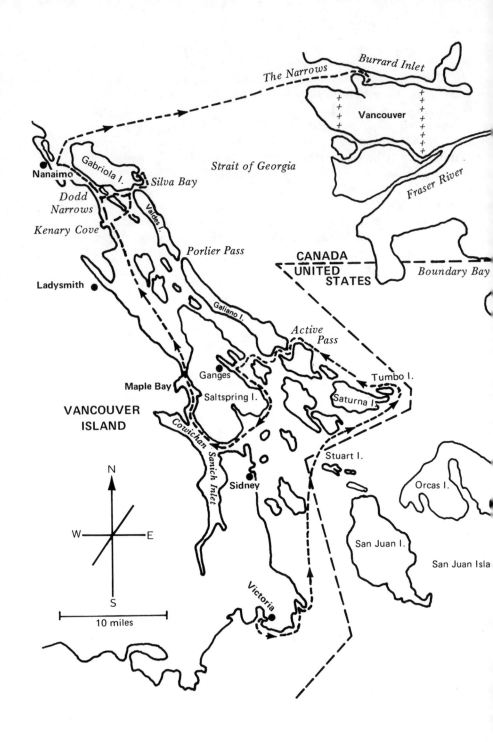

The Narrows

Burrard Inlet

Vancouver

Strait of Georgia

Nanaimo

Gabriola I.

Silva Bay

Dodd
Narrows

Valdes I.

Kenary Cove

Fraser River

Porlier Pass

CANADA
UNITED
STATES

Boundary Bay

Ladysmith

Galiano I.

Active
Pass

Tumbo I.

Maple Bay

Ganges

Saturna I.

VANCOUVER
ISLAND

Saltspring I.

Cowichan

Sanich Inlet

Stuart I.

Orcas I.

N

W   E

S

Sidney

San Juan I.

San Juan Isla

10 miles

Victoria

Victoria to Vancouver, B.C.

Victoria is the provincial capitol of British Columbia, typically British and considerably more so than Vancouver. Situated on the southeastern end of Vancouver Island, it overlooks the Strait of Juan de Fuca to the south, and Haro Strait to the east. Victoria is linked to Port Angeles on the Washington state side of the Strait by ferry and to Seattle and Vancouver by the venerable Princess steamers.

In the very heart of Victoria, nearly a mile within a completely landlocked waterway, is one of its two fine yacht harbors. The other is at Cadboro Bay, to the northeast of Victoria proper, and enroute to the Gulf Islands that border the Georgia Strait side of Vancouver Island.

The inner harbor has slips and moorings, and all the necessities for cruising are within easy walking distance of the harbor. At the nearby Customs House, the required cruising permits for boats arriving from the States can be quickly obtained. Only a few minutes walk from the inner harbor is the stately Parliament House, stone-built in true Old-English style. On the Causeway, directly across from the harbor, is the impressive Empress Hotel, which has hosted Kings and Queens, Presidents and Ambassadors, from all over the world.

Cruising eastward out of Victoria's snug harbor puts one immediately into the waters on which Capt. Vancouver sailed in the era of his discovery and survey of Puget Sound and the Strait of Georgia, some 180 years ago. Hugging the island coastline, we pass close by Trial Island light and turn north into Cadboro Bay where the Royal Victoria Yacht Club has its facilities. Slips and anchorage are available to visiting yachts, and fuel and supplies obtainable if they were not taken aboard in Victoria's inner harbor. To the east of Cadboro Bay, across Haro Strait, it is less than 10 miles to San Juan Island, the

Victoria, British Columbia, Haro Strait and the San Juan Archipelago. Far background is continuously snow-capped Mount Baker.

westernmost of the San Juan Archipelago. Our cruise takes us into Haro Strait, but to the northwest around Cadboro Point toward the first of the Gulf Islands, frequently called Canadian San Juan Islands (which are virtually a continuation of those in the state-side waters). We will remain in Canadian waters until past Prince Rupert, nearly 450 miles toward Alaska.

The choice of routes through the Gulf Islands, toward Nanaimo, is as varied as the hundreds of islands that make up the group. They cover an area that is 20 miles in width at the widest point, and roughly 50 miles long in a northwesterly direction. The larger ones, and many of the smaller ones, are like a mountain range with their ridges extending up from the clear waters of the Strait of Georgia; between their ends are narrow passages from the inner channels to the broad Strait.

One of the many quiet coves on Portland Island, which is about 5 miles north of Sidney.

Many of the smaller islands are privately owned.

We left Cadboro Bay early in the afternoon, cruised northerly past Stuart Island of the San Juan group, headed for Bedwell Harbour on South Pender Island. This is the site of Canadian Customs Office and is frequently the point at which boats cruising from the U.S. San Juans into Canadian waters obtain their clearance papers, fuel from the barge anchored near the slips, supplies from a well-equipped store, or enjoy the heated swimming pool and dining facilities at a rustic-log lodge overlooking the Bay.

A pleasant afternoon and evening was spent at Bedwell, meeting old friends and making new acquaintances, one of whom was an Indian: Chief Pelkey of the Songhees tribe. He loaned us his clam rake and showed us where the best oyster and clam beds were along a part of his eight-acre property. "There used to be plenty big crabs along here," he told us; "now all gone. Too many people." A familiar refrain, we reflected. He told us, too, of a watersnake that used to glide down from its woodsy home to eat fish or plankton from the beach. "Then earthmover came to clear land. It killed snake.

After that fresh-water stream dry up. Make watersnake-god angry."

We smiled and asked: "But now you get heap-good water from pipe?" Chief Pelkey laughed, as though to say he didn't think much of his act either. At least he tried.

Later in the week we were invited to spend a few days with the then-owners of Tumbo Island. This lies to the east of Saturna Island, with a narrow channel between it and Saturna, and on the opposite side, the wide expanse of the Strait.

Our instructions were very explicit: "Approach Tumbo Island from the east, keeping Rosenfelt Rock buoy to your port side; when abeam the islet with the tall firs, stop a few hundred yards off shore and we will send a pilot out in a small boat to guide you into the inner harbor." As we left Bedwell Harbour we once again reviewed the instructions, and after passing the eastern end of Saturna Island, Rosenfelt Rock buoy came in sight. Rounding it from the eastward we proceeded as directed for another two miles, and soon saw a launch coming out from the islet.

When hailed by the lad who was running the launch, we stopped and welcomed aboard an elderly gentleman whom he had brought to act as our pilot. His first statement when stepping on deck was: "Please take me to the pilot house"— which seemed odd, and when there he told us to take a heading of 340 degrees "until you see the white rock on the far side of the inner channel." When it came into view, he continued: "When you see the white rock, turn left to 250 degrees until the patch of kelp is close by your starboard side." Just when we were coming to the kelp and within a hundred feet of a group of rocks on our port side, he said: "When you pass the kelp, make a slow, easy turn to head you toward the barn on the bank of the channel."

By now all of us were becoming curious as to why he should be wearing dark glasses in the late afternoon cloudiness, but we were too concerned about his instructions to ask any questions. When nearly within touching distance of the channel bank, his next order was: "Head her toward the floats at the head of the Bay, and drop your anchor when opposite the tallest tree on the point just off your port bow." This we did, and anchored in two fathoms of water, with towering trees on all but the open channel side. It was not till then that he introduced himself, and apologized for his gruffness, but added "you certainly do a fine job of obeying orders from the only blind pilot in Canadian waters!" Were we relieved to be at anchor!

Two days with our friends and owners of the island were filled with clam digging and oyster picking, intermingled with some salmon fishing in Tumbo channel. We wanted to prolong our stay at Tumbo, but friends were to meet us at Maple Bay on Vancouver Island, for the trip to Nanaimo and Vancouver. This led us to Active Pass, 10 miles from Tumbo Island, on the northwestern end of Mayne Island, as a means of getting from the Strait of Georgia to the westward of Saltspring Island—largest of the Gulf Island group. Active Pass is well-named because it carries both a tremendous volume of water into and out of the Strait of Georgia each change of tide, and much of the pleasure and commercial traffic between Vancouver and Victoria. It is an S-shaped channel, well-marked, relatively narrow, and breathtakingly beautiful with tree-covered hills and peaks as high as a thousand feet within a mile of the passage.

Enroute from Active Pass to Maple Bay (and only three miles off our most direct route) is the very complete harbor of Ganges on Saltspring Island. There we took on fuel, water and replenished the larder with fresh vegetables and fine meats; we could have played golf on their attractive course if time had permitted. Retracing our course out of Ganges Harbor, we kept Saltspring Island on our starboard hand, passing Fulford Harbor on the Island; passed Sanich Inlet which cuts deeply into Vancouver Island with its southern end almost reaching the outskirts of Victoria; and turned northwest past Cowichan Bay to the narrow channel that leads to Maple Bay. A small bight off the north side of Cowichan Bay named Genoa Bay is the site of the Cowichan Bay Yacht Club with floats and fine shoreside facilities. Genoa Bay is also well-known for its summer resort attractions that include an outdoor, heated swimming pool, lodges, pitch and putt golf course, tennis courts, restaurants, rental boats for local fishing—in addition to fuel and ship's stores.

Many have cruised past Maple Bay without realizing it exists, tucked as it is into a small inlet off the main route toward Nanaimo. We had it well circled on our *Northwest Cruising Atlas* and a specific date with friends to meet them at the Maple Bay Yacht Club. Although there are floats for visiting boats, a more startling view of the evergreen timbered mountains rising from the water edge can be had when anchored in the Bay. We

Fulford Harbour near Ganges on Saltspring Island is the terminus
for one of the many car ferries that ply these waters. The ferries

operating in the U.S. and Canadian San Juan Islands have opened
many boating areas for trailed-boat owners.

had been towing our dinghy, which presents no problem in these protected waters, and in a few strokes of the oars were ashore. Later we rowed not over 200 yards to the south end of the Bay, rather than disturb the quiet of the evening with even the small noise of our outboard engine. There, in the crystal clear waters, were all manner of fish leisurely swimming under the dinghy and almost challenging us to tempt them with a trolling line.

Twenty miles northwest of Maple Bay, past countless islands to our right and the coal-mining town of Ladysmith on Vancouver Island to our left, we had another date with friends. It was at Boat Harbor, also known as Kenary Cove, where, on one of our earlier trips, we were greeted with the firing of cannons and serenaded with music from our host's high-fidelity amplifiers that could be heard throughout the entire half-mile-wide cove. Many years ago this harbor was used for log-rafting by lumber operators who would tow their rafts to mills in Nanaimo or Ladysmith. Now, the only reminders of its commercial days are the remains of a pier and a few pilings that were used to corral the logs dumped into the cove.

Across from Kenary Cove is a chain of small islands beyond which are big Valdes and Gabriola Islands which separate this cruising region from the Strait of Georgia. Between Valdes and Gabriola Islands is Gabriola Pass, one of the three main passes between the Strait and the area we have been cruising. Like Porlier and Active Passes to the southeast, Gabriola is a winding one through which currents up to eight knots will flow during ebb and flood tides.

Taking leave from our host at Kenary Cove, we made an easterly side trip through Gabriola Pass to Silva Bay—less than 10 miles away—to rendezvous with a group of predicted loggers. Silva appeared to be a large bay until the fleet arrived. It then became a wonder how they could all squeeze in. Across the Bay from the fuel docks, Royal Vancouver Yacht Club's outstation clubhouse on Tugboat Island was gaily swathed in welcoming flags. As first arrivals appeared, horns and sirens blew—the climax coming from a venerable 90-foot steam tugboat. Its deep, mournful whistle outdid them all, and ended in a shower of mist from her polished brass whistle.

Retracing our course through Gabriola Pass, we timed our arrival at Dodd Narrows for slack water. This is one of the narrowest in this island group, and unless one wants a thrill of

Royal Vancouver Yacht Club's out-station on Tugboat Island in
Silva Bay, on the eastern side of Gabriola Island.

shooting-the-rapids, or trying to buck them, it is prudent to use
the tide tables to establish the time of passing Joan Point in
Dodd Narrows. The biggest danger in going through the
Narrows at other then reasonably slack water is the risk of
tangling with driftwood or floating logs which will be gyrating
with the current and eddies, and are completely unpredictable
as to direction, combined with the problem of maneuvering
one's own boat, in the 10-knot currents, to avoid the logs.

It is only six miles from the Narrows to Nanaimo. This fine
harbor is frequently the first official stop for those cruising
from the States to British Columbia, where cruising permits are
obtained at the Customs House. Their officers may make a brief
inspection of the boat checking on firearms and any oversupply
of "spirits." Substantial floating docks that can accommodate
as many as a dozen visiting boats at one time are directly below
the main street of Nanaimo, and it is only a few minutes walk
to any type of desired store—for foods, Canadian spirits, ship's
supplies or other cruising necessities.

One of the Nanaimo's many small craft moorages, all within walk-

ing distance of shops and restaurants in the town.

Overlooking the harbor is the old Block House, once heavily fortified to defend Nanaimo from Indians and pirates. It is both a landmark and a museum. Shipyards, oil docks and additional visitor-boat floats are a mile to the northwest of the city-center floats, on the west side of Newcastle Island Passage. The Nanaimo Yacht Club also has its splendid facilities in this Passage, which leads to Departure Bay where there is ample room for those wishing to anchor instead of tying to floating docks.

Thirty-three miles to the northeast, across the Strait of Georgia, is the largest of British Columbia's cities—Vancouver, named after the Captain whose sailing ship *Discovery* first entered the harbor in 1792. The main links between Nanaimo and Vancouver are high-speed ferry boats, coastal-type freighters and towed barges. To the south of Vancouver the 500-mile-long Fraser River empties into the Strait through three mouths, the largest and most used being about 10 miles from the Burrard Inlet entrance to Vancouver. During spring and summer run-offs, silt carried down the river is evident in the Strait for many miles from its mouths.

For powerboats, the trip across the Strait is best made in the mornings, because afternoon winds from either the northwest or southeast through the Strait can create a miserable beam-sea condition. For sailing, the afternoons are better.

After passing under Lions Gate Bridge, at the first narrows, the inner harbor of Vancouver rudely awakens one from his cruising thoughts. It teems with traffic—luxury liners on world cruises, outboard-powered fishing skiffs, freighters destined for far-off ports, power and sailing yachts, tugs pulling mile-long log rafts to the mills in the upper reaches of the harbor.

Burrard Inlet, spanned by Lions Gate Bridge, extends more than 20 miles past Vancouver. It creates current conditions that can pose steering problems for long tows or large vessels. Once inside the Narrows, it is only 3 miles to the extensive docks and floats of the Royal Vancouver and Burrard Yacht Clubs—both situated on the edge of Stanley Park.

Unique to Vancouver harbor are the fueling barges anchored in the bay about one mile from the two yacht clubs, which handle a large proportion of the fueling for Vancouver's large pleasure-boat fleet as well as much of the smaller-size commercial craft. The barges are roughly 60 to 80 feet square, with enormous rubber tire fenders around the four sides to protect

Coal Harbor is center of yachting activities at Vancouver, B.C.,
where the Burrard and Royal Vancouver Yacht Clubs have their
facilities. It adjoins scenic Stanley Park, at the right, and is only a
short distance into the heart of Vancouver, on the left.

the boats taking on fuel from the considerable amount of
motion created by the nearly continuous water traffic passing
them. Besides fuel, they also dispense bottled gas for galley
ranges, and fresh water. When the oil barges (as they are called)
are busy with boats tied to all four sides of each barge, the
traffic jams created by the boats waiting to tie alongside can
test the skill of the most competent skipper!

After fueling, we proceeded to the Burrard Yacht Club where
we were greeted with the deep-throated whistle of a steam tug
that had been converted to pleasure cruising. The clanging of its
engine-room bells, as it maneuvered to make room for us, was
reminiscent of an era when steam was supreme. All aboard our
cruiser expressed admiration for the owner of the steamer for
his interest in keeping alive the type vessel which had played
such an important part in building the northwest.

Rivers
Inlet

Calvert I.

BRITISH
COLUMBIA

Cape
Caution

Hope I.

Allison

Knight Inlet

Bute Inlet

Cape
Scott

Port
Hardy

Queen Charlotte
Strait

Yaculta
Rapids

Port
Harvey

Toba
Inlet

Campbell
River

Refuge
Cove

Princess
Louisa
Inlet

VANCOUVER
ISLAND, BC

Powell
River

PACIFIC
OCEAN

Howe
Sound

Vancou

N

W——E

S

Victoria

Cape
Flattery

Strait of Juan de Fuca

50 miles

WASHINGTON

Vancouver, B.C. to Cape Caution

The cruising waters in the lee of Vancouver Island, between Vancouver and Cape Caution, are ones that should be enjoyed on a leisurely basis. The direct route is about 250 miles, but on the indirect routes one could cover 10,000 miles and never anchor twice in the same bight, cove or inlet. Traveling at only 10 knots, the round trip could be made in four days—but forty days could be spent in exploring these protected waters and only part of them would be visited.

It is within the lee of Vancouver Island that there are such well-known inlets as Jervis, Princess Louisa, Toba, Bute, Knight, Belize and Seymour—just to name a few—all on the mainland side to the northeast of the Island.

Our most recent cruise through these waters was with a group of other powerboats from Seattle and Vancouver, with a destination of Skagway. The daily runs were from 40 to 90 miles, and at the end of each day everyone had the same feeling: "If we could only have taken time to go up this inlet or that inlet, or to have laid over for a week in just one of the many groups of islands."

Heading westward from Vancouver's Lions Gate bridge, there is a contrast of views that should be noted. Looking astern, past the bridge, are city skyscrapers; to the north are snow-capped mountains that literally jump out of the Strait of Georgia; to the west is the entrance to Howe Sound; and to the south the 30-mile span of Georgia Strait.

Howe Sound has become one of Vancouver yachtsmen's favorite cruising and resort areas. It is only six miles from the bridge to the eastern side of the entrance to the Sound. Extending 22 miles into mountains, it is filled with four large islands and a dozen smaller ones, all heavily timbered and indented with some 30 anchorages. Many of the anchorages or

Looking westward over a small portion of West Vancouver Yacht
Club's facility, situated on Howe Sound. Access to the slips is

around either side of the island (upper left corner) giving complete
protection during winter storms.

Floats are provided for pleasure craft at Princess Louisa's terminus of Chatterbox Falls.

coves have visitor floats, and there are more than a half-dozen fueling stations for local and visiting craft. During summer months, many Vancouver businessmen commute to their summer homes on the Sound, tying their boats to floats or mooring them on buoys.

Thirty-five miles northwest of Howe Sound, with Halfmoon Bay and Thormanby Islands enroute, is Pender Harbour which might easily be passed without noticing the three-mile-deep indentation into the surrounding hills, from the Strait of Georgia. A mile inside the Harbour, on the north side, is a cove that provides excellent anchorage—close to floats that lead to the lodge on the shore. On one side of this cove is a marine railway and boat repair facility, with a high-roofed shed over the ways for protection from their heavy winter rains. The village of Pender Harbour is on the north side of the channel just after entering the bight. This is frequently the point where those cruising through Jervis Inlet will take on their extra fuel and other ship's needs, because it is easy to cruise 150 miles between Pender Harbour and Westview, near Powell River, without passing another major supply depot.

One of the most photographed waterfalls in British Columbia is Chatterbox Falls, at the extreme upper reaches of Princess Louisa Inlet. To reach it from Pender Harbour takes us through the Agamemnon Channel with Seechelt Peninsula close by our starboard. On the eastern side of the Peninsula is Seechelt Inlet with its Skookumchuck Narrows four miles from the Inlet's convergence with Agamemnon Channel. Passage through the Narrows should only be made at or near slack water because a body of water 40 miles in length must pass through the 1/8-mile-wide Narrows with each change of tide. Velocities reach as high as 12 knots. A convenient place to wait for slack water is at Egmont, where fuel and supplies are available, and substantial floating docks are maintained.

One of the few sand beaches in this area is a mile northeast of Egmont Point, on Wales Reach, an extension of Jervis Inlet. Anchorage can be taken close to shore, off the sand beach. Another good anchoring spot is behind Sydney Island, across Wales Reach from Egmont Point. From here, up through Wales, Princess Royal and Queens Reaches, the water is deep and most boats will tie alongside log booms, instead of trying to anchor.

Princess Louisa Inlet is six miles from the northwestern limits of Queens Reach, and extends four miles northeasterly between

Looking south to Strait of Georgia, across Buccaneer Bay on Thormanby Island.

5- to 8-thousand-foot mountains. Entrance to it should be timed with slack water, to avoid the challenge of going with or bucking 8- to 10-knot currents through its narrow S-shaped channel, at the mouth of the Inlet. Once inside, and to port, is Malibu Lodge with guest accommodations, restaurant, some provisions for boats and a fuel dock. This inlet, too, is extremely deep—in many places over 1000 feet deep—but at its end are floats for visiting boats and virtually the only spot in the Inlet where anchoring is practical. The roaring Chatterbox Falls have created a small sandbar that extends a few hundred yards from the water's edge, with depths shallow enough for anchoring. The current created by the Falls holds an anchored boat with its bow toward shore.

For nearly 30 years, much of Princess Louisa Inlet was owned by James F. Macdonald, an ardent boatsman and lover of wilderness beauty. During the summers he lived aboard his houseboat, tied to the floats he had built, and was the genial host to yachtsmen from every port of the Pacific Coast. In 1953 he deeded the property to The Princess Louisa International Society, which was formed by a group of Canadian and American yachtsmen to preserve the area in its natural state. The Society deeded it back to the Canadian government in 1964 with the stipulation it could never be commercialized, and must always be kept "in natural" as a marine park.

Returning downstream to the Strait of Georgia, we head northeast toward Powell River, across from the northerly end of 30-mile-long Texada Island. The largest pulp and paper mills in British Columbia are located here, and much of their output is shipped to publishers in the United States as newsprint paper. The actual port of entry for Powell River is Westview, two miles to the southeast, where there is a government-built, small-boat harbor with fuel, supplies, marine railway and repair facilities. It is a short ride by taxi to Powell River and visitors are invited to go on the conducted tours through the pulp and paper mills.

From Powell River, or Westview, to Cape Caution there is the choice of the inside-Inside Passage route through the Yaculta Rapids or the shorter route through Seymour Narrows. If the Seymour Narrows route is chosen, a straight run of about 30 miles is made across the Strait of Georgia to Cape Mudge on Quadra Island; if the inside route is chosen, it will be close by the mainland shoreline to the eastern side of Cortes Island and through Lewis Channel. Our last trip was through the inside route and, even though considerably longer in distance, it provided greater opportunities to visit back-channel communities and anchorages.

An easy run of about 22 miles takes us from Westview to Refuge Cove on Redondo Island. The first to arrive ties alongside floats, and those arriving later merely put over fenders and raft to the first, second or third boat out from the floats. Typical of so many of these British Columbia anchorages, there will be floats for a half dozen or more boats, gasoline and diesel fuel, and a small supply store, either on a barge or built on pilings at the water's edge. Not infrequently, high-octane aviation fuel is also available for the many float planes that are flown in this area. Generally there will be a few commercial trollers also in the anchorage and almost without exception the opportunity to buy, for only a nominal price, a freshly caught salmon.

A small islet in the entrance to Refuge Cove gives it protection from winds, and assures a mirror-like water condition in the Cove. Five miles to the east is Deep Bay, where at low tide some of the finest clams are to be had; and to the northeast is Toba Inlet that stretches over 20 miles into the mountains.

On one of our earlier visits to Refuge Cove, their well-stocked general store was in a building perched on the Cove's steep bank, with an inclined ramp down which blocks of ice could be slid, or cases of food supplies. Our needs were meat for the evening's barbecue. The young girl "butcher" went into a walk-in refrigerator, hefted down a huge side of meat nearly as large as she was, plunked it down on a chopping block, and with saw and an enormous cutlass hewed out a splendid steak. The next minute she was down on the dock fueling a boat and bare-handling 25-pound blocks of ice to her customers. After fire razed the store a few years ago, a barge was brought into the cove and on it is now the supply center for fishermen and yachtsmen who make Refuge Cove their base of operations while in Desolation Sound.

Some 18 miles northwest of Refuge Cove is Stuart Island where another choice must be made—whether to enter 35-mile-deep Bute Inlet on the east side of the Island, or stay on schedule to meet the slack water in Yaculta Rapids. The latter requires considerable figuring, because there are a series of rapids in the five-mile distance between Stuart Island and the

Dent Islands to the west; there is also a difference of about a half hour in the time of slack waters at the two ends of the rapids. When correctly calculated, the passage can be as smooth as glass, albeit one with considerable traffic during the cruising season because pleasure, fishing and commercial boats all wait for the slack water to go through Yaculta Rapids.

Westward of the Rapids a myriad of channels can be taken to Port Harvey, roughly 60 miles distant. Ever since the 1964 earthquake which did so much damage to western Alaska (nearly 1000 miles from the area we are now cruising), the times of maximum currents have been considerably changed from what they were before the earthquake. The times of maximum flood velocities have not been changed as much as maximum ebb, which occurs now about 1½ hours later than formerly. For those on predicted log contests through this route, this has thrown another variable into their predictions.

Leaving the inner-Inside Passage through Sunderland Channel puts us on a 15-mile stretch of Johnstone Strait, which is also part of the Vancouver-to-Cape Caution route through Seymour Narrows. A turn to the north, however, leads us into Port Harvey and again on the waters of the inside-Inside Passage. Within Port Harvey is a near-deserted lumbering operation, with a group of government-provided floats for tying alongside. From this cove to Minstrel Island, where fuel and ship's stores are available, a winding course through Chatham Channel must be made. It is one of the few channels in this region where the shoreline does not rise abruptly from the water—instead there are marshy flats for a quarter mile or more on the easterly side of the channel. Also unusual is the kelp which grows in the shallower waters, despite the currents that range as high as seven knots.

Minstrel Island is a jumping-off point for cruising Knight Inlet, which reaches 50 miles northeasterly into snow-capped mountains. In the opposite direction, Knight Inlet extends 15 miles before reaching Queen Charlotte Strait. Twelve miles from Minstrel, on the northern banks of Knight Inlet, is Hoeya Sound, which is reported to have exceptionally fine crabs. From there to its headwaters, there are few clearly defined anchorages, due to the depths in the Inlet—but being so deep, it is not an infrequent sight to see a boat with bow and stern lines tied to trees on the banks of a slight indentation. Literally hundreds of waterfalls cascade down the steep ravines, and the amount of fresh water pouring into the Inlet maintains a slight down-channel current at all times.

To travel the 60-mile distance between Minstrel and Allison Harbor takes us through 45 miles of Queen Charlotte Strait. Since leaving Vancouver, this is the longest stretch of open water we have covered; yet it is reasonably protected by the northwestern end of Vancouver Island. It can be a rough stretch of water if a strong northwest wind is blowing, and a test of navigational skill if fog exists in the area before reaching the Strait.

One particular trip stands out in our minds, aboard a 30-footer with but the barest of instrumentation. We had left Minstrel Island, with wisps of fog in Knight Inlet and around the island. We were headed toward the Carey Group of islands that spanned some 10 miles on either side of our route, our day's destination being Allison Harbor. Another boat of our fleet, cruising at the same speed, was close by and within sight until the fog cut visibility to a point where our own bow staff could hardly be seen. We throttled back and conferred. Turn back? No. Perhaps it will clear when the sun is further up. It didn't clear. If anything, the day turned darker. Jack steered, with eyes glued to the compass. I sat beside him on the flying bridge with watch, paper, pencil and chart. At a certain rpm we should be making so many knots. Fortunately we had calculated a speed curve earlier. But was it exact? Time would tell. It was tense going, especially so in this area of islands, islets and X-marks-a-rock, on all sides.

There's an eerie feeling when moving through fog—we *should* be paralleling Village Island, but not even a darker shadow marked its portside position. Then some crows cawed, just to port. The island was there. We were on course, but timing not quite right. A bit of kelp lay ahead, and something black. We stopped. We had arrived at another course-change two minutes early (Later we found out that the speed-indicator had been calibrated in fresh water rather than salt. It made a difference.) At one point we noticed an angular ripple to starboard. One half of some boat's wake. Faintly we heard an engine purring. When we blew our horn, the other boat responded, uncomfortably close. By now four hours had elapsed. We both wanted to stop, have coffee, and stretch. A 90-degree turn to port should lead us right up to an island where we hoped to find anchorage. More crows scolded as we moved slowly into a small shoreline

Typical of the thousands of islets dotting Inside Passage waters is
this one near Allison Harbor, British Columbia.

indentation. Until we were almost on the rocky shore, depths
were 60 to 100 feet. Finally we found a small shelf, anchored
and looked about us. What a ghostly and melancholy place!
Long festoons of moss hung from every tree branch. The silence
was only broken by crows cawing and intermittent surge
splashing against the shore.

After a brief rest we moved back again on our time and
distance navigation, virtually feeling our way through the murk.
When our chart showed we should have the Carey Group of
islands abeam, we turned again shoreward for a lunch stop. It
was then that we suddenly burst into blinding sunlight with
stunning visibility. All about us were dozens of little green
islets. Our surroundings looked nothing at all like the charts.
Both Coast & Geodetic chart and *Marine Atlas* showed only a
few islets in this area, but if we could believe our eyes there
were over a score of rocks and islets in sight. We cruised around
in the sunny patch awhile, relaxing and enjoying the warmth
and beauty around us. Meanwhile, we made note of our
small-scale chart's lack of space in showing only a third of the
number of islands in the Carey Group. Here, if ever, was no
place to be fog-bound! By afternoon, however, a warm sun
burned off the last of the fog in Knight Inlet, enabling us to

press on at our normal cruising speed.

Allison Harbor is no more than a small, wooded cove, with floats for a few visiting boats. Some years there is fuel and a general store on a barge tied to the banks of the cove. A path leads into the forest for those who like hiking, and wild berries of many kinds can be picked within a few yards of the shoreline. When all of our fleet had arrived from the Minstrel Island take-off point, it filled the harbor. Before long, wisps of smoke from galley ranges or barbecues filled the evening air with the aroma of cooking steaks and salmon. An early morning departure was agreed upon by the skippers to make the run through Schooner Passage to Nakwakto Rapids.

Turning westward from the Rapids, our route was through 5-mile-long Slingsby Channel to open waters of Queen Charlotte Sound, eight miles from Cape Caution. This ended the inside-Inside Passage from Vancouver to the Cape; the alternate to the more direct route from Powell River to the Cape through Seymour Narrows.

As mentioned earlier, the distance from Powell River across the Strait of Georgia to the southern end of Quadra Island is about 30 miles. From there northwestward is again the Inside Passage. It is the route taken by commercial traffic and pleasure craft bent on reaching Alaska in the shortest time. The famous salmon fishing waters of the Campbell River region are to port, as we pass April Point and its hidden harbor. Six miles past Campbell River are Seymour Narrows, which until a few years ago, were a threat to navigation because of Ripple Rocks in the narrowest part of the Narrows. The Canadian government tunneled under the Narrows and detonated the largest non-atomic explosive charge in history, to remove the Rocks. Although the currents through the Narrows still reach 4 to 6 knots at maximum flow, there are not the violent eddies, whirlpools and cross currents that there were before removal of Ripple Rocks.

Once above Seymour Narrows, Discovery Passage and Johnstone Strait average from a mile to three miles in width along their 70 miles from the Narrows to Queen Charlotte Strait. There are only a few harbors on the Vancouver Island side of the channels; the principal one is Kelsey Bay from which a car-passenger ferry operates to and from Prince Rupert. To the northeast, however, there are scores of inlets, arms and bays which provide good anchorage or the opportunity to tie to

Single-filing through Schooner Passage to its headwaters of Nak-wakto Rapids, where currents race up to 24 knots at full ebb or rise.

government floats.

At the entrance to Queen Charlotte Strait is Malcolm Island, with its well-protected Mitchell and Rough Bays on the south side of it. On the latter is the Finnish community of Sointula, nestled behind a breakwater that protects its small-boat facilities. It is a haven for many cruising north or south because of the hospitality of its residents, sauna baths and fine Finnish foods at their restaurants.

Four miles before reaching Malcolm Island is Alert Bay on Cormorant Island. It is the largest community along this portion of the Inside Passage, with more than a thousand residents, about half of whom are Indians of the Kwakiutl Tribe. A number of shipyards and machine shops are available for repair of transient boats or those that make this their home port.

Any cruise through this area should include a visit to the Kwakiutl Big House at Alert Bay. Indian Chiefs Henry Speck Ozistalis, James Sewid and Charlie George, with the help of many others from their Tribe, started construction of the Big House in 1963. It now stands as a monument to the proud race of Indians who pioneered this region. Measuring 50 by 70 feet, two huge logs run the length of it to support the roof; each is

At Alert Bay, Indians perform their tribal dances in a replica of
their original Big House. A fire burns (right foreground) for
warmth and illumination, its smoke ascending through a square
opening in the high-vaulted ceiling. The entertainment is usually
held weekly for summer tourists.

three feet in diameter and weighs five tons. Intricately carved
and brilliantly painted totemic designs are a part of the
supporting posts, beams and rafters. Indian ceremonial dances
are frequently held in the Big House and visitors to Alert Bay
are invited to witness them.

After leaving Malcolm Island, it is 16 miles to Port Hardy, the
northernmost community of any size on Vancouver Island.
Fishing and lumbering are its principal activities, with well-
stocked stores for most all types of supplies. Port Hardy is
frequently the jumping off point for those cruising northward
past Cape Caution, on the mainland side of Queen Charlotte
Strait, or for those cruising the west coast of Vancouver Island.

To use it as the point of departure for either route leaves unvisited a group of islands to the northwest that deserve a number of days time to explore.

God's Pocket on Hurst Island, about 10 miles from Port Hardy, is one of many small coves that leaves a visitor with the feeling that he is a million miles from civilization. A float with space for a half dozen medium-size craft has, at the shore end of it, an incline to what was a store that carried supplies for fishermen. Abandoned when we were last there, the fishermen and few visiting yachtsmen now spin yarns about the day's fishing while exchanging beers on their respective boats.

Sixteen miles further northwest Hope Island, with its excellent Bull Harbor, has an attraction not duplicated on other islands—a cemetery-in-the-trees. High in trees surrounding small Village Bay are cedar coffins, with shakes over them for protection, lashed to the boughs of the trees with rope made from bark. This was a custom of the Indians many years ago, and is unique to this area.

During the salmon fishing season Bull Harbor is alive with gill-netters and trollers. In the center of the harbor is a fish-buying barge which also is the principal supply depot for fishing gear, ice, canned and fresh galley supplies, fuel and water; nearby, along the shoreline, a government dock has fuel, ice and water available.

At the head of the harbor is the government weather-reporting station, from which weather reports are broadcast or can be obtained by going ashore. Unless the weather has been good for the preceding few days, it is prudent to get the latest reports before leaving for the west coast of Vancouver Island, or northbound across Queen Charlotte Strait. The 40-mile run to the lee of Calvert Island, with aptly named Cape Caution about midway from Hope to Nigei Islands, can be mean and most skippers choose to round the Cape as early in the day as possible to avoid the normal afternoon buildup of seas that can be expected even during the best of summer weather. If heading westward for Cape Scott on the northwestern end of Vancouver Island, the full impact of the Pacific Ocean is met in the channel separating Hope Island from Vancouver Island. Strong currents run through this passage and, if there is a choice, it should be run in the morning with a flood tide when it will be smoother, rather than later in the day—particularly if the currents are running toward the west against the prevailing winds and swells.

Rivers
Inlet

Calvert I.

BRITISH COLUMBIA

Cape Caution

Hope I.   Allison

Knight Inlet

Cape
Scott   Port
Hardy

Queen Charlotte Strait

Bute Inlet

Coal
Harbor

Yaculta Rapids

Quatsino
Sound   Port
Alice   Port Harvey

Toba Inlet

Refuge
Cove   Princess
Louisa Inlet

Campbell River

Kyucout Sound   Zeballos

Powell
River

Esperanza Sound

VANCOUVER
ISLAND, B.C.

Nootka

Ho
Sou

PACIFIC OCEAN

Tofino   Vancouv

Claycout Sound   Port
Alberni

Barkley Sound   Bamfield

N

Victoria

Cape Flattery   Strait of Juan De Fuca

W   E

WASHINGTON

S

50 miles

West Coast of Vancouver Island

Cruising the west coast of Vancouver Island is in sharp contrast to days or weeks that may have been spent along the eastern shores of the island, or further eastward through the inside passages along the British Columbia mainland. While small sailboats or powerboats can do the latter with ease, the west coast is not the ideal place for them. Those who do cruise the Pacific side of the island usually do so starting from its northwestern tip to take advantage of prevailing winds and seas that most of the time will be on the stern quarter.

From Cape Scott on the northwestern end of the island to Victoria at its southeastern extremity, the point-to-point distance is about 300 miles. But the nearest lee shore is thousands of miles to the west across the Pacific.

Along this rugged coastline there are six major Sounds or Inlets: Quatsino, Kyuquot, Esperanza, Nootka, Clayoquot and Barkley. Their shorelines add hundreds of miles that are ideal for cruising, once inside the headlands. Their quiet waters are much like those on the British Columbia mainland between Vancouver and Cape Caution. But between the headlands, such as from Cape Sutil on the northern end of the island to Kains Island at the entrance to Quatsino, a distance of about 50 miles, there are only a couple of small bays that could be used as harbors of refuge. Or between Kains Island and around Cape Cook to Kyuquot Sound, roughly 40 miles, the only inlets offering protection are tricky to enter even in broad daylight and perfect visibility because of the rocks and islets at their entrances. Without the years of local knowledge acquired by fishermen who make their home ports along this coast, radar becomes the most important navigational tool, even in clear weather; in fact, weather is the most unpredictable factor while on the west coast. No two seasons follow the same pattern.

The fish-buyers barge in Bull Harbor, Hope Island, is also the general store with fishing gear, foul-weather clothes, food, engine repair parts and fuel sold from it, as well as ice to chill the holds of the salmon trollers that use the barge as a base of operations during the short salmon-fishing season.

Because of this, frequent reports are broadcast on 1630 kHz by Canadian Government weather stations, and they provide more frequent information than is available along other areas of the Pacific Coast. In contrast, however, is the uniform and consistantly fine hospitality of the residents at the fishing villages. Even if compelled to stay a few days in a small harbor waiting for improved weather, they can be pleasantly spent visiting with those on other pleasure boats or with the commercial fishermen. When going from one major Inlet or Sound to the next, early morning departures tend to be smoother passages than later in the day when prevailing winds pick up.

On our most recent trip down the west coast of Vancouver Island, we were fortunate to have two weeks of bright, clear weather. Only while leaving Tofino and again in Barkley Sound was there any fog, and then for but a few hours. We kept counting our good fortune, because only 100 miles to the north of the Island gale warnings were posted, and to the south through the Strait of Juan de Fuca small craft warnings had been up for days.

Our fleet numbered four powerboats, and we timed our early morning departure from Bull Harbor on Hope Island to take advantage of the last of the ebb tide that flows westward across the northern tip of Vancouver Island. The 22-mile run to Cape Scott put us there shortly after the tide had turned, and before the tide rips that can be serious around the Cape had a chance to build up. To the west the Scott Islands were the last pieces of land between ourselves and the Orient.

The 35-mile run from Cape Scott past Kains Island to Winter Harbor, just inside Quatsino Sound, was as pleasant as cruising in Puget Sound. The only differences were that land was to our port side, and nothing but the ocean to starboard, and an easy ground swell from the northwest boosted us toward our destination.

Typical of nearly all of the small fishing villages on Vancouver Island, Winter Harbor has a government pier for handling supplies delivered by coastal freighters, and floats for a large fleet of fishing boats. It also has facilities for seaplanes that are the only means, other than by boat, of reaching the "outside world." Lashed alongside the pier and resting on a grid was grim evidence of the navigational perils of this coastline: a coastal freighter that had hit a rock while entering Quatsino Sound. It had been salvaged and was now having its bottom replanked during periods of low tide that allowed work on the hull. To add insult to injury, the exhaust of one of the many engine-driven emergency pumps on deck caught fire to the superstructure, and what the rocks had not done to the bottom the fire nearly did to the deckhouses before it was extinguished.

Leaving Winter Harbor for the upper reaches of Quatsino Sound, we reluctantly passed by the 12-mile-long inlet leading to Port Alice. The inlet looked beautiful but our time was limited and geared to the tides.

The small size of this mini-fisherman can be judged by its two
Indian occupants. Even though the boats are small, they troll for
salmon many miles to sea from harbors in Barkley Sound.

To reach Coal Harbor, we timed our passage through
Quatsino Narrows coincident with slack water. This two-mile-
long channel is only a few hundred yards wide. Through it the
waters of 23-mile-long Holberg and Rupert Inlets must pass—at
terrific velocities during maximum ebb and flood stages. We
were all prepared for the aroma from the whaling station, which
we had experienced on a previous trip, but to our surprise we
found that it had been closed. For many years this was one of
the largest whaling operations on the Pacific Coast. Upward of
550 whales had been processed in one of their more productive
years. Even though as much as 95 percent of the whale was used
for one purpose or another—most of it as frozen meat shipped

to Japan—whaling became unprofitable. The rusting remains of two whaling ships, one built in Norway and the other in Japan, were tied to a pier waiting for some enterprising firm to convert them into sea-going tugs.

Lumbering operations are now the community's industrial activity. Some timber is trucked across the island about 14 miles to Port Hardy; the balance is shipped overseas aboard large freighters that regularly negotiate Quatsino Narrows.

A week could easily be spent in this area, with scores of bights affording good anchorage. And for those who like to mix golf with their cruising, the course at Port Alice is available. Our schedule, however, compelled us to steam past inviting coves, westward to the Pacific, then south around Cape Cook to a rendezvous point in Walters Cove, in Kyuquot Sound. Again we were favored with fine weather and smooth seas during the 45-mile run.

The last four miles before reaching Walters Cove is definitely one that should be made in clear weather. A winding course between reefs, islets and rugged rocks finally leads to a 100-yard-wide opening into the lovely landlocked cove between Walters Island and the mainland of Vancouver Island. Fortunately a small commercial fishboat was heading into the harbor, and we simply stayed on his stern, at times losing sight of him as he made sharp turns around the small islets protecting Walters Cove. For navigating these waters there is nothing better than taking advantage of "local knowledge"!

Once within Walters Cove, where fuel and any needed supplies are available, we rafted together for the balance of our stay. Scores of salmon trollers came in, unloaded their fish at refrigerated barges, and then moved to nearby floats in front of their well-kept homes around the perimeter of the Cove.

North and eastward of Walters Cove are inlets that extend 12 to 15 miles, with such Indian names as Tahsis, Kashutl and Cachalot, surrounded with timber-covered mountains 3 to 4000 feet high. One of the most attractive anchorages is on the eastern side of Hohoae Island, locally called Dixie Cove, but not even named on charts. Like so many of the other coves and inlets along the west coast of Vancouver Island, Dixie Cove has a narrow entrance that can easily be missed if the crew is not alert or specifically looking for it.

It was in Dixie Cove, a few years ago, that we heard history being made. The occasion was the astronaut's first moon

The fishing boat we are following is headed for Walters Cove in Kyuquot Sound. After 4 miles of S-turns around islets and rocks, of which this view shows one of the last, we reached our destination—one of the most beautiful spots on the entire Pacific side of Vancouver Island.

landing. The nearest broadcast station that we could hear was hundreds of miles away in Vancouver, B.C. We shut down all machinery to eliminate the slightest trace of noise or static, and with ears glued to the radio, heard the now-famous remark: "That's one small step for a man, one giant leap for mankind." (Neil Armstrong, astronaut, Apollo 11, August 1969).

From Kyuquot Sound to Esperanza Inlet, another open ocean passage of about 15 miles was enjoyed in good weather. Our destination was Queen Cove, where again we were surrounded by commercial fishermen whose immaculate and well-equipped boats were the envy of us all. Many had radar and Loran; all had the finest of depth-sounding equipment; the majority had CB radiotelephones which they used for inter-fleet communications. A highlight at Queen Cove was the gift of freshly baked bread from the kitchen of the general store operator.

Queen Cove can be the starting point for days of cruising within the arms and inlets that carve their ways into towering, timbered mountains. Distances are not great. The arms range from five or six miles in length to as much as ten miles; but the scenery is so spectacular it calls for slow-speed running to have time to thoroughly enjoy the unspoiled natural beauty of the area. A specific destination within this region was Zeballos, a community of only 250 to 300 persons but with good docks and floats for visitors. Among the community's virtues was its government liquor store, of which there are not many along the entire west coast of Vancouver Island. It and Tahsis, 15 miles away and at the upper end of another arm, are the two principal ports-of-call in this area. Fuel, supplies, repairs, air service, even hospital facilities, are available. Zaballos also has a large commercial pier for loading ore carriers, since mining is its principal industry; while Tahsis is a lumber town and a home port for many commercial fishermen.

Twenty miles south through the narrow Tahsis Inlet, with mountains climbing skyward on both sides, is the historic community of Nootka. Captain James Cook of England's Royal Navy is credited with charting much of this area during his third expedition which left England in 1776. Drawings of his ship *Resolution* and the *Discovery,* which accompanied him, showing both ships at anchor in Friendly Cove, just south of Nootka, are in the British Museum, along with other drawings made during his explorations of the Pacific Northwest. Ten years later, Captain Charles W. Barkley, who had sailed his *Imperial Eagle* half way around the world from England, spent a month in this region trading with the Indians, before moving southeast to discover the Sound that now bears his name.

Nootka is no longer the active port that it was in earlier years. Its docks and cannery buildings are being eaten away by weather; although a coastal freighter makes stops to unload supplies for the fishermen who make Nootka their homeport. The preferable anchorage in this area is at Friendly Cove, where there is good protection in the small bay, and a Government dock with floats for small craft. On the southern point of the bay is a lighthouse which marks the entrance to Nootka Sound. Ashore are a dozen or so homes of Indian fishermen, on the

Queen Cove, in Esperanza Inlet, is another fishing village nestled in a quiet protected cove. Whether the boats were newly painted or not, they all carried the finest of electronic equipment—sounding equipment for spotting schools of fish, as well as radiotelephones and direction finders.

sites of the first Spanish settlement on Vancouver Island. Monuments honoring Captains Cook and Vancouver add to the historical lore of Friendly Cove.

Clayoquot Sound is entered at Sydney Inlet, roughly 28 miles from Friendly Cove. Like Nootka Sound, it is a labyrinth of arms and inlets, with countless bights and bays inviting one to drop a crab trap or to troll for salmon. First stop for any who cruise these waters is Hot Springs Cove, whether for fuel, restocking the galley, getting fish-ice for the refrigerator (a finely chopped ice used to ice-down salmon in fishing boat holds, and quite practical for use in refrigerators if compacted and put into buckets or pans) or to enjoy the hot springs about a mile toward the Cove's entrance. The sulphur water flowing out from the rocks and down into the pools is near-boiling, keeping the pools at a comfortable but warm temperature year-round.

Only five miles northerly up Sydney Inlet on the eastern side, are two small coves that we visited where water was sufficiently warmed by the sun to make swimming enjoyable. Entrance to one of them was only about 75 feet wide, but the bight opened up inside with plenty of room for a dozen boats at anchor in 40-foot depths. In the other cove, remains of the foundations of a pilchard reduction plant, abandoned many years ago, are mute evidence of the changes in commercial fishing operations.

Tofino is at the southern part of Clayoquot Sound, reached through winding channels past a myriad of timbered islands. Enroute we stopped at Ahouset in Matilda Inlet to take on fuel and water. There was plenty of fuel available, but we were asked to take as little water as possible because of its shortage. The summer was a dry one, and reservoirs were nearly exhausted from supplying the scores of commercial boats that use Ahouset as their operations base. While there, a cannery tender arrived with the weekly supply of fish-ice which was loaded onto the fish-receiving barge; then tons of salmon were loaded aboard the tender for delivery to a distant cannery. In the earlier years of this century, most of these small communities had their own canneries, but it has proved more practical and economical to use cannery tenders to pick up and transport the fish to larger canneries that are more efficiently operated.

The last five miles of the route to Tofino require careful navigation. Although reasonably well buoyed, a 100-yard zig instead of zag can put a boat onto a sandbar in short order.

Friendly Cove at the entrance to Nootka Sound
is marked with a lighthouse and radiobeacon.

The mountains to the east across the
Sound are 3000 feet and more in height.

Tofino is one of the larger of the communities on this coast, and has good docks, floats, fuel and supplies. One of its major industries is crab packing, and crab can be bought by the case from the cannery during the season. Well worth the time and nominal taxi fare is the drive south to Wickaninnish Bay. Its five-mile crescent of sand beach is a driftwood-collector's bonanza.

Twenty-three miles from Tofino, southeastward to Ucluelet Inlet, is mainly open ocean cruising again. Ucluelet boasts nearly 2000 population, between the communities on each side of the mile-wide inlet. It is the best equipped harbor of any so far, with marine railways, Government liquor store, and all other services needed by pleasure and commercial boats. Between it and Bamfield, on the southeast edge of Barkley Sound, those cruising this island-studded, 100-square mile Sound would never want for mechanical or comfort-aboard-ship supplies. Aside from these two communities, and Port Alberni some 30 miles up Alberni Inlet, the area is little changed from the days when Captain Charles W. Barkley discovered it in 1787 and named it for himself.

Many of the islands, points of land and channels carry the names given them by Captain Barkley—such as Imperial Eagle Channel, for his ship; Loudoun Channel for a former ship of his; Grances Island, Hornby Rock, Trevor Channel for his wife's maiden name. Contrasts of time are apparent on all sides, with inboard-engine-driven, cedar log dug-outs trolling for salmon with a modern fiberglass runabout within yards, doing the same. In Poett Nook, where we reaped a harvest of clams during low tide, there was our fleet of diesel-powered cruisers, and nearby on the beach a number of Indian dug-outs with only paddles for propulsion and tied to a float was a small flotilla of inboard/outboard-powered mini-cruisers that had been trailed from Victoria over the paved highway to Port Alberni and launched from modern ramps.

Accessibility of Barkley Sound by highway from the eastern shores of Vancouver Island is making it more popular each year for small boat owners. And it is becoming increasingly popular for larger powerboats and sailboats which must transit the Strait of Juan de Fuca from Puget Sound and Strait of Georgia communities. For the first time in nearly two weeks, since leaving the northern end of Vancouver Island, we saw other pleasure boats flying the U.S. or Canadian ensigns.

Tidal range at Bamfield Inlet is more than enough to allow repairs
on bottoms while careened against or away from the dock.

Several boats cruising together leave Poett's Nook after an overnight anchorage, chiefly to gather clams and oysters at an early morning low tide.

It is nine miles northeast of Cape Beal,
enroute toward Alberni.

The trip up Alberni Inlet was somewhat anti-climatic after the hundreds of miles of cruising the near-virgin waters along the west coast. Alberni is a major lumbering town with smokestacks belching pollution into an otherwise clear sky; ocean-going ships and enormous barges loaded with uncut logs being towed toward other mills or reshipment points; froth covering the water from acid byproducts of the mills. After a brief shopping expedition, we beat a hasty retreat downstream toward Bamfield.

On our copy of Frank Morris' *Marine Atlas* is a penciled reminder of a narrow-entrance bight off the northeastern end of Uchucklesit Inlet—about two-thirds the way down Alberni Inlet, on its northern side. Once within the basin it was hard to realize that we had only recently left a maelstrom of industry at Alberni—it was so quiet, protected and green.

Bamfield was once the terminus for transpacific cable communications. The abandoned buildings of the company still stand on the shores across from the fishing community. Again, good facilities and supplies were available, cordial hospitality from store-keepers, and pleasant exchanges of information on the fishing areas with the fishermen.

The 90-mile run eastward through the Strait of Juan de Fuca to Victoria was timed with an incoming tide to avoid the seas that can be created with a westerly wind blowing against an ebb tide. Principal topic of conversation was when could we make another cruise around Vancouver Island, and the agreement that a month should be planned to more thoroughly explore the inlets and arms that we had only briefly enjoyed.

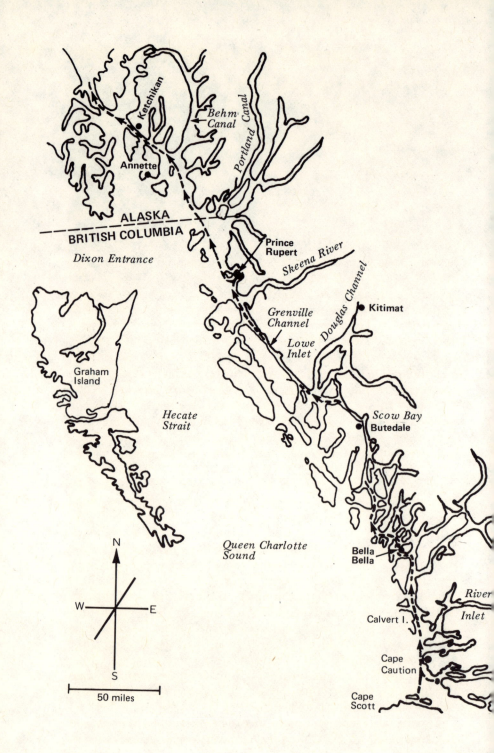

ALASKA
BRITISH COLUMBIA

Ketchikan

Behm Canal

Portland Canal

Annette

Dixon Entrance

Prince Rupert

Skeena River

Grenville Channel

Douglas Channel

Kitimat

Lowe Inlet

Graham Island

Hecate Strait

Scow Bay
Butedale

Queen Charlotte Sound

Bella Bella

River

Inlet

Calvert I.

N

W — E

S

Cape Caution

Cape Scott

50 miles

Cape Caution, across from the northwest tip of Vancouver Island, is used as a take-off point for the cruise to Ketchikan more for geographical convenience than for the practical requirements of cruising. It is the natural end to the inside passages that lie to the east of Vancouver Island, and in a way is the beginning of a somewhat different type of boating, through more open waters and straighter channels.

Popular overnight anchorages before passing Cape Caution are on the mainland side at Allison Harbor, or any one of the dozen or more coves in that immediate area, or from the harbors on either Hope or Nigei Islands snuggled next to Vancouver Island. Cascade Harbor on Nigei Island provides a straight run to the Cape, and from this anchorage Queen Charlotte Sound can be seen. If it looks rough, delay departure; if smooth, get underway as soon as possible! It is about the same distance to Cape Caution from Allison Harbor, although the open water run is a few miles shorter.

From either Allison or Cascade Harbors, there is a 40-mile stretch of Queen Charlotte Sound that must be covered before reaching the lee of Calvert Island and protected waters that are beyond it in Fitzhugh Sound. Even before reaching Calvert Island, however, there are a number of inlets to the east that are both good refuge and magnificent cruising. Time permitting, 55-mile-long Rivers Inlet, with its entrance about 14 miles past Cape Caution, should be cruised. It is filled with little bights, coves and sub-inlets. At Wadhams, just after entering Rivers Inlet, there is a cannery with fuel and supplies, and on some occasions the opportunity to have the salmon canned that was caught while cruising in this area.

Moving up Fitzhugh Sound in the protection of Calvert and Hecate Islands to port, the biggest navigational hazards are the

Rivers Inlet is reported to be one of the greatest salmon
fishing areas along the British Columbia coast.

At the peak of the season, the gill-netters at the mouth of the Inlet require vigilant watching in order to avoid their mile-long nets supported by hard-to-see buoys.

gill-netters, with their 1000-foot-long gill nets streamed across the channels. In a distance of possibly 10 miles we passed scores of these small commercial fishermen, and had to be on constant alert to avoid nets that are marked only with small floats. Tucked into coves, such as at Namu, are canneries operated only a few weeks a year during the salmon fishing season. Highly mechanized, they are the lifeblood of the economy in this area. During the government-controlled, short fishing season, a stream of cannery tenders from Prince Rupert and Vancouver supply the canneries with empty cans, supplies, fuel, personnel, and bring back to their home ports cases of canned salmon for reshipment to the markets of the world.

From Cape Calvert to within a few miles of Bella Bella, the cruising is through well-protected waters with only a minimum of chart work necessary. We merely steer through the middle of deep channels, with mountains rising from the water on each side.

Bella Bella on the east side of its channel (and New Bella Bella, an Indian village across the channel) is another of the typical fishing communities. Government floats that will accommodate 20 or 30 boats at one time, a fuel dock, and a fish-buying station on a barge are the scene of tremendous activity for a few months of the year—then lie quietly for the balance of the year. At the head of a steeply inclined ramp is the general store where everything (nearly literally) from frozen foods to wearing apparel is available. Even a radio station for communication from this isolated community to mainland metropolises is among its modern facilities.

We had occasion to use their radio to order a new air compressor from Seattle to replace one that failed, and which left us without windshield wipers or horns. Until it reached us at Juneau, we improvised a system of lines and pulleys around the flying-bridge structure and to the three windshield wipers on the forward windows. When we had to use the wipers, two of our crew would alternately pull on the port and starboard lines to give the helmsman the clear visibility he needed.

An easy run of 38 miles, of which about half were nearly straight courses, took us from Bella Bella, through Milbanke Sound, to Klemtu on Swindle Island. The last five miles were through a channel sometimes only a ¼-mile wide, with timbered mountains rising so fast from the water's edge that it was a continuous wonder how the trees could hang onto the

Our fleet, tied to the Government floats at Bella Bella, British Columbia.

precipitous terrain. We called this "canyon cruising."

An alternate route to Klemtu that avoids crossing the open waters of Milbanke Sound commences at Ivory Island, about 16 miles from Bella Bella. Just before reaching the island which is on the eastern side of the Sound, the narrow channel between Cecilia Island and Don Peninsula comes into view, and must be negotiated with caution. A northerly course is cruised until reaching Jackson Passage, which can be easily missed because it is narrow, and an S-turn at its eastern end makes it appear to be no more than a very small cove. Timing should be arranged to reach the entrance to Jackson Passage at high slack water in order to avoid strong currents that flow through it, and to gain a few extra feet of water for deep-draft boats. Its 6-mile cut between forrested islands opens to the west, only 2 miles from Cone Island.

Fuel and supplies are available at Klemtu, or one can continue past Klemtu for another 40 miles to Butedale.

Rounding a point just before reaching Butedale brought into view a cascade of water tumbling down a cut in the hills behind Butedale. The falls come from a lake about a mile back from the cove and possibly 500 feet higher. Besides providing a spectacular sight, the lake is also the source of hydro-electric

Fishing or crabbing by American boat owners in B.C. waters now requires a license based on the size of boat. Our fleet cruising to Juneau made a crabbing stop at Scow Bay near Butedale.

power at this village.

Only five miles away was Scow Bay on Klekane Inlet. That was our destination for the night, where our fleet tied to the remains of a log-rafting boom that had seen many years of profitable service when logging operations were the principal activities of this cove. Now, only the cries of birds or the splashing of jumping fish break the silence.

A small stream empties into Scow Bay, and the crystal-clear water showed crabs practically covering the sand bottom below our rafted cruisers. It was not long before traps were over the sides, and within minutes they were filled; only the largest were kept, and females tossed back. For some strange reason, within an hour the crabs moved away, and those first caught were the last.

Leaving Scow Bay we continued the canyon cruising toward Grenville Channel, which is over 40-miles long and only in a few places more than a mile wide. At the entrance to Grenville

Propeller and shaft repairs are frequent when cruising the Inside
Passage, because of the amount of driftwood in those waters.
Prince Rupert, like many other ports of call, has grids that take
advantage of the 10 to 20-foot tide ranges.

Channel, branching off to starboard, is Douglas Channel.
Forty-five miles up this winding body of water is the largest
industrial community along all of the British Columbia coast
north of Vancouver. It is Kitimat, which has grown from
nothing to more than 10,000 population since 1951 when the
first buildings were erected. The Aluminum Company of
Canada has one of the world's largest aluminum plants at
Kitimat, and it is said that upwards of 25,000 persons will be
living and working here within the near future. It is a "company
town," with piers for ocean-going freighters, floats for small
craft, shipyard and repair facilities for those in need of them.

It is not an unusual sight in Grenville Channel, or the many
other channels like it, to see two and sometimes three fishing

Looking southerly over Ketchikan, showing one of their small-craft harbors; another is near the center of town and a third is further south.

Annette Island is in
far right on horizon.

boats lashed together and proceeding full speed with only one man at one of the wheels. Engines on the boats will be working full-bore, but the crews will be sleeping or catching up on rest while traveling between fishing areas.

There are five inlets on the mainland side of Grenville Channel, each with its own brand of secluded charm. Lowe Inlet is one of the most often visited because of the waterfall that pours from the lake at the head of the inlet and which draws to it salmon of enormous size. Aside from one fisherman's cabin in the cove, there is no evidence that man has ever found this sanctuary of calm, tree-encircled water.

Roughly 30 miles northwestward of the end of Grenville Channel is Prince Rupert. Approaching it from the south takes us across a 10-mile, open stretch of the lower portion of Chatham Sound. To the west are the open waters of Dixon Entrance. This area can be rough but if too much so, there are scores of anchorages after leaving Grenville Channel and before reaching the Sound.

The change from uncrowded cruising waters to the activity at Prince Rupert forces one to realize that there must be commerce and business to make possible the enjoyment of cruising. Passenger steamers, ocean-going freighters, cannery tenders, fishing boats of all types, mingled with pleasure craft, stream in and out of the harbor. It is the fishing industry's center for upper British Columbia waters, and is well-provided with natural protection from nearby islands. Marine railways, a grid for boats up to 110 feet in length, and supply stores of all types are near the small craft basins. (On Wednesdays the city's business establishments are closed, so cruising itineraries should contemplate this custom, one which is also observed in most British Columbia cities.)

The city is on an island only four by six miles in extent, with seven peaks on it between 1000 and 2300 feet high. Railroad and automobile bridges connect Prince Rupert with the mainland to the east. Across the harbor is a modern airport, on Digby Island.

A narrow, winding, but well-marked channel around the north end of Digby Island can be used when leaving Prince Rupert. It is well to follow local fishing boats through this channel, until past the Indian village of Metlakatla, because of their knowledge of the best parts of the channel to use. For larger boats, the better route away from Prince Rupert is south through the main entrance channel until clear of the many islets off the south end of Digby Island, then into the open waters of Chatham Sound. This is the route used by the Alaska Highway System's passenger-car ferries, which link the trans-Canada highway with Alaska's highways at Haines.

The first half of the 85-mile route to Ketchikan is through open waters, although there are islands to the westward which give fair protection to otherwise straight running. But like most of the other sounds and wider straits, there are anchorages in coves along the islands or on the eastern shores, never more than 5 miles distant. Thirty-five miles north of Prince Rupert is the International Boundary between Canada and the United States, much of which is shown on charts as running mid-channel up Pearse Canal and Portland Inlet to its headwaters, then from mountain peak to mountain peak.

To within 25 miles of Ketchikan, the courses are straight for distances of 10 to 20 miles at a time, until the south tip of Revillagigedo Island is reached. It is on the southwest side of this island that Ketchikan is situated, on Tongass Narrows. The other three sides of the 45-mile-long island are surrounded by Behm Canal, with hundreds of miles of shoreline created by the many deep inlets running into either the island or the mainland. Near the northern turning point of the Canal is Bell Island Hot Springs, with mineral baths, resort accommodations and limited supplies.

Annette Island is to the west of the south entrance to Behm Canal. On it are two extremes that are typical of Alaska: a modern jet airport for trunkline passengers destined for or leaving Ketchikan, and the nearly 100-year-old Indian fishing community of Metlakatla with its well-protected harbor behind a breakwater. An additional $2 million was approved by the Federal Government in 1970 for a second small-craft facility adjoining the older one. Within a two-mile walking distance of Metlakatla are a dozen lakes ranging in elevation from a few hundred feet to over 1000 feet, that are favorite fresh water fishing spots for both residents and visitors to this region.

Across Clarence Strait to the west of Annette Island is the 110-mile-long Prince of Wales Island, which gives protection to these waters and beckons one to explore it instead of turning northeast to Ketchikan. Further to the west is the wide-open Pacific, until it reaches the shores of Russia from which came the early explorers of the region we are now cruising.

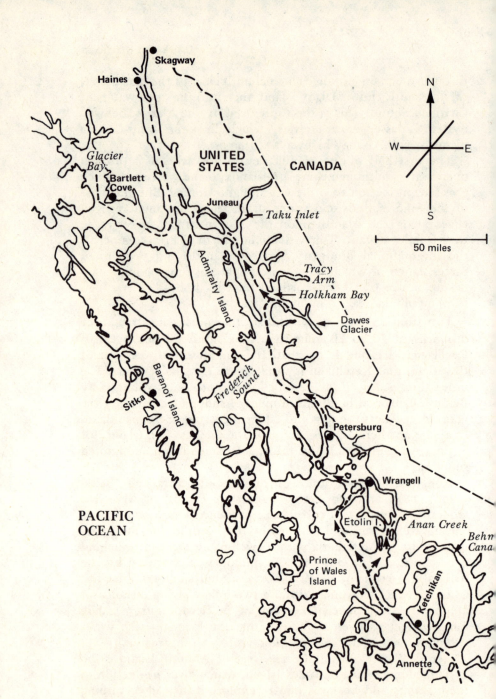

N

W   E

S

50 miles

Skagway

Haines

Glacier Bay

Bartlett Cove

UNITED STATES

CANADA

Juneau

Taku Inlet

Tracy Arm

Holkham Bay

Dawes Glacier

Admiralty Island

Frederick Sound

Baranof Island

Sitka

Petersburg

Wrangell

Etolin I.

Anan Creek

Behm Canal

PACIFIC OCEAN

Prince of Wales Island

Ketchikan

Annette

After several days of cruising the more primitive waterways of British Columbia and those of southeastern Alaska, the city of Ketchikan appears on the scene almost as a surprise. Settled beneath the brow of a vast icefield and neatly shelved at sea-level along the Tongass Narrows, the city bustles with activity, as do its small craft moorages that can accommodate over 1000 craft. For many years Ketchikan was the salmon capital of the world, but the lumber and pulp industries are rapidly becoming runners-up in Ketchikan's economy. These rich but more prosaic industries are counterbalanced by reflections of a unique past, such as the world's largest collection of brightly painted totem poles and Indian community houses which are landmarks in town and in adjoining forest clearings outskirting Ketchikan.

Another contrast we encountered during a recent July cruise was that of watching water-skiers skimming across sunflecked waters directly below the perpetual snowfields that cover the city's mountain backdrop. Along the main business thoroughfare, contrasts continue in the shopping area. Alaskan gems, jewelry and costly furs are featured in one store, perhaps alongside a miner's outfitting concern or rifle shop. Adjoining these, another store will specialize in carved ivory, Indian mucklucks, extravagantly furred parkas or totem replicas—while interspersed will be the ubiquitous bait and tackle supplier.

Many of Ketchikan's totem poles have been moved from more remote regions and brought to a point on Tongass Narrows, just three miles south of town. Since the end of the 19th century the art of totem carving has become lost and the remaining poles will be kept on display for posterity through the efforts of the United States Forestry Service. Unfortunately many of these historic Indian treasures were destroyed by

Indian ceremonial house, near Ketchikan, Alaska.

well-meaning but uninformed missionaries who thought the totems were heathen idols. There is, in fact, no religious significance attached to these carvings. Because these Indian tribes had no written language, the totems told a story in hieroglyphs of certain events that occurred in his or in ancestors' lives; and in part served somewhat as a family crest or coat-of-arms.

Ketchikan and Juneau to the north, are centers for south-eastern Alaska's network of flying-boat, seaplane and helicopter transportation. Trunk airlines operate from Annette Island's

Taking the dinghy ashore at Anan Creek, for a glimpse of salmon-
fishing black bears.

airport and passengers make the 20-mile flight to Ketchikan's
waterfront in amphibians. Scheduled and charter air services
link the scores of fishing villages, cannery ports, hunting and
fishing areas in the quadrangle formed by Ketchikan, Sitka,
Glacier Bay and Skagway. If time permits, those cruising these
waters should make a round-trip flight from Ketchikan to some
of the other communities to see from the air a portion of
Alaska that can be viewed by no other means of transportation.

Out of Ketchikan, there are two water routes that may be
taken to reach the next major town of Wrangell. The shortest
(about 88 miles) is a northwesterly course up Clarence Strait,
leaving Etolin Island to starboard, then heading north through
Stikine Strait. A few miles longer, but the more picturesque
route which we prefer, is northeasterly through Ernest Sound
between Etolin Island and Cleveland Peninsula, along Seward
Passage to Anan Creek and north along the eastern shoreline of
Wrangell Island.

One of our main reasons for taking this narrow back-route to
Wrangell (other than "it was there") was an opportunity to see
and photograph the Alaskan black bears fishing for salmon
below the falls at Anan Creek.

This is an area reserved for hunting with cameras only, and because these bears have been protected it is said they have increased in numbers around the Falls area and pay little attention to tourists who come to watch them feeding. We arrived at Humpback Bay, the anchorage into which Anan Creek flows, in the midst of a driving rainstorm. But the moisture did nothing to dampen the enthusiasm of our party for a short overland hike to "the bear place."

Once ashore we found ourselves in a true rain forest. The trail was dark and wet under a dense canopy of trees. It was quiet, with only a faint sound of distant falls and the occasional shriek of a bird alerted by our approach. Suddenly our leader stopped. "A bear track!" There was no mistaking the big paw print impressed in the mud before us. We paused. "I thought the bears were on the *other* side of the creek." "Black bears won't hurt you, only brown ones are mean," someone said unconvincingly. Finally curiosity overrode our apprehension and we hurried along the trail which opened at a series of rushing falls. A few yards below us, thousands of salmon were flinging themselves upstream on their headlong rush to spawn. Masses of them hurtled through the air to land in slacker waters, pausing only momentarily before jumping again and again to reach their destination. Then an enormous black bear emerged at streamside, ambled slowly over the rocks to a shallow pool, and then stretched out a huge paw toward a jumping fish. I should have copied the bear's measured movements when I adjusted my camera. Just as the bear successfully picked a salmon from the water and held it in his mouth (the perfect picture) I hit the wrong button. The shutter would not work. Meanwhile the bear padded off into the woods with his fish, and my picture.

Out of Humpback Bay, a northwest heading leads to Blake Channel, through the 100-yard-wide narrows to Eastern Passage, at which terminus is Point Highfield, the northerly tip of Wrangell Island. The city of Wrangell lies on the westerly side of Point Highfield in a nearly landlocked harbor which has become the largest lumber shipping port in Alaska. This is also a port of call for all cruise ships and since the late 1800's has been an outfitting center for those seeking gold, fish, or wild game near the banks of the Stikine River. Through one of Alaska's major gold mining areas, the Stikine winds into the northeastern mountains for over 160 miles.

A popular tourist attraction also enjoyed by cruising yachts-

Totem poles are preserved in perfect condition on an islet near the
small-boat harbor at Wrangell.

men who have the extra time is a 3½-day round trip up the Stikine River, the fastest navigable river in North America, aboard the *Margaret Rose*. During the cruise upriver the Stikine rises 560 feet, sometimes through 10-knot riffles, out of the rainforests and into a semi-arid climate of lodgepole pine and poplar trees. In the gold rush of 1899 and 1900, Stikine River sternwheeler traffic became so heavy that boat signalmen were stationed at narrow canyon gorges to direct traffic. Today the modern 65-foot *Margaret Rose* and her passengers cruise the River alone, revisiting the scene of a once tempestuous era.

Wrangell has about 1600 residents and is Alaska's third oldest community. First settled by the Russians in 1834 as a fur-trading post, its steep-roofed buildings huddle together as if for protection against the magnitude of its bordering mountain terrain. We stopped at their well-built, small boat harbor and walked the short distance into town for a fresh crab and shrimp lunch, and later inspected some of Wrangell's fine collection of totem poles.

In early afternoon we cast off for the 40-mile run to Petersburg on Mitkof Island, heading westerly between several islets and the two large islands of Zarembo and Mitkof. At Point Alexander to starboard, our course swings north to cruise up famous Wrangell Narrows. Here, if ever, a sharp watch is necessary, both for drift and for the many buoys marking the winding but well-dredged channel; the only dredged channel, in fact, between Victoria, B.C., and Skagway. But the watcher cannot complain, whether in Wrangell Narrows or in any of these magnificent waterways. The scenery is so compelling in color and form, in sunshine or rain, that to watch is not the duty but rather the privilege of cruising this Inside Passage.

All the green shades of the spectrum line the Narrows' undulating corridor, turning the watery labyrinth to a matching hue. Now and then we pass a small clearing where a cabin and a few outbuildings bespeak of the trapper or the homesteader hewing his livelihood from this rugged, still-new land.

Before we are even ready to end our day's cruise, we round a bend in the Narrows to find the vista ahead has suddenly opened to a greater water expanse backed by 4000-foot, snow-capped mountains. We've arrived at Petersburg.

Our arrival that evening at Petersburg was well timed. The tide was ebbing and taking out with it a giant iceberg which had, for most of the day, been blocking the small-boat harbor.

As we moved into our slip we could see the great berg moving slowly down the Narrows, shimmering rose-gold and blue in the waning sunlight. Nearby, fishing boats were unloading their cargoes of salmon, halibut, cod and crab. And though midday had been warm, as the sun dipped below the western mountains, air temperature sank to 37 degrees.

Petersburg, often called the "Little Norway of America," is a base for a number of scenic guided tours by comfortable charter cruisers, to such points of interest as Leconte and Baird Glaciers, only a few miles to the southeast or north, respectively. It is from these tremendous ice-fields that such bergs as we had recently seen, are sloughed off, occasionally to drift into Petersburg's snug harbor. It is reported that Leconte is the fastest moving glacier in the world. Baird Glacier, which heads Thomas Bay, is the most southerly nesting colony of the Arctic tern and other sea and shore birds, affording an interesting cruise-tour for the bird watcher. Other tours by land are arranged for those who wish to visit Petersburg's fish processing plants, to explore the nearby muskeg with its acres of brilliant wild flowers, to inspect an experimental fur farm or to hunt on bountiful Mitkof Island for deer, brown, black and grizzly bears, mountain goats or waterfowl.

At Petersburg and at most of Alaska's major southeastern cities, a new activity is becoming popular with those who wish to hunt, fish or camp in virgin areas inaccessible except by air. Inexpensive charter flights from principal southeastern Alaskan communities will carry a party and their gear to any one of the scores of wilderness cabin sites which have been built by the United States Forest Service and native Alaskan sportsmen. These modern A-frame cabins are well-stocked with utensils, firewood and cookstoves, and for those at a lake site, a boat is also provided for the visitor's use. Food and bedroll, and possibly a 3-h.p. outboard, is all the traveler need bring. There is a $5 per day charge for the use of these cabins, but an occupancy limit of 5 days to a week is maintained during the summer and autumn seasons. In other words, one's air-fare for flying in and out of the campsite (which may run from $50 to $100 per party, depending on the distance covered) is the only other cost for such a 5-day vacation.

Much credit is due the Alaska Sportsmen's Council for their efforts and donations toward the development of the wilderness cabins. Part of construction costs are derived from the Golden

Looking north toward Fredrick Sound over Petersburg.

Wrangell Narrows, used to reach Petersburg from the south,
is at left of the cannery docks and boat harbor.

North Salmon Derby held annually in Juneau; other contributions of time and money are donated by private enterprise. Those who have sampled luxurious living in wilderness cabins are extravagant in their praise of this adventure. As one guest remarked, "At last I've found a mountain cabin where the office can *never* call me, and where the trout *never* get away!"

The distance between Petersburg and Juneau is just over a hundred miles, and could well be covered in a day's cruise. But even the most fleeting glance at a chart shows a wealth of arms and bays branching off Stephens Passage. One of the most picturesque, but easily passed without noticing its opening from Stephens Passage, is Hobart Bay, about 45 miles northward from Petersburg. In the center of the bay's entrance is aptly named Entrance Island. A small cove with government-built floats will accommodate a dozen cruisers, and ashore is a cabin that was once the home of a fur farmer. Only a few miles further north is Windham Bay, at the head of which are the abandoned structures of the first gold mine in Southeastern Alaska.

Entry to these bays only hint of the culminating grandeur awaiting those who cruise a little further to explore, particularly, Endicott and Tracy Arms extending off Holkham Bay. This area, also referred to as Fords Terror Scenic Area, embraces nearly 14,000 acres of tidewater valleys bordered by abruptly upthrust mountains. The fiords terminate in their eastern extremities with mammoth glaciers, pieces of which break away in midsummer to move majestically with the changing tides, often out into Stephens Passage and beyond.

Our first cruise into Holkham Bay and Endicott Arm occurred in a late afternoon. There was a high overcast with skies and water both the exact color of dull steel. But the grayness which seemed to extend into infinity, only served to intensify the refracted brilliant blues of icebergs floating all about us. This awesome seascape might well have been captioned: "The Bitter End of Nowhere," so did its coloring depict a feeling of coldness and isolation.

We dropped anchor for the night at a small indenture called Sumdum Bay which lies a few miles to the southeast of Endicott's entrance. On the following morning, however, we awakened to brilliant sunshine, exposing the wooded and granite walls of Endicott's fiord and its bergs sparkling, this time, under cloudless skies. The scenic metamorphosis was from

Sumdum Glacier moves down to Holkham Bay through the valley between 6660-foot Sumdum Mountain to the north (left) of it and the 6100-foot unnamed peak to the south. The Bay is filled with icebergs calved from the many glaciers in Tracy and Endicott Arms.

Ice chipped from these bergs is so dense that it will last for days, even when left on deck.

winter to summer, making the balance of the cruise southeast in Endicott Arm, to Fords Terror, another splendid day of sightseeing.

According to Frank Morris, co-author of *Marine Atlas*, Fords Terror earned its name by early adventurers who may have referred to it as the "Terror of the Fiord." The current rushes through the entrance at over 16 knots, and sometimes there are large icebergs which come tumbling through the 200-yard-wide channel to be smashed into bits as they hit the rocks and shoal water near the entrance. He describes it as one of the seven wonders of the world, because of its sparkling green waters, high precipitous marble cliffs and gigantic waterfalls. Passage through the narrows should only be made during neap tides or slack water, which lasts for about 30 minutes.

Extending north and east from the entrance to Holkham Bay is the 22-mile length of Tracy Arm, with Sawyer and Denali Glaciers at its headwater vying with each other to produce greater and more beautiful icebergs. Numerous others, unnamed, are on either side of the fiord, interspersed with waterfalls to indicate many more beyond sight in the higher valleys.

From this mid-point along Stephens Passage, and before continuing through Gastaneau Channel to Juneau, there are at least three other inlets or arms that deserve a day each for exploring. The first northerly of Holkham Bay is the three-armed Port Snettisham. Its northern arm is the site of a long-abandoned pulp mill, and a new hydro-electric plant that will, when completed, supply Juneau with its electric power.

The only other activity in the area is gill-netting during the fishing season. Seven miles further toward Juneau is nearly landlocked Taku Harbor. Once the headquarters for Father Hubbard, whose home still stands there, a government float provides moorage for scores of fishermen and there is usually room for cruising boats. Crabs are bountiful in this bay, as well as good fishing off the entrance points. Along the shores by the abandoned cannery are oil drums laid on their sides, and used by native fishermen for smoking salmon. Sixteen-mile-long Taku Inlet, with its world-famous Taku Glacier, can be visited . before reaching Juneau, or included in the many daycruises one may have on his itinerary while using Juneau as a base port.

Here at the State's capital city, the pleasure boat visitor will find excellent facilities awaiting him at Juneau's small-boat harbors or at Douglas marina across the channel. Fuel, supplies and good restaurants are all within walking distance of these excellent facilities. Moored in the same harbors are comfortable cruisers for charter for those wishing guided hunting or fishing trips to some of the prime fish and game areas surrounding Juneau. Land tours by taxi or sightseeing buses may be arranged with Travel Services in town, as well as airplane or helicopter scenic flights which are becoming more popular.

Although Juneau is not Alaska's oldest city, it was the very first Territorial white settlement founded under the American flag. Other principal southeastern Alaska communities had diverse early settlers. Sitka and Wrangell were originally Russian inhabited; Petersburg has Scandanavian ancestry and others were first settled by the Finnish—all, of course, preceded by Indians. Not yet a hundred years old, Juneau first became a gold-mining camp in 1880, a year after gold was first discovered by Joe Juneau and Richard Harris. Three years later it had risen to the status of Alaska's gold center, and flourished as such for many years. In 1917 the mines on Douglas Island across from Juneau, were flooded, and in 1944 the last of Juneau's big mines were depleted, thus ending a colorful era so well-marked in history.

Replacement of the lusty gold-seeking days, however, has been toward an increasingly stable economy, not the least of which is due to the vast network of waterways and airways radiating from Juneau. Commercial fishing and forestry are today's major industries of the area, with tourism a rising challenge.

Juneau lies on the eastern shore of Gastineau Channel
and is well-endowed with two large marinas.

Bridge at right connects Juneau to Douglas Island, on which is another excellent marina about two miles southeast and down the channel from Juneau.

Auke Bay, some 14 miles northwest of Juneau and within sight of
Mendenhall Glacier, is the site of the annual salmon-fishing derby.

One of the most popular side-trips for newcomers to Juneau
is the 13-mile drive from town to Mendenhall Glacier. This
slowly receding glacial moraine still contains remnants of the
great forest it sheared off in its long-ago descent to Auke Lake
Valley. Footpaths have been carved along the side boundaries of
this nearly two-mile-wide glacier, to permit the hiker to look
down into some of its massive crevasses. From a flight over
Juneau, Mendenhall is but one of a dozen glaciers that can be
seen in this immediate vicinity.

Going from cloud tops to underground, visitors may wish to
tour the historic Alaska Juneau Gold Mine where a train ride
through a mile-long tunnel takes one out to the face of Mt.
Roberts, high above the city. From this point a reconditioned
road and bridge lead to some of the old mine buildings where
ore samples are on display, along with tools and conveyers used
during the days when millions of dollars in gold ore was taken
from the A.J. Mine and sent to Juneau's mill for refining.

Early in August the annual Golden North Salmon Derby
attracts thousands of residents and visitors to vie for heaviest
salmon brought to dock. Over $25,000 in prizes are given to
winners in this popular fishing contest. Revenue from the sale
of fish caught is donated to a host of worthy enterprises,
ranging from scholarships to materials for wilderness cabins.

Leaving Juneau's mini-metropolitan atmosphere, puts us back
into wilderness cruising, with Skagway 100 miles to the north;
but Glacier Bay to the west beckoning us to add nearly 200
miles to our cruise. Retracing our course down Gastineau

Channel to round the southern end of Douglas Island, we continue through protected waters of Stephens Passage on a northwesterly heading to Point Retreat, about 38 miles from Juneau. From here, we can go north to Skagway with a stop at Haines-Port Chilkoot, or head westward for Icy Strait and Glacier Bay. We chose the latter.

The weather had been excellent for many days, and knowing that Glacier Bay is overcast or rainy for about 70 percent of the time, we decided not to press our luck and cruised the 55 miles to Glacier Bay's Bartlett Cove without stopping at the many inviting harbors enroute. Glacier Bay Lodge is only a short walk from the pier where small boat floats are attached to it. Fuel and water are available from the pier, and it is the sole source of supplies in the 4600-square-mile National Monument.

While entering Glacier Bay from Icy Strait, we could not help wondering what Capt. George Vancouver would have said if he had been aboard our fast cruiser. In 1794, when he passed a small indentation that is now the entrance to the Bay, a towering wall of ice marked the seaward outlet of an immense glacier that completely filled the Bay. It extended over 100 miles to the north, was 20 miles or more wide, and up to 4000 feet deep. During the following century the ice front retreated 40 miles from the mouth of the inlet; by 1916 the terminus of Grand Pacific Glacier was 65 miles from the mouth, and it has continued to recede. Since 1900 the spectacular John Muir Glacier has receded more than 18 miles. What was once a single glacier extending to Icy Strait, is now 16 active tidewater glaciers of varying sizes. It is said by authorities that nowhere else in the world have glaciers receded at such a rapid rate.

To the north and west of Glacier Bay are the loftiest mountains in the U.S. Mount St. Elias reaches 18,000 feet and feeds Muir Glacier, among others. Muir is nearly 2 miles wide at its terminus, and although it is moving toward tidewater some 20 feet per day, its face continues to recede.

We were well-advised by the National Park Service rangers at Bartlett Cove not to approach Muir or Johns Hopkins Glaciers closer than two miles. When they "calve," the resulting wave and the floating ice from previous calvings can seriously damage a boat. Smaller glaciers can be approached within a half mile. An alternative way to cruise the inlets of Glacier Bay is to take a day-long cruise aboard an especially built boat operated by the National Park Service.

Two odd facts stand out in our minds about Glacier Bay. First, the inability to judge distance because of the total lack of objects with which to draw a comparison—such as docks along the shoreline, or structures of any kind. What appeared to be an islet or an iceberg which we would guess to be a mile away, would often prove to be many miles away when measured by radar. The other was the density of the ice. When brought aboard with a fishnet, it would take days to melt, whereas manufactured ice would be gone in only a few hours. We surmised that the thousands or millions of years that it took to compress the snow into glacial ice made a more durable product than that which is man-made in a few hours within a refrigerator.

Taking leave of Glacier Bay, still with good weather, we reluctantly passed both Excursion Inlet and Port Frederick (to north and south, respectively, of Icy Strait) in order to reach Haines-Port Chilkoot in time for a dinner date at its renowned Halsingland Inn. After leaving Icy Strait, the 70-mile run took us northward into Lynn Canal, with its towering snowcapped mountains climbing high on either hand.

In 1904 the first military post in Alaska was built adjacent to Haines. Originally named Fort William H. Seward, it was later renamed Haines-Port Chilkoot and in 1946 was abandoned by the Army. A group purchased the buildings, officers quarters and barracks, some of which are now used by Hotel Halsingland.

Haines is primarily a fishing community, with a breakwatered mini-harbor for the fleet that operates in the area. It is also one of the ports-of-call for the Alaska State Ferry System, since the Haines Highway connects with the Alaska Highway in the interior. Cruise ships and air service also bring tourists to the area, the principal attraction being the Chilkat Dancers. An authentic Potlatch House of the Chilkat Tribe has been built where regular performances are scheduled during the summer months by the Chilkat Dancers. The costumes worn by the dancers are reproductions of traditional dance dress. Under the auspices of Alaska Indian Arts, a non-profit organization, not only do the young people dance but they are also trained in totem pole carving, silver smithing, soapstone carving and the creation of the ceremonial items which they use in their performances.

Fourteen miles to the north, Skagway beckoned us as it did

The upper reaches of Glacier Bay are filled with mini-icebergs. Unless one is moving slowly, even small ones (seven times deeper in the water than their height above) can do serious damage to a boat.

those in search of gold in the late 1890's. Little changed, except for a shrinkage of population from 20,000 to around 1000 inhabitants now, Skagway is the terminus of pleasure and commercial boat traffic from the "lower 48" through the Inside Passage. It is also the starting point of the White Pass and Yukon Railroad that climbs through the mountain passes to Lake Bennett and Whitehorse in the Yukon Territory. This narrow-gauge railroad was completed in 1900, paralleling the "trail of '98" used by the thousands headed for the Klondike.

At one point along the railroad's route, the grade is so steep and the curves so sharp that it takes two hours to go 20 miles. Economy of Skagway is largely dependent on the railroad, which carries thousands of visitors each year over the gold stampeeders' route. It also is the commercial link for freight between Canadian and U.S. ports and the entire Yukon Territory.

The town has done a remarkable job of keeping the atmosphere and color of the gold rush days. Alaska's first granite structure, which now houses the Trail of '98 Museum, is filled with mementos of the early days; originally it was the

Skagway is nestled into a valley at the northern end of Lynn Canal. Its harbor facilities include modern cargo cranes for handling freight, a ferry terminal for the Alaska Ferry System ships, and a breakwater-protected, small-boat harbor.

Federal Court Building. "The Shooting of Dan McGrew" is part of a variety show staged by townsmen, which includes performance of the Can-Can Dance Girls.

Even the recently built hotels are styled and decorated as they were 70 years ago. Now billed as the "friendliest town in Alaska" by its residents, during the gold rush days unbridled lawlessness and terror characterized early-day Skagway. With cruise ships, pleasure boats and airplanes bringing new generations to the area, it may be hard to keep alive the old days of the gold rush era—and possibly it is best that lust for gold is suppressed in favor of the more enjoyable activities that are available to us when cruising.

For those who bring their own boats up from the south for a period of sightseeing and exploring, there remain innumerable return routes other than those taken cruising north, each of which presents new vistas of never-ending interest. As for us, book pages are running out. Regretfully, we must make Skagway the end of our cruise.

TYPES OF BOATS SUITABLE FOR NORTH COAST CRUISING

Nearly all types of power boats are suitable for cruising British Columbia and Alaska waters along the inside passages. Fast day-cruisers are used extensively because their speed shortens the time for runs between fuel and supply depots and attractive campsites or hotel accommodations. Larger and heavier powerboats seldom encounter water passages too shallow for their hulls, and again, the wealth of overnight facilities precludes even the slowest of such craft having to seek anchorages after darkness. Each year finds a larger number of people trailing their boats from distant ports to launch them in northwest waters for extended summer vacations in these scenic waterways. Although sailboats are encountered occasionally, the Canadian and Alaskan regions are not conducive to good sailing simply because the waters are protected by mountains and other land windbreaks. Moreover, strong tidal currents often necessitate greater hull speed than the average sailboat's auxiliary can manage.

FACILITIES AND SUPPLIES

There is no scarcity of fuel and supplies along the more direct routes between Victoria, B.C. and the northwest end of Vancouver Island; even along the inside-Inside Passages, it is seldom more than 50 miles between them. Some of the longer inlets may require 100 miles of cruising, considering the distance up and back to a lumbering operation or fisherman's supply depot. Once past Cape Caution, to the northeast of the extremity of Vancouver Island, the distances between fuel and supply depots become greater. The longest distances between them are roughly 100 miles, as one is heading northwest toward Skagway, Alaska.

Unique to this area is the completeness of supply stores that are usually adjacent to fueling docks—with apparel, fishing gear, food and common engine-repair parts. These are stocked for the operation and provisioning of commercial tugs and fishing boats. In some of the most remote areas there will be a marine railway or grid for boats up to 30 or 40 feet in length. The latter is simply a heavily built platform on piling, five to seven feet below high-water level, with a bulkhead along the shore side. A boat in need of bottom repairs ties to the vertical bulkhead, or in some cases to a group of piles, and waits for the tide to go out. With the range of tide between low and high water as much as 25 feet in the more northern reaches of this area, a good many hours of repair work can be performed before the next rising tide floats the boat off the grid. In some of the larger harbors, grids are available for boats up to 100 feet in length.

APPROXIMATE DISTANCES IN NAUTICAL MILES

BETWEEN BRITISH COLUMBIA AND ALASKAN PORTS:

Victoria, B.C., to Nanaimo 64
Victoria to Vancouver 72
Victoria to Campbell River 142
Victoria to Cape Caution 270
Vancouver to Powell River 68
Vancouver to Campbell River 99
Vancouver to Yaculta Rapids 110
Vancouver to Cape Caution via Yaculta 237
Cape Caution to Bella Bella 68
Bella Bella to Butedale 80
Butedale to Prince Rupert 100
Prince Rupert to Ketchikan, Alaska 85
Ketchikan to Wrangell via Anan Creek 98
Ketchikan to Wrangell via Stikine St. 88
Wrangell to Petersburg via Wrangell Narrows 40
Petersburg to Holkham Bay 74
Holkham Bay to Juneau 46
Juneau to Bartlett Cove, Glacier Bay 90
Juneau to Skagway 100

ELECTRIC/ELECTRONIC EQUIPMENT

Anchor Windlass— In British Columbia and Alaska, although the ground tackle needed is little different from that required for anchoring along the California, Oregon and Washington coasts, the depths of the coves, inlets and harbors dictate the need for more than average lengths of chain and anchor rode and an electric-power anchor windlass.

Radio navigation aids are few and far between, and basically of no great need because of the canyon-channels. Depth sounders, on the other hand, are of great assistance in anchoring, due to the steep slopes of beaches and the depths that are common even close to shore.

Radio communication to shore-based public telephone operators is not as reliable as along the coasts of California, Oregon and Washington, because terrain and canyon-like channels limit the range of the average marine radiotelephone. The British Columbia Telephone Co., has stations at Vancouver and Prince Rupert, and the Alaska Communication System—formerly operated by the U.S. Air Force but now by a division of RCA—has stations in Ketchikan and Juneau. Weather reports are broadcast by both groups. In addition, many British Columbia communities are equipped with radio links using VHF equipment and repeater stations high atop the hills and mountains and will handle radio traffic to mainland cities.

Other electronic equipment helpful in cruising these waters include automatic pilot, radiotelephone and radar. The latter is particularly helpful if one plans to run at night, even though no fog is present, because the topography of the area gives sharp definition to the inlets and channels and shows them on the radarscope as precisely as they are seen on charts.

FENDERS

When tying alongside log booms and log-supported floats, pneumatic fenders should be used. In addition, it is helpful to lash a lead ball of the type used on seine nets, to the lower end of each fender to keep them in a vertical position between the hull and the log. Without the sinker-weight, the fenders will float horizontally and be of little value.

BOAT CHARTERING

As we have brought out in the Introduction to this book, there is no Pacific Coast boat chartering on a large commercial scale, as is done from south-Atlantic ports. A few private boat charters are available from such British Columbian harbors as Vancouver and Victoria, and in Ketchikan and Juneau, Alaska. Advertisements of these operators and details of their services can be found in such magazines as *Alaska Sportsman* and *Sea,* and in certain other outdoor or hunting-and-fishing periodicals. An alternative source of charter information would be through yacht brokers in Seattle, Washington, and Vancouver, B.C.

CLOTHING

Summer temperatures in British Columbia and southeastern Alaska will vary from the high seventies to occasional lows of around 40 degrees. There have been occasions when no rain has fallen for a three-week span, but this is not to be depended upon. Several warm sweaters, wool slacks and a water-repellent jacket should be included in clothing brought for this climate, as well as shorts or summer dresses for sunny afternoons. A basic wardrobe of informal, sports-type clothes are the rule—the only areas where dinner clothes are generally worn for evening are in Victoria and Vancouver at their larger hotels or restaurants. For those planning special hunting, fishing or hiking expeditions, the individual pursuit will indicate suitable apparel such as might be taken for other outdoor areas having comparable temperature variations.

CUSTOMS CLEARANCE IN AND OUT OF CANADA AND THE UNITED STATES

There is no duty on merchandise up to $100 brought from Canada into the United States. There is no limitation on cigarettes for personal use, but not more than 100 cigars may be included. Not over one quart of alcoholic beverages per person may be brought from Canada into the United States, or taken from the U.S. into Canada.

Entry ports into British Columbia of concern to those cruising the Inside Passage include Vancouver, Victoria, Nanaimo, Sidney, Powell River, Bedwell Harbour, Campbell River, Courtnay and Prince Rupert. There is no charge at Victoria or Sidney between the hours of 8 am and midnight, nor at Nanaimo between 8 am and 5 pm. At Bedwell Harbour the hours are 8 am to 10 pm up to Labor Day, and 9 am to 5 pm until the end of September. At Campbell River, Courtnay and Port Alberni (on the Pacific side of Vancouver Island) the hours are 8:45 am to 5 pm Monday through Friday. If clearance into British Columbia is required at other than these hours, a minimum charge of $20 plus transportation costs will be charged. No passports are required for U.S. citizens going into Canada, but it is well to have one's proof of citizenship available. Firearms and animals require special handling. Before departing from the last port of call in British Columbia, one must surrender the cruising permit obtained when entering.

For those returning from Canada, the U.S. entry ports nearest Canadian waters are Bellingham, Blaine, Port Angeles, Port Townsend, Anacortes, Friday Harbor, Roche Harbor, Everett and Seattle. During weekdays between 8 am and 5 pm there are no Customs charges, but on holidays, Sundays and after those hours an overtime charge of $25 will be collected. Through the efforts of the Interclub Association of Washington, clearance through Roche Harbor and Friday Harbor can be made on holidays and Sundays between the hours of 8 am and 7 pm for a charge of only $3, the balance of the overtime charges being handled by the Association.

For entrance to the U.S. at Port Townsend on holidays or Sundays the City's Chamber of Commerce prepays the Customs Officer, who will clear a boat between the hours of 10 am and 6 pm for a charge of $5 instead of the full overtime charge.

Both the Canadian and U.S. Customs Officer schedules cited above were applicable during the 1972-73 boating season, and are subject to change from year to year.

CANADIAN FISHING LICENSES

The Canadian Department of Fisheries has established a schedule of fees for fishing licenses, applicable to any U.S.-owned boat, based on boat length.

Up to 15 feet	$15
15 to 28 feet	25
30 to 39 feet	50
40 feet and over	75

A Salt Water Fishing License is required for taking any sports fish, bottom fish, crabs, shrimp, clams or oysters, whether taken from the boat itself or from the shore by anyone from a non-resident boat. A dinghy will not be licensed but the larger boat bringing it across the border must be licensed if the crew aboard will be fishing. Licensed craft must display a decal. Maximum penalty for violation, $1000 fine or a year in jail. The license may be obtained from the Canadian Department of Fisheries or at Canadian Customs stations at ports of entry.

BOOKS AND CHARTS

Tide and current tables published by the United States and Canadian Governments, in addition to the charts available from the U.S. Coast & Geodetic Survey, U.S. Hydrographic Office and Canadian Hydrographic Office, are essential to safe and enjoyable cruising in these waters. The tide and current tables will serve to determine times of departure from one harbor to the next, to take advantage of favorable currents and to avoid areas where maximum floods or ebbs can create turbulent and sometimes dangerous water. Publications and charts are available at all the principal ports, such as Victoria, Vancouver, Nanaimo, and Prince Rupert, British Columbia; and Ketchikan, Wrangell, Petersburg and Juneau, Alaska. It requires more than 50 charts to cover the route from Victoria, B.C. to Skagway, Alaska, so detailed are many of them.

Northwest Passages, Volume II, Bruce Calhoun, Sea Publications, Inc., Book Division, 1499 Monrovia Ave., Newport Beach, California.

Alaska, monthly magazine, 130 Second Avenue South, Edmonds Washington.

Marine Atlas, Volume 2, Frank Morris, W.R. Heath & Amos Burg, P.B.I. Co., P.O. Box 54, Seattle, Washington.

Index

EDITOR   Ed Reading

DESIGNER   Leo Bestgen

Copy editor Janet Taylor. Art
assistants Bob Price, Lois Greene
and Conrad Schwable. Photos
supplied by the authors.